Common Information Model

Implementing the Object Model for Enterprise Managment

Common Information Model

Implementing the Object Model for Enterprise Managment

Winston Bumpus

John W. Sweitzer

Patrick Thompson

Andrea R. Westerinen

Raymond C. Williams

Wiley Computer Publishing

John Wiley & Sons, Inc.

NEW YORK · CHICHESTER · WEINHEIM · BRISBANE · SINGAPORE · TORONTO

Publisher: Robert Ipsen

Editor: Marjorie Spencer

Assistant Editor: Margaret Hendrey

Managing Editor: Micheline Frederick

Text Design & Composition: Thomark Design

Designations used by companies to distinguish their products are often claimed as trademarks. In all instances where John Wiley & Sons, Inc., is aware of a claim, the product names appear in initial capital or ALL CAPITAL LETTERS. Readers, however, should contact the appropriate companies for more complete information regarding trademarks and registration.

This book is printed on acid-free paper. ∞

This publication is designed to provide accurate and authoritative information in regard to the subject matter covered. It is sold with the understanding that the publisher is not engaged in professional services. If professional advice or other expert assistance is required, the services of a competent professional person should be sought.

Library of Congress Cataloging-in-Publication Data:

ISBN: 0-471-35342-6

Printed in the United States of America.

10 9 8 7 6 5 4 3 2 1

*To my loving wife Carole, who tolerated the weekend
and evening hours I spent on the creation of this
book. I also dedicate this book to the technologists
and visionaries who come together to develop
industry standards. These people make our everyday
lives better by developing standards that improve the
interoperability of our tools and our toys.*

—Winston Bumpus

*To my three wonderful children Jason, Jennifer, and
Laura; and my loving wife Sara; for their support
and encouragement.*

—John Sweitzer

*Dropping red petals
And golden green leaves
All the beauties and gifts of our days.*

-Patrick Thompson

*I dedicate this to my husband, Jeff, and my
daughters, Samantha, Stephanie, and Becky, who
helped me through many long nights working on
CIM and this book. Also, to the many System and
Device Working Group team members (past and
present) who helped design the models.*

—Andrea Westerinen

To my long-suffering wife Pam.

—Raymond Williams

CONTENTS

T he Common Information Model (CIM) (*pronounced sym*) is a collaborative work of the world's leading experts on management technology, information modeling, and information systems architecture. Over the short number of years of its existence it has already achieved broad industry support and adoption. It is the basis of management architectures for the foreseeable future. Out of the seeds that developed within the minds of a few visionaries, the industry has come together to develop one of the most important pieces of technology since the creation of the World Wide Web.

The model and its ancillary standards are being developed within the Distributed Management Task Force (DMTF). This organization is made up of the leading companies in today's computing industry and its membership reads like a who's who of high technology companies. The membership consists of operating system vendors, systems manufactures, network systems, and services vendors as well as the leading manufactures of systems management technology. This book was written by the active participants from within this organization and will give the reader the most accurate view of the intent of the model as well as reason that it was developed the way it was.

This book, like the technology, is also a collaborative effort. It has been written by the pioneers of CIM and provides insight into the intent as well as the inner workings of the model. Early in its evolution the team of engineers and architects from the leading companies in the computer industry met every two weeks at locations around the world to develop CIM. The authors of this book were members of that original team and are still actively participating in its ongoing development. Working together on the creation of CIM close bonds were formed making the creation of this book an enjoyable task.

This book provides the reader with an inside view of the Common Information Model starting from modeling basics, for those that are new to information modeling, to how to implement this into a management or managed system.

Concepts (Chapters 1 – 3) This section of the book is designed to familiarize the reader with the concepts behind information modeling and the fundamentals of CIM. It is a good introduction to this model and provides a general overview for anyone that is new to object oriented data design. It also describes how the information can be represented graphically using UML (Universal Modeling Language).

In-depth (Chapters 4-8) These chapters take a detailed look at the model itself, the Common portion of the model, and sections of the model that are used to represent managed elements and their associations. There is also a discussion on those areas of CIM that are still under development. These sections were developed by the folks closely involved with the development from within the DMTF working groups.

Design (Chapters 9-11) These chapters are for those who have a need to extend the CIM schema. It is filled with ideas, concepts, and methodologies that should be considered and followed when building extensions to the Common model.

Implementations (Chapter 12) The book also includes a section on how to implement the model into a management system. This section explains that there is more than turning a logical database into a physical database. This section covers many issues that need to be considered including performance and usability

For further information on CIM and the current state of the model you should go to the DMTF web site at www.dmtf.org. The Web site also contains a self-paced tutorial that will help the reader to better understand the model and the terms and how to develop your own extensions to the model. Also as new models get completed and approved they will be posted there as well.

This book will provide you the reader with a good working knowledge of the common information model. It should be of assistance when you need to implement a management system using CIM or you are extending the model to implement into a managed. From beginner to the advanced data modeler this book should be a guide and a reference to using the Common Information Model.

The task of writing this book was made easier with the help of many others, including the chairs and members of the DMTF working committees, who provided many diagrams and works-in-progress. In particular, we would like to acknowledge David Simons, for his insightful comments and suggestions, and Julie Schott, for supplying several figures for Chapter 5.

The book would not have been possible without the support and guidance from the folks at Wiley Computer Publishing, in particular our editor Marjorie Spencer. She believed in the team from the very beginning, and it is due to her patience and prodding that we completed this book.

A big thanks also to everyone who worked to create the Common Information Model (CIM); it entailed a lot of extra work from people at competing companies. It takes both vision and fortitude to complete such a monumental task. This model will be an integral part of all information management technology for the foreseeable future. We also want to thank the executives of the companies that funded this development; without their support and belief in the benefits enabled by a common model, none of this would have been accomplished.

Finally, and especially, we thank Patrick Thompson for his undying dedication, vision, and brilliance, which gave birth to such a model, and for his belief, which led to the proof that it could be improved by developing it in an open standards environment. And we acknowledge Ray Williams, who through leadership and perseverance drove the establishment of the internationally accepted industry standard data model for distributed management.

Winston Bumpus has more than 30 years' experience in the computer industry. He participated on the DMTF Common Information Model (CIM) development, and was chair of its Application Management Working Group. He is currently the Director of Open Technologies and Standards at Novell, Inc.; he also serves as President of the Distributed Management Task Force (DMTF), and is Novell's representative on the DMTF Board of Directors. Bumpus is also coauthor of the recently released book *The Foundations of Application Management*, published by John Wiley & Sons, Inc.

John W. Sweitzer is a Distinguished Engineer for Tivoli Systems. He has more than 18 years' experience in the IT industry. Sweitzer has been involved in a variety of technical and management positions associated with systems, network, and application management dating back to 1981. Currently, he is focusing on managing applications in distributed environments and investigating how pervasive computing changes management. Sweitzer is also interested in developing technologies that will facilitate the integration of software systems, using techniques pioneered in the database and the artificial intelligence disciplines. He has a BS in Computer Science from Penn State University and an MS in Computer Science from North Carolina State University.

Patrick Thompson is a program manager in the Microsoft Windows Management Instrumentation group. His background is mainly in the area of database management systems, database design, and online transaction processing. He is the author of a book on database design and transaction processing called *Data with Semantics*, published by Van Nostrand Reinhold in 1989. Formerly, he worked for Unisys, where he played a major role in the design and implementation of the award-winning Semantic Information Manager (SIM) database management system; he also taught database administration and design. Thompson was responsible for formulating the models on which CIM was originally based, and provided much of the initial impetus to the formulation of the CIM standard, in particular regarding modeling formalisms and practices.

Andrea R. Westerinen has worked in the computer industry for more than 20 years, the last six years primarily in the areas of enterprise, systems, and server management. She chaired the CIM System and Devices Working Group at DMTF for the last two years. This group created and published CIM's Core, System, Devices, and Physical Models—object models of the managed environment. Westerinen is currently the Technical Director of the Storage Networking Industry Association (SNIA) where she works with the association's technical teams, customers, and various other standards organizations to achieve well-defined and interoperable storage solutions. Before joining the SNIA, she was employed by Microsoft, Intel, NCR, IBM, Johnson Controls, and the Medical College of Wisconsin.

Raymond C. Williams is Director of Standards for Tivoli Systems, Inc., in the Corporate Technical Office, where he is responsible for defining and executing Tivoli Systems Standards Strategy. He has more than 41 years' experience in the computer and networking industries. He joined IBM in 1957; and in Britain, he worked on some of the early computer systems, including satellite data transmission. He transferred to the United States in 1967 to work on the IBM System 370. He became Senior Technical Staff Member in 1988, the highest technical level in IBM. He joined Tivoli Systems in 1996.

Williams currently serves as the Vice President of Technology for the DMTF, and is responsible for the technical programs there, including the Common Information Model (CIM) and the Emerging Web Based Enterprise Management (WBEM) architectures. Williams is well known in the standards arena as a result of his work on OSI and the OpenGroup. Educated at Lancing College and London University in England, he has certificates in Mechanical, Electrical, and Production Engineering.

CHAPTER 1

CIM Introduction

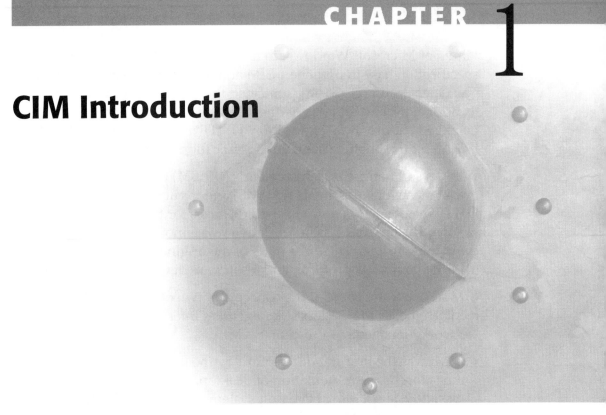

To help meet the business objectives of an enterprise, network and system resources are connected and closely related. In a perfect world, devices and resources have infinite precision and unlimited capacity and require intervention only for administrative or business reasons. But the world isn't perfect, and devices fail and resources reach saturation. System management is often superimposed (instead of integrated) to track usage of resources.

The Common Information Model (CIM) describes management information and offers a framework for managing system elements across distributed systems. CIM is not bound to a particular implementation, and this flexibility allows different systems and applications to exchange and interpret management information. (The CIM specifications, schemas, and tools are available via anonymous ftp from the Distributed Management Task Force (DMTF) at www.dmtf.org.)

CIM History

CIM is implementation- and architecture-neutral, which means you can use it in Intel-, Alpha-, or Risc-based computers running UNIX,

Linux, or Microsoft Windows, to name a few. The open nature of the specification has strengthened CIM and its acceptance in the industry. The OpenGroup (TOG) has published the CIM Specification as part of its normal process and has defined CIM as a key component of its management program. In addition, DMTF intends to submit CIM to ISO under the publicly available specification (PAS) process.

Web-Based Enterprise Management's (WEBM) proposal for a hyper-media management schema (HMMS) and input from a number of DMTF member companies formed the basis for the final CIM specifications. The original WBEM initiative was announced by a group of companies in 1996. The three parts of the original WBEM program included HMMS, a protocol, and a software development kit (SDK).

CIM incorporates some of the concepts of two other network management protocols: the Desktop Management Interface (DMI), and Simple Network Management Protocol (SNMP).

- DMI was the first standards effort by the DMTF to provide guidelines for the instrumentation of desktop, mobile, and server PC-based systems. Most PC-based systems shipping today have implemented DMI only in the system hardware. Though provision for software applications was part of the DMI Master Management Information Format (MIF), application management using DMI has not been well received.

- The IETF's SNMP, over many versions, has provided network administrators with management information for network elements. SNMP is not without its shortcomings; nevertheless it is deeply entrenched in many enterprises and likely to remain so for the foreseeable future.

How CIM Works

A common management axiom states, "Management is only as good as the agents will allow," or, more pragmatically, as good as the data presented by the agents. You can have the finest graphics with 3D, color, virtual reality, fuzzy logic, and so on, but without the appropriate information from the device (or its agent), the management application can't function.

Within the CIM model, *agent-to-manager* and *manager-to-manager* communications form the basis for *distributed system management*. The *man-*

ager/agent paradigm provides robust management capabilities for network systems and resources. The *manager* (or managing system) supports dialog with a *resource* (or managed system). Since the resource may not be outfitted to support the management dialog, an agent represents the resource to the manager. The agent is local, and provides command/control and monitoring, externalizing functions through support of *management protocols* that flow between the manager and the agent.

CIM is a hierarchical, object-oriented paradigm with relationship capabilities; the complex relationships that exist in the real world can be depicted in the schema, thereby linking information from different sources. As a result, you can easily track and depict the often-complex interdependencies and associations among different managed objects. Interdependencies may exist between logical network connections and underlying physical devices, or between an e-commerce transaction and a Web database server. CIM schemas describe the gamut of managed elements: servers and desktops (operating systems, components, peripherals, and applications), all layers of the network (from Ethernet switches to IP and HTTP connections), and even end users. Schema properties describe the attributes that apply to objects, such as the type of printer or storage medium, RAM and CPU capacity, and even information about Border Gateway Protocol support on a switch. CIM will also define management functions and disciplines, such as application performance measurement and policy-based networking.

In a fully CIM-compliant world, it is possible to build an application such as service-level agreement (SLA) tracking using management data from a variety of sources and different management systems, including Tivoli Management Software, HP OpenView, Novell's ManageWise, Microsoft's SMS, Manage.Com's FrontLine e.Manage, and others. The management data would be collected, stored, and analyzed using a common format (CIM) while the extensions offered by the particular management package would provide added value.

CIM Specification and CIM Schema

The CIM specification describes the language, naming, metaschema and mapping techniques from other management models such as the IETF's Simple Network Management Protocol (SNMP) Management

Information Base (MIB) models, and DMTF Management Information Format (MIF) files. The *metaschema* is a formal definition of the model. It defines the terms used to express the model and their usage and semantics. The elements of the metaschema are *classes*, *properties*, and *methods*. The metaschema also supports *indications* and *associations* as types of classes, and *references* as types of properties.

The CIM schema provides the actual model descriptions along with a set of classes with properties and associations that establish a well-understood conceptual framework, within which it is possible to organize the available information about the managed environment.

The CIM schema is structured into three distinct layers.

Core schema. An information model that captures notions applicable to all areas of management

Common schema. An information model that captures notions common to particular management areas but independent of a particular technology or implementation. The common areas are systems, applications, databases, networks, and devices (see Figure 1.1). The information model is specific enough to lay the foundation for the development of management applications. This schema provides a set of base classes for extension into the area of technology-specific

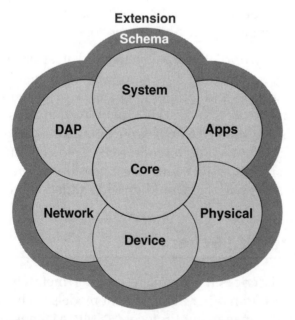

Figure 1.1   The areas of the Common schema.

schemas. Currently, there are six approved common schemas: systems, applications, physical, devices, networks, and distributed applications performance (DAP). More schemas are planned for definition by the year 2000 in the areas of databases, policy, and service-level agreements, and users.

Extension schemas. Technology-specific extensions of the Common schema relating to environments, such as operating systems (for example, UNIX, Linux, or Microsoft Windows).

The formal definition of the CIM schema is expressed in a *managed object file* (MOF), which is an ASCII file that can be used as input to an MOF editor or compiler for use in an application, or encoded with the Extensible Markup Language (XML).

Note that the Unified Modeling Language (UML) is used here to illustrate the structure of the schemas (see Figure 1.2). Therefore, you should be familiar with UML notation (go to www.rational.com) and with basic object-oriented concepts in the form of classes, properties, methods, operations, inheritance, associations, objects, cardinality, and polymorphism.

Techniques to develop UML (Visio) files from MOF files have been developed so that information can be depicted graphically. In the discussion that follows, italicized words refer to objects in the figure.

Core Schema

The Core schema defines classes of elements in a managed environment; these include the Managed System Element class and the related classes such as Usage Statistic and Service (see Figure 1.3). Managed System Element classes represent management-significant system elements. Service classes are functions provided by systems and elements of systems and the Usage Statistic classes are all statistical views or groupings of the Managed System Element classes.

Because the Core schema is a framework for the class structures that make up the overall schema, it is very stable. Alterations to the structure or content of the Core schema indicate a shift in interpretation of the classes and methodology that underlie the schema as a whole.

More classes will be added to the Core schema over time; however, major reinterpretations of the Core schema classes are unlikely. Possi-

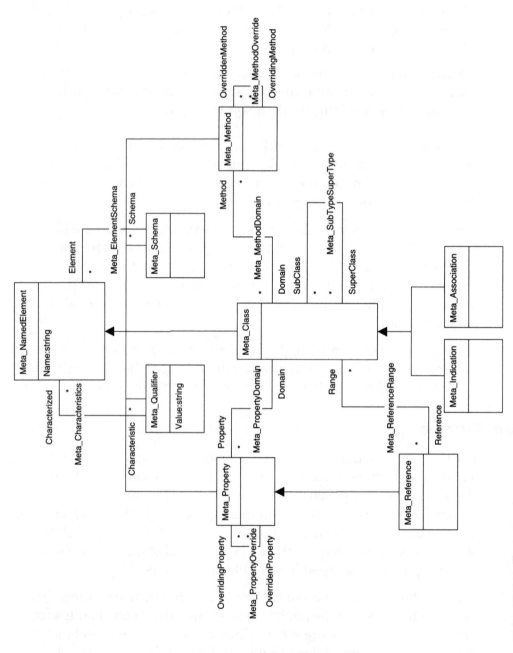

Figure 1.2 Using UML to illustrate schema structure.

ble extensions include the addition of a Managed Element class as an abstraction of the Managed System Element class. Descendents of the Managed Element class (classes that represent objects outside the managed system domain), may be added to the Core and possibly the Common schema. For example, it will be desirable in some applications to model objects such as organizations and users.

It is essential to the conceptual integrity of the model that organizations and users be supported as objects outside the system domain, and not as subtypes of the Managed System Element class. For example, in the model, in no sense can an organization or user be considered an element of a system, but they may have associations with systems, such as ownership or placement relationships.

The Managed System Element (MSE) class and its subclasses provide a detailed catalog of the systems in the managed environment. The following are subclasses of MSE:

- Subclasses of the System class represent systems.
- Descendents of the Network Element class represent network topologies.
- Descendents of the Logical Element class represent applications.
- Descendents of the Device class represent the functional capabilities of devices; descendents of the Physical Element class represent a device's physical packaging.
- *Settings* and *arrangements* describe the configuration of systems and system elements. Arrangements are groups of dependencies, and settings are groups of parameters.

Common Schema

The Common schema, or resource-specific schema, is a conceptual framework of organizing principles for schema designers, used to interpret and analyze the information requirements of management applications. The Common schema contains a set of abstract and concrete classes that define the basic characteristics of systems, networks, applications, databases, and devices. In parallel to the Common schema are various groupings of statistical and other management-related data such as classes required to model organizations, locations, and classes that provide a *recast mapping* (that is, a direct

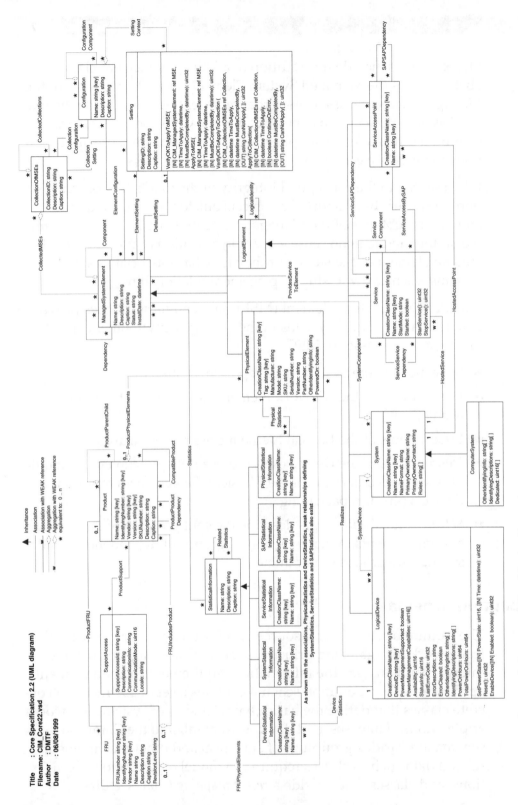

Figure 1.3 Classes of elements defined in the Core schema.

representation) of existing sources of management data such as DMI, SNMP, or CMIP.

Methodology and Structure

Typically, to design a schema, you systematically identify the information requirements it must support. Together, the applications that will use the schema define the set of requirements. This design approach is based on two assumptions:

- The set of applications that will use the schema is known, and each application can clearly articulate its information needs.
- The applications will not change over time, and no new applications will have to be supported by the schema.

For the Common schema, neither condition applies. You can expect new applications to be created to take advantage of the schema, but no one can predict the new set of requirements. Current management applications evolve from release to release, and so cannot articulate requirements that will have to be met in the future. Information requirements must be defined as general characteristics of the system to be managed, rather than as the specific requirements of any particular management application.

Information schemas normally model a specific domain for a particular application or set of applications. The Common schema is both an information schema and a framework for the future development of management information schemas. A framework, as defined by the object-oriented community is a "reusable, semi-complete application that can be specialized to produce custom applications." Unlike class libraries with more general uses, frameworks are targeted for particular business units (such as accounting or human resources). Similarly, to extend the CIM schema, you must establish specializations of the provided classes that fit the Core schema, which establishes the basic terminology, types of associations, and classifications available to the schema designer. In this way, the Core schema resembles a framework since it establishes a compulsory structure that requires individuals extending it to use a common information-modeling approach.

The Common schema is an extension of the Core schema into the following domain-specific areas:

Systems, in the form of the Managed System Element hierarchy.

Applications, in the form of the various application-related elements of the Managed System Element hierarchy.

Networks, in the form of the Network Element hierarchy.

Databases, in the form of a collection of database-related classes, mainly in the software package area of the schema.

Devices, in the form of the Device hierarchy.

Each domain area represents an aspect of the system that will be a common focus for a wide range of applications.

In addition to these domain-specific hierarchies, a nonspecific hierarchy in the form of the Usage Statistic class and its descendents sets up a location for statistical data and application-specific aggregations. These aggregations either extend or regroup other areas of the schema to accommodate the requirements of specific applications or groups of applications. Examples of these are the "perfmon" and "sysmon" groupings in Windows 95 and Windows NT and the SNMP MIBs. There are also various peer classes such as those required to model organizations and locations. Locations are represented in a rudimentary fashion; organizations are not represented in the schema.

Extension Schemas

The Extension schemas are technology-specific extensions to the Common schema. The Common schema is likely to evolve as a by-product of the promotion of objects and properties defined in the Extension schemas.

Managed Object Format

Management information is described in a language based on the Interface Definition Language (IDL), called the Managed Object Format (MOF), using Augmented BNF (Backus-Naur Form) notation. We use the term "MOF specification" to refer to a collection of management information that conforms to the MOF syntax and introduce elements of MOF syntax on a case-by-case basis with examples.

The MOF syntax is a way to describe object definitions in textual form and establishes the syntax for writing definitions. The main components of a MOF specification are textual descriptions of classes, associations, properties, references, methods, and instance declarations and their associated qualifiers. Provision is made for the inclusion of comments to help with the understanding of the schema.

In addition to specifying the managed objects, a MOF specification can be processed using a compiler, with the assistance of a series of compiler directives.

CIM in the Management Industry

The acceptance of CIM marks the first time in this industry that a common method of describing management information has been agreed upon and followed through with implementation. Other efforts have failed because of the lack of industry support. Because it is implementation independent, the model itself does not provide sufficient information for product development; rather, it is the specific product areas, applications, system, network, database, and devices and their product-specific extensions that enable workable solutions (see Figure 1.4).

As more organizations deploy CIM in the desktop, mobile, and server systems, we will need to create new management applications that can exploit the new management model and the related information. For example, where scanners and the like have to be written to look for information, this information will be available through CIM and its implementations.

Two major areas will implement the Common Information model:

- As a source for management information from desktop and server systems: agent-to-manager flow.

- As the method to describe management information among elements of a truly distributed management system: manager-to-manager.

Relationship to WBEM

Web-Based Enterprise Management (WBEM) was introduced by a number of companies in 1996 as an initiative to promote the use of Internet technologies for the management of desktops, servers, and all other Internet-related devices. The formal definition adopted by the DMTF upon acceptance of the initiative is:

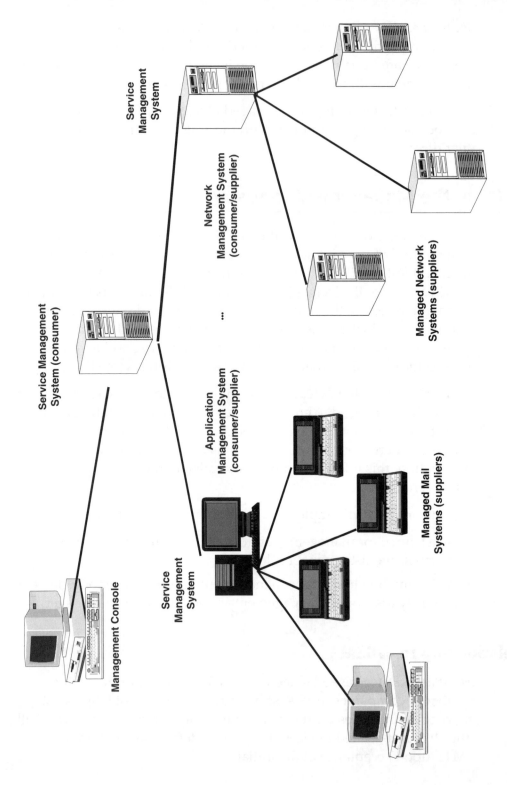

Figure 1.4 CIM in the enterprise.

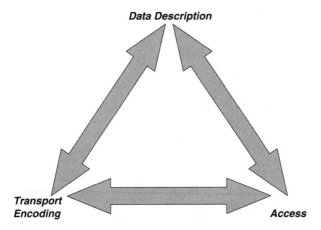

Figure 1.5   Management architectures.

Web-Based Enterprise Management is a set of management and Internet standard technologies developed to unify the management of enterprise computing environments.

There are three fundamental requirements for any management environment:

- A data description
- On-the-wire encoding
- A set of operations to manipulate the data (get, set, action, event)

These three—along with some form of identification mechanism that enables manager and agents to know who to talk to—are the requirements for a management environment (see Figure 1.5). The quality, and to some extent the quantity, of the management data determines how comprehensive or sophisticated management is. A system that returns only the fact that it exists, but does not tell the manager who it is (identification), what it is (configuration), and how it is (status), will be of limited value.

The current technologies that have been adopted, defined, or in the process of WBEM definition are (See Figure 1.6):

- A data definition format (CIM)
- An encoding for transport (xmlCIM)
- A set of HTTP operations that define how a management application acquires the management data (and how an agent has to respond to the operations).

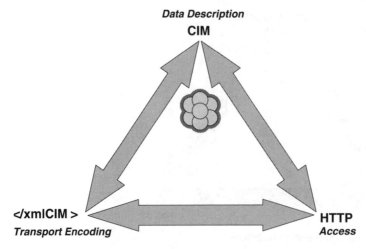

Data Description
CIM

</xmlCIM >
Transport Encoding

HTTP
Access

Figure 1.6 The WBEM triangle.

In addition, a management type definition (MTD) template is being defined that can be used by a location methodology such as the proposed IETF Service Location Protocol.

xmlCIM

The Extensible Markup Language (XML) is a simplified subset of SGML that offers powerful and extensible data-modeling capabilities. An *XML document* is a collection of data represented in XML. An *XML schema* is a grammar that describes the structure of an XML document.

There are two fundamentally different models possible for mapping CIM in XML:

Schema mapping. The XML schema is used to describe the CIM classes; CIM instances are mapped to valid XML documents for that schema. (Essentially this means that each CIM class generates its own document type definition (DTD) fragment, the XML element names of which are taken directly from the corresponding CIM element names.)

Metaschema mapping. The XML schema is used to describe the CIM metaschema, and both CIM classes and instances are valid XML documents for that schema. (In other words, the DTD is used to describe in a generic fashion the notion of a CIM class or instance. CIM element names are mapped to XML attribute or element values, rather than to XML element names.)

Although there are obvious additional benefits to employing a schema mapping (more validation power and a slightly more intuitive representation of CIM in XML), metaschema mapping was adopted for the following reasons:

- It requires only one standardized metaschema DTD for CIM, rather than an unbounded number of DTDs. This considerably reduces the complexity of management and administration of XML mappings.

- XML DTD does not allow an unordered list of elements. In a static mapping this would mean either fixing an arbitrary order for property, method, and qualifier lists (making it harder for a receiving application to process), or; defining a very unwieldy mapping, to take account of all list orderings explicitly (whose size would grow exponentially with the number of list elements).

- In a schema mapping, the names of CIM schema elements (class, property, qualifier, and method names) populate the XML element namespace. In order to replicate the scoping rules on CIM element names within XML DTD, it would be necessary to employ XML namespaces to define XML schema to per-property level of granularity. This would be extremely cumbersome to administer and process. A metaschema mapping introduces only a small, fixed number of terms into the XML element namespace (such as "class," "instance," "property," and so on). As an alternative to the introduction of additional XML namespaces, some renaming of CIM elements could be done (for example, prefixing a qualifier name with the name of its owning property and its owning class), but this would result in verbose XML documents that were difficult to understand.

- Although a schema mapping could allow XML-based validation of instances against classes, this would be possible only if the entire class hierarchy were flattened before mapping the CIM class to an XML schema. If this flattening were not performed, then inherited properties might be absent from the DTD, which would cause validation to fail against an instance that included the value of an inherited property.

CIM Operations over HTTP

The DMTF has defined a mapping of CIM operations onto HTTP that allows implementations of CIM to operate in an open, standardized manner. This mapping also defines the notion of conformance in the context of HTTP mapping and describes the behavior an implementation of CIM must exhibit in order to be described as a conforming CIM implementation. The HyperText Transfer Protocol (HTTP) is an application-level protocol for distributed, collaborative, hypermedia information systems. It is a generic stateless protocol, which can be used for many tasks through extension of its request methods, error codes, and headers.

Potentially, there are many different ways CIM operations could be represented within XML, and those operations encapsulated within HTTP messages. In the interest of interoperability among different implementations of CIM, there is an obvious requirement for standardization of both XML representation and HTTP encapsulation. The DMTF document uses XML representation to define the HTTP encapsulation.

The following criteria have been applied to the representation of CIM operations over HTTP.

- Each CIM operation is described completely in XML—completeness is favored over conciseness.

- The set of CIM operations provide sufficient functionality, which enables implementations of CIM to communicate effectively for the purposes of management. It is not a goal of the first release of the mapping to provide a *complete* set of operations, rather to allow for straightforward extension (addition of further features) in future versions.

- The CIM operations are classified into functional profiles to allow for a range of implementations (varying from complete support of all operations to support of a minimal subset). The number of functional profiles is kept as small as possible to encourage interoperability, and mechanisms are provided by which CIM implementations can declare their level of support.

The following criteria have been applied to the HTTP encapsulation of CIM operations:

- In recognition of the large installed base of HTTP/1.0 systems, the encapsulation is designed to support both HTTP/1.0 and HTTP/1.1.

- The encapsulation does not introduce any requirements that are in conflict with those stated in HTTP/1.0 or HTTP/1.1.

- The encapsulation should be usable in a straightforward manner over the current base HTTP infrastructures. Certain features are intended to anticipate and exploit enhancements to this base, but no aspects of the encapsulation should make any such enhancements mandatory.

- The encapsulation avoids the use of pure HTTP *tunneling* or URL *munging* (for example, the use of the question mark (?) character) in favor of a mechanism which allows existing HTTP infrastructures to safely control content.

- The encapsulation exposes key CIM operation information in headers to allow efficient firewall/proxy handling. The information is limited to what are considered essentials, so that the size of the header will not be significantly affected. No CIM-specific information appears in a header that does not also appear within the CIM operation.

- There is a clear and unambiguous encapsulation of the CIM operation payload within the HTTP message. Conciseness of the encapsulation is of secondary importance.

Common Data Representation

To repeat, sufficient, accurate, and timely data is key to management. Without it, any management architecture is of limited value. Administrators need management data to effectively carry out management tasks. It does not matter if the information is a visual display of raw data, a summary for management purposes, a simple automated solution to a system problem, or a very complex programmed analysis of a set of problems using artificial intelligence. All require accurate input information.

A great deal of academic work has been done on the classification of management data. ISO/IEC 7498-4 (Management Framework) defines five system management functional areas:

Accounting management

Configuration management

Performance management

Fault management

Security management

Accounting Management

Accounting management allows charges to be established for the use of resources in an OSI environment, and for costs to be identified for the use of those resources. Accounting management includes functions to:

- Inform users of costs incurred or resources consumed.
- Enable account limits to be set and tariff schedules to be associated with the use of resources.
- Enable costs to be combined where multiple resources are invoked to achieve a given objective.

Configuration Management

Configuration management identifies, exercises control over, collects data from, and provides data to open systems for the purpose of preparing for, initializing, starting, providing for continuous operation of, and terminating interconnection services.

Configuration management includes functions to:

- Set the parameters that control the routine operation of the open system.
- Associate names with managed objects and sets of managed objects.
- Initialize and close down managed objects.
- Collect on-demand information about the current condition of the open system.
- Obtain announcement of significant changes in the condition of the open system.
- Change the configuration of the open system.

Performance Management

Performance management enables evaluation of the behavior of resources in the OSI environment, as well as the effectiveness of communication activities. Performance management includes functions to:

- Gather statistical information.
- Maintain and examine logs of system state histories.

- Determine system performance under natural and artificial conditions.
- Alter system modes of operation for the purpose of conducting performance management activities.

Fault Management

Fault management encompasses fault detection, isolation, and the correction of abnormal operation of the OSI environment. Faults cause open systems to fail to meet their operational objectives, and they may be persistent or transient. Faults manifest themselves as particular events (for example, errors) in the operation of an open system. Error detection provides for the recognition of errors. Fault management includes functions to:

- Maintain and examine error logs.
- Accept and act upon error-detection notifications.
- Trace and identify faults.
- Carry out sequences of diagnostic tests.
- Correct faults.

Security Management

The purpose of security management is to support the application of security policies by means of these functions:

- Create, delete, and control security services and mechanisms.
- Distribute security-relevant information.
- Report security-relevant events.

When you expand these functions into traditional management topology such as in Figure 1.7, you can see that the same data can be used for a number of different management applications.

The key significance to using CIM for management definition across the various applications required to meet customer needs is that, in many cases, the data only has to be entered, retrieved, or transferred once; furthermore, because of the objected-oriented approach to data representation, complex relationships can be portrayed in a meaningful manner.

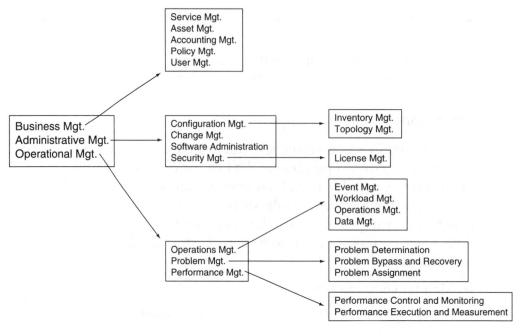

Figure 1.7 The multiple use of data in management.

References

Fayad, M., D. Schmidt, and R. Johnson. 1999. *Building Application Frameworks: Object-Oriented Foundations of Framework Design.* New York: John Wiley & Sons, Inc.

CHAPTER 2

CIM Basics— Concepts and Models

Object-Oriented Modeling

There is a tremendous amount of confusion over what is and what is not object-oriented (OO). Much of the confusion arises from the common insistence on a "what is . . ." approach to defining it. It is a common mistake to insist on correct definitions as opposed to accurate usage. The questions that need to be answered about OO are not what is it but rather what and who is it for and when should it be used. What object-oriented means will change from one context to another and will shift depending on whom you ask and when you ask. These three questions of what, who, and when will be covered in this and following chapters. Chapters 3 and 4 deal with the "what" question, chapters 9 and 10 deal with "who" and "when."

The Purpose of OO

The object-oriented paradigm can help you develop large complex systems by providing languages and associated environments that enforce well-established software engineering principles, including:

- Modularity
- Reuse
- Loose coupling
- Evolutionary development

In recent years, the consequences of using software development methodologies that do not enforce object-oriented principles have become increasingly serious. Systems have become more complex as a result of the increasing demands and sophistication of both administrators and end users. Many management information systems (MIS) organizations face the problem of managing old systems that were developed in an ad hoc and disorganized fashion using system development methodologies that fail to produce changeable, reliable, and maintainable systems. The object-oriented paradigm helps developers avoid such design pitfalls.

Increasing breadth and complexity of data-intensive applications in development further complicate the management landscape. Improvements in memory and disk capacity and raw processing power are leading to a whole new crop of complex applications. In the systems management area, this translates to an increase in the number and types of objects that must be represented and managed.

Industry evolution is leading to *data-intensive programming in the large*. A data-intensive program is one that produces and/or requires large amounts of data, and programming in the large refers to the software engineering process required for multiple programmers to produce large and complex programs. It is becoming increasingly important to be able to characterize the programming task as an engineering discipline that can be learned, not as an art to be mastered. By adhering to the principles of software engineering, the object-oriented paradigm, holds out such a promise.

Three fundamental concepts characterize the object-oriented paradigm:

Object orientation. The object is the basic unit of data. All values are objects. All sets are collections of objects. The system is object-oriented both in the data that the user stores in the system and in the data used to manage the system.

Inheritance. Provides support for the notion of classes and subclasses. Both structural and behavioral inheritance are provided within the system. That is, properties and operations declared for a superclass are inherited by all of its subclasses. If manager is a subclass of employee and employee has a name, it necessarily follows that all managers also have a name.

Data abstraction and encapsulation. An object has an interface part and an implementation. The interface consists of the operations supported by the object. The implementation comprises the data structures and algorithms provided to support those operations.

Other object-oriented concepts, such as polymorphism, can be derived from and are implied by these three concepts.

Traditionally, analysis produces two separate outcomes. One is a collection of data structures, records, fields, and so on, which captures the data needed to manage the application. The other outcome is a collection of algorithms that represent the behavior of the application. The object-oriented data model captures both the behavioral and structural semantics of applications.

For example, in Figure 2.1, a UML diagram of a gas pump, the pump object has operations IncAmount, ReadAmount, and so on, as well as state reflected by AmountDispensed and DeliveryCost. The intention of the model is to provide a view of the way the information is represented that closely corresponds to the way the user perceives the corresponding objects in the real world.

The UML model captures all aspects of an application; this includes both persistent and nonpersistent objects. It offers a reverse engineering tool that enables the expression of the semantics of an existing system; in addition, its software architecture allows an object-oriented layer to be placed on top of a traditional record-based system.

We can describe the advantages provided by the object-oriented paradigm in terms of its major features:

Object identity. Every object has a unique identifier. The system recognizes the identifier and is responsible for ensuring that it is unique. In all cases, given an identifier, the system can efficiently locate the corresponding object.

Types and classes. Objects are grouped into classes. A class corresponds to the natural idea of a collection of similar things. The process of classification, whereby we assign an object to a class, and

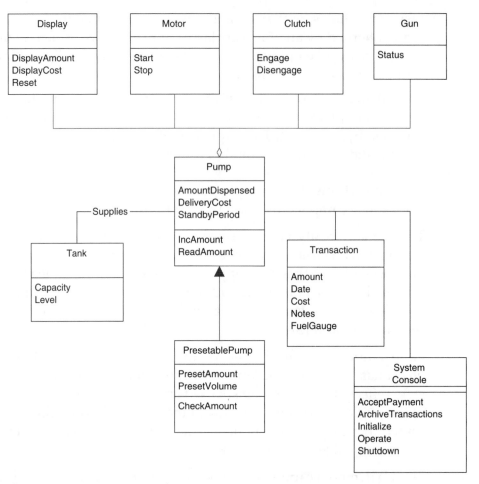

Figure 2.1 Gas pump example.

the implied process of identifying the class itself are fundamental to understanding the world around us. The object-oriented paradigm directly captures this process. It allows the analysts to represent their insight and understanding in a language that closely mirrors the terms in which they formulated the understanding in the first place.

Classes and subclasses. These, too, mirror natural modes of dealing with the real world in the form of generalization and specialization. If, for example, in the class of managers, every manager must be an employee, then manager is a subclass of employee (see Figure 2.2). Generalization refers to the process whereby a series of specialized objects—for example managers, contractors, part-time workers and foreign workers—are generalized to the class of employee. That is,

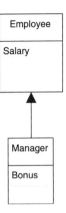

Figure 2.2   Classes, subclasses, and inheritance.

all of these descriptions are special cases of employees. For many purposes it is important to be able to deal with them simply as employees, and not have to be concerned with the variations among the types. The reverse of generalization is specialization. Here we must be able to look at a particular employee as a manager, not forgetting that he is also an employee. Being able to focus on a specific type of employee may again be an important simplification of an otherwise intractable problem. It is essential to be able to restrict the scope of an inquiry as the inquiry becomes more detailed.

Inheritance. Inheritance provides a view of the subclass/superclass hierarchy, which automatically presents to the user the complete set of properties applicable to any given class. In CIM, inheritance is a consequence of the presence of classes and subclasses. Where a class, for example, Manager, inherits from some other class, such as Employee, inheritance ensures that the properties applicable to employees are also available for managers. This is a natural consequence of the fact that every manager, by definition, is an employee. It follows that anything that applies to an employee must also apply to a manager because a manager is an employee. Inheritance is sometimes referred to as an "is-a" relationship. This follows from the common English usage in which "is a" defines the relationship between a subclass and its superclass, for example "a manager is a person."

Complex objects. A complex object is an object perceived as made up of other objects. The object-oriented paradigm supports complex objects by representing relationships using references to other objects. There is an explicit statement of the existence and interpretation of any relationships between objects. The language of the model uses the relationships themselves as data. For example, the component relationship between a pump and the parts that make up the pump is a feature of the pump. It is then natural to look at and manipulate a pump as an object made up of a group of related parts. This idea of parts and wholes represents a fundamental mode of understanding the world around us. In addition to classifying objects, people naturally group objects into complex wholes. A major simplification can be achieved by dealing with the whole rather than with the detail and complexity represented by the separate parts that make up the whole.

Encapsulation. An object has an interface and an implementation. The interface consists of the operations supported by the object. The implementation comprises the data structures and algorithms provided to support those operations. Encapsulation is the isolation of the internal details of the management of the object. Through encapsulation, the object-oriented paradigm provides direct support for the software engineering principles of modularity and loose coupling. For example, the property location of employee may be stored for each employee or it may be derived from the location of the employee's department. Any process not directly concerned with the maintenance of the location property does not have to be aware of these details. Encapsulation implies that the analyst is always dealing with a problem of limited scope. Objects are grouped into classes; classes may be specialized into subclasses; and related groups of objects may be dealt with as a single complex object. Through encapsulation, all of these different groupings appear as different contexts within which the analyst can formulate algorithms and understand the behavior and characteristics of data structures without worrying about other extraneous features of the system.

Polymorphism. The implementation of the same operation may vary from one object to the next depending on the type of the object. Salary of manager, for example, may include a bonus computation that does not apply to regular employees. The object-oriented paradigm separates an operation from its implementation. The implementation is often referred to as a *method*. The operation is the public interface that remains the same across all objects. The method is the actual algorithm used to derive the result of the operation. As a result of polymorphism, it is possible to provide different methods for the same operation in different classes. Salary may be defined as an operation *on* Employee. There may be a default salary method that will be used if an object is just an employee. Each subclass of Employee may provide its own salary method, allowing managers to have bonuses, and hourly workers to be paid overtime.

Overriding, overloading, and late binding. Subclasses and inheritance imply polymorphism. Polymorphism in turn implies several other concepts. Overriding is the process whereby the method for a superclass is replaced by, or overridden by, a method supplied by a subclass. The superclass method will only be overridden if the object involved is a member of the subclass. Late binding is required because it is not always possible to determine in advance to which subclasses an object may belong. If a user requests the average salary of all employees, the salary operation will be invoked for each employee. The method used will depend on the type of each employee. It is not possible then to produce code ahead of time for the computation of salary that represents a single, simple expression. The choice of method must be delayed until a particular object is interrogated. Overloading is a special form of overriding whereby the primitive operations of the model may be overridden. For example, EQL may be redefined for strings allowing for case-insensitive string comparisons.

Extensibility. An object-oriented system is extensible in that the user can add new classes and types to the system. The new features can be manipulated using the standard operations of the model. The classes and types themselves can be further extended with operations of their own, allowing structural and behavioral extensions to be added to the model.

Through its fundamental concepts and the set of features derived from those concepts, the object-oriented paradigm provides support for well-established software engineering principles that support a reliable, controllable application development process.

CIM Concepts and Terminology

The following sections will describe the main concepts of the Common Information Model. These all flow from the object-oriented concepts described in the first part of the chapter and include:

- Schemas which are a collection of definitions
- Classes which are object types and their instances
- Various relationships between classes and instances such as inheritance and association
- The mechanisms used for identifying instances in the form of keys

Schema

The term "schema" has been defined variously in the context of the object-oriented paradigm. The following are most pertinent to the discussion at hand:

- A namespace and unit of ownership for a set of classes. Schemas may come in forms that include text file, information in a repository, or diagrams in a CASE tool (see, for example, the CIM Specification to be found at www.dmtf.org).
- A collection of class definitions that describe managed objects in a particular environment.

Before beginning to extend or design a schema, it's helpful to be cognizant of its purpose. A schema is deemed essential when there is a need to model things that exist in the real world; and so that others can understand us when we refer to these real things, we formalize them into statements in a language of some sort. The rules and procedures that link the real world to the formal world are known as *operational semantics*.

People use operational semantics to interpret the information supplied by a schema. For example, an operator, seeing that a database audit file is 70 percent full, switches to a new audit file, backs up the old one, and removes it. The operator's interpretation of the information ("audit file is 70 percent full") is what gives it meaning. Without the interpretation—or, to put it another way, if the schema has no consequence—the schema and the information it provides are literally meaningless. Simply put, meaning can be measured only in terms of consequences; a piece of information that has no consequences in the real world is, by definition, meaningless.

A schema is dependent on the existence of operational semantics; on its own, the schema is not meaningful. It acquires meaning only if someone is willing and able to interpret it. As a schema designer, you are dependent on and restricted by the level of understanding of the users and programmers who will use your schema. A schema is worthless if no one understands it or is willing to use it. The operational semantics (i.e., the ability of someone to interpret the schema) is an integral part, possibly the most important part, of the schema and should always be in the forefront of your mind when putting a schema together.

When designing a schema, keep in mind that you are creating a language by which to communicate the structure of things (both physical and logical elements) within an information system. This structure will grow over time and will be interpreted by its various users. In the nature of things, you cannot define the absolute meaning of the structure; nevertheless, you must strive for a reasonable balance between level of detail and comprehension. You need to provide enough detail to be useful, but not so much as to make the schema overwhelmingly complex.

Schema Modification

The following list supports schema modifications, some of which, when used, will result in changes in application behavior. Changes are all subject to security restrictions; in particular, only the owner of the schema, or someone authorized by the owner, can make modifications to the schema.

- A class can be added to or deleted from a schema.
- A property can be added to or deleted from a class.
- A class can be added as a subtype or supertype of an existing class.
- A class can become an association as a result of the addition of an Association qualifier, plus two or more references.
- A qualifier can be added to or deleted from any Named Element.
- The Override qualifier can be added to or removed from a property or reference.
- A class can alias a property (or reference, if the class is a descendent of an association), using the Alias qualifier. Both inherited and immediate properties of the class may be aliased.

- A method can be added to a class.

- A method can override an inherited method.

- Methods can be deleted, and the signature of a method can be changed.

- A trigger may be added to or deleted from a class.

In defining an extension to a schema, the schema designer must operate within the constraints of the classes defined in the Core Model. With respect to classification, any added component of a system should be defined as a subclass of an appropriate Core Model class. The schema designer should address the following question for each of the Core Model classes: Is the class being added a subtype of this class? Once the Core Model class to be extended has been identified, the designer should answer the same question with respect to each of the subclasses of the identified class. This process, which defines the superclasses of the class to be defined, should be continued until the most detailed class has been identified. The Core Model is not a part of the metaschema, but is an important device for introducing uniformity across schemas intended to represent aspects of the managed environment.

Schema Versions

Certain modifications to a schema can cause failure in applications that operated against the schema prior to modification. These modifications include:

- Deletion of classes, properties, or methods

- Movements of a class anywhere other than down a hierarchy

- Alteration of property type or method signature

- Alteration of a reference range to anything other than the original specification

Other alterations are considered to be interface preserving—that is, the introduction of the change will not impact a program or query that worked against the schema prior to the change. Using the schema changes just listed implies the generation of a new major version of the schema (DMTF 1999).

Classes

A class is a collection of instances, all of which support a common type, that is, a set of properties and methods. The common properties and methods are defined as features of the class. For example, the class called Modem represents all the modems present in a system. In the WBEM context, a class defines the basic unit of management. Each class is a template for a type of managed object; all instances of the type use the template. Classes can contain properties, which describe the data of the class, and methods, which describe the behavior of the class (DMTF 1999).

A class may participate in associations by being the target of one of the references owned by the association. Classes also have instances and can be static or dynamic. Instances of a static class are stored by the object manager using some persistent data store and retrieved on request, whereas instances of a dynamic class are generated by a provider. Third-party developers can define custom classes to support managed objects that are specific to their managed environment. For example, a custom class can be defined to represent a specific database or type of tape drive. Developers can use the object manager API to define new classes or the MOF language. For example, in WBEM, Win32_DiskDrive is a class. All devices that fall under the category of disk drive on a Win32-based system belong to this class.

Classes can be thought of as nothing more than a mechanism for classifying objects encountered in the real world. We use the term "class" in the same sense as in the science of biology. The essential characteristic of such a class is that it must always be possible, given some object from the real world, to answer the question: Is this object a member of the class?

There are two recognized ways of identifying an object as a member of a class:

- *Establish a condition that an object must satisfy to be considered a member of the class.* For example, a condition may specify: "has three sides, and one of the internal angles is 90^0." The condition defines the class of right triangles.

- *Provide an exhaustive list of the members of the class.* For example "Clinton, Nixon, and Andrew Johnson" define the class of impeached presidents. A database would store and provide the list of instances of the class on demand, thereby giving an operational definition of the class in terms of its current set of instances. This method is typical of data management systems.

It is very important to recognize that the accuracy and consistency of the classifications that the data model represents largely determine its integrity and usefulness. Each time you define a class, it is essential to have an absolutely clear idea of its membership criteria.

It is also important to recognize that classes are really just logical constructs and may not correspond to any aspect of the real world. There are innumerable ways to divide the world into entities and classify them. No one way is mandatory or absolutely correct. Any classification scheme will only be valid within the frame of reference it was devised and is likely to be quite meaningless outside of that frame.

The class defines a set of properties and other features that can be thought of as part of the defining criteria for the class. For example, the class Person may have the property Name. This statement simply translates to: If something is classified as an instance of the class Person then it must have a name. Each of the properties and methods defined for a class is assumed to apply to or be supported by each of the instances of the class. In a sense, support for the features of the class is what makes something an instance of the class. As the saying goes, "If it smells like a pig, feels like a pig, and looks like a pig, it is a pig!"

Abstract classes are those that do not have instances directly. Instead, they may have instances as a result of a subclass having instances; but the class never has an instance that is not a member of any of the subclasses of the class. A second possibility is that the abstract class may define a type, not a class in the sense of an enumerable set of instances.

Generally, object systems make the assumption that instance types are immutable, meaning that once an instance is defined as a particular type, never will the same object become some other type. In reality, however, this happens all the time. Consider for example a person in a university database. The person may begin as an applicant, then become a student, and eventually become an instructor. The difficulty in most systems is that the identity of the object is tied up with the type of the object; if the type changes, the object identity changes as well.

This process of changing the type of an object is known as *metamorphosis*. There is nothing in CIM to prevent it. In fact, metamorphosis is effectively required in an instrumentation scenario. It is unlikely that all of the information about a device or system will be discernible when the object is first encountered. For example, the operating system may be able to determine that a device is attached to a bus and has a specific device identifier; but the system may require specialized instrumentation, which can only be added at a later time, to determine that the device is of a specific type. So the cycle begins with an abstract notion of a device as a generic type and adds specializations as more information becomes available.

Instances

According to the CIM specification, an instance is a unit of data; it is a set of property values that can be uniquely identified by a key. Instances represent the members of a class. A given instance can be a member of more than one class, provided the classes have a subclass-superclass relationship. For example an instance of CIM_Modem is also an instance of CIM_LogicalDevice because one is a subclass of the other.

In object-oriented terminology, instances are sometimes referred to as objects. The use of the term "object" is equivocal because "object" is also used to refer to a class. For example in "a person is an object; the first president of the United States is an object" the first use of the term "object" refers to a class; the second use refers to an instance.

Superclasses and Subclasses

A subclass is derived from a superclass. The subclass inherits all features of its superclass, but can add new features or redefine existing ones. superclass is the class from which a subclass inherits (DMTF 1999).

A class is said to be a subclass of another class if all the members (or instances) of the first class are also members of the second class. Put another way, a subclass cannot have an instance that is not an instance of all of its superclasses.

Inheritance, Subsets, Venn Diagrams, and Boolean Logic

Inheritance is a relationship between two classes in which all members of the subclass are required to be members of the superclass. Any member of the subclass must also support any method or property supported by the superclass. For example, Modem is a subclass of Device. Venn diagrams are a common convention for representing class relationships. The relationship between Modem and Device would appear as in Figure 2.3. An instance, indicated by X, contained in the region marked Modem is necessarily in the region marked Device because the Modem region is contained in the Device region.

It is important to recognize that inheritance is a relationship between *classes* not between instances. Not making this distinction results in bizarre hierarchies, such as the X500 schema in which a Computer is classified as a Person. There are, no doubt, good reasons why this was done, but a computer is clearly not a type of person, and it is inappropriate to interpret the relationship between them as one of inheritance (as the term is being used here). Relationships between instances are illustrated by Figure 2.4, again in the context of a Venn diagram. It illustrates the idea of relationships between instances, in this case between a modem labeled x and a COM port labeled y.

A similar idea can be communicated using predicates; for example, the idea that modem X is a member of the class Modem and, by implication, a member of the class Device could be defined as:

$$(\forall (x) \; \text{Modem}(z) \; \rightarrow \; \text{Device}(z) \; \& \; \text{Modem}(x)) \; \rightarrow \; \text{Device}(x)$$

Or given that for all z: z is a modem implies z is a device and the instance x is a Modem; it follows that the instance x is a device. In this fashion, there is a very close, if at times complex, relationship between data models and logic.

Domain, Range, and Type

Classes in the model provide sets of instances, each of which must be distinguishable. Instances can be distinguished by using an arbitrary object identifier (OID) or by designating some properties of the instance as keys. In the case of a keyed object, any two instances with

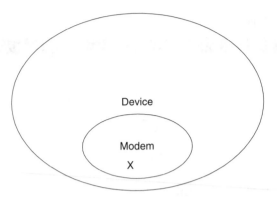

Figure 2.3   Classes and Venn diagrams.

the same key values are considered to correspond to the same underlying object.

The idea of a class as a set of instances can be understood in terms of the idea in set theory of the fundamental definition of a class. In set theory, there are two ways of defining a class: by providing a comprehensive list of the members of the class, or by providing clear criteria that can be used to recognize members of the class. The critical idea is that to have a usable definition of a class, it is necessary to be able to distinguish objects that belong to the class from objects that do not belong to it. These two techniques for defining classes are sometimes referred to, respectively, as *definition by extension* (providing the list of members or the extent of the class) and *definition by intension* (providing an algorithm that can be used to recognize members of the class).

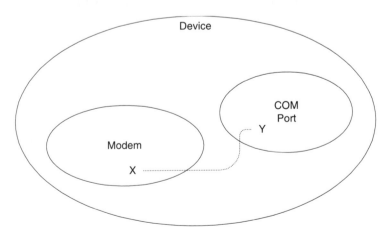

Figure 2.4   Relationships between instances.

Table 2.1 Class of n and n^2 Integers

n	n^2
1	1
2	4
3	9
4	16
5	25

When designing a class, it is important to understand that you must be able to provide a good definition of the class, preferably an extensional definition. If you cannot provide an extensional definition, you must establish criteria that allow a competent user to understand when an object belongs or does not belong to the proposed class—often a very tricky task. For example, in CIM, it is very difficult to provide a good positive definition of the members of the LogicalElement class. In practice, traditionally it has been defined by exclusion; that is, a LogicalElement is any element of a system that is not a PhysicalElement, since physical items are much easier to distinguish.

The distinction between classes defined by extension and intension is well illustrated by the distinction between a type and a class. In CIM, classes are always enumerable—it is always reasonable to ask for the current set of members of a class. Furthermore, classes do not have an algorithmic criterion that can be used to determine the members of the class (other than enumerating the current set of members). By contrast, it is generally difficult to ask for the members of a type; consider, for example, enumerating all the possible temperatures between 0 degrees

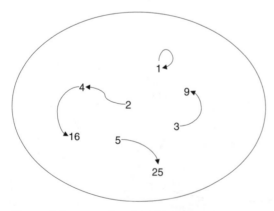

Figure 2.5 Mappings integers to squares.

Table 2.2   Employee and Employee Number

EMPLOYEE NUMBER	FIRST NAME
31731	John

Celsius and 100 degrees. Admittedly, if the granularity of the enumeration admits only one-degree intervals, there are only 100 values and enumeration is not too difficult. But in reality, temperature is a floating-point value, and a wide range of discrete temperature values between one degree and the next exist; the limit is dictated only by the precision of the variable we choose to use.

Types then are sets of values defined by intension; classes are sets of values that are defined by extension. Classes and types can be characterized by mappings between them. For example Table 2.1 provides a mapping between the class of integers n and the class n^2. The mapping is purely positional, provided by the correspondence between rows and columns in the table. The same information could be given as in Figure 2.5, where the mapping is indicated by lines between the relevant numbers.

Note in the figure that the information provided by the line between 5 and 25 in the diagram is the same as the row in Table 2.1 pairing 5 and 25; this is equivalent to saying that the square of 5 is 25. In the same way we can represent the idea that the first name of employee number 31731 is John either in a tabular form (Table 2.2) or as a mapping between sets (Figure 2.6).

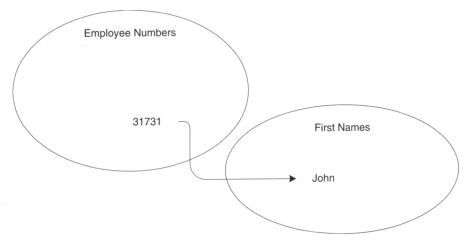

Figure 2.6   Mapping employee numbers to first names.

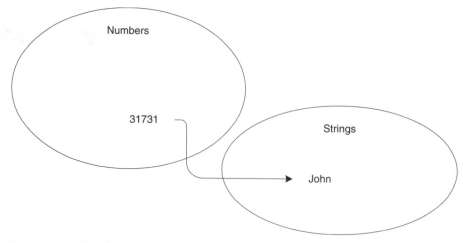

Figure 2.7   Mapping numbers to strings.

An interesting point raised by the diagram in Figure 2.6 is that Employee Numbers are not in the same set as First Names. In some ways, Figure 2.7 is an equivalent diagram; the two sets have just been relabeled. In Figure 2.7, we have a mapping between numbers—in this case employee number and strings—and first names. We could also have a mapping between employees and departments, as in Table 2.3.

Some interesting issues arise out of this. First, again the table is clearly a mapping between numbers and strings although the table description led us to expect a mapping between employees and departments. Presumably, what is happening is that the numbers in some sense stand for or represent the employees, and, similarly, the string stands for the department. These values are being used as surrogates or stand-ins for the objects in question. We represent the case as a Venn diagram in Figure 2.8. Here again we are dealing with mappings between sets of objects, but in this case both objects are classes—they are defined by extension not by intension. The diagram also emphasizes the idea that the employee and department objects are not the same thing as any one of the mappings used to characterize them. You cannot say that a department is the same as its name or that an

Table 2.3   Departments and Employees

EMPLOYEE NUMBER	DEPARTMENT NAME
31731	Toys
54729	Furniture

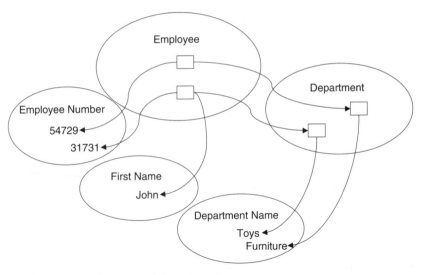

Figure 2.8   Employees and departments.

employee is the same as their employee number; this is represented graphically by the unlabeled rectangles for basic objects that cannot be identified with a single instance of some simple type (that is, a string or a number).

Figure 2.8 also illustrates the idea that these mappings are directional. The diagram can be read as "John is the name of an employee," or as "31731 is the employee number of an employee." In these statements, employee is sometimes referred to as the *domain,* and the related value is referred to as the *range.* Strictly speaking, the domain is a set of values, as is the range.

The existence of mappings between sets provides the basic mechanism for defining information within a data model. It is very important to understand that all relationships, all techniques of characterizing objects, are nothing more than mappings of one kind or another. In designing a model, you should be careful not to think in terms of specific types of mapping. Definition is more than just the decision about whether a set will be defined by intension or extension (that is, whether to use types or classes). That decision is often intimately bound with the details of how the information will be stored and used; often, however, this is not understood in the early phases of model design. Indeed, any modeling technique that requires such information in the early phases of the design process is probably itself poorly designed.

Consider, for example, dates. The set of valid dates is naturally thought of as a set defined intentionally. It is unlikely that anyone would establish a system in which all of the possible dates were explicitly stored as instances in a permanent store of some kind. This becomes even more obvious if clock time is taken into account. Dates are much more likely to be treated as primitive types within the system. Imagine for a moment a systems administration application intended for use as a part of a scheduling system; in this system, events occur on specific dates, and the operator must be able to schedule jobs that are to be run on specific dates. Given that a date is just a characteristic of a job, there seems little point in treating it as anything other than a nonenumerable type. Another way of saying this is: Dates are not interesting except in the context of a specific job.

If it later turns out that an operator needs to be able to see all the jobs due to run on a specific date, dates become more interesting in their own right. This could of course be represented simply by sorting the jobs in date order, to enable the operator to see which jobs will occur on a given date. Perspective alone is not enough to force us to consider a date as an object, in the same sense that a job is an object—one that is defined by extension. Take the case where an operator has to be able to block a date. Here, information must be associated with the date itself, independent of how it will be used elsewhere. The date must be stored, in some sense, independently of any specific job to allow the required date association. See Figure 2.9 for a graphic representation. The figure introduces the set of Blocked Dates as a subset of the set of Dates. Blocked Dates are defined by extension; that is, the system keeps an explicit list of Blocked Dates, but dates are defined intentionally. There is no explicit list of dates, though the system can recognize a valid date when it is presented with one.

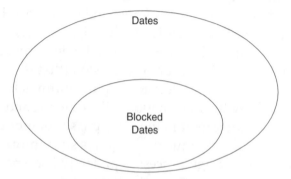

Figure 2.9 Blocked dates.

Properties

Properties are simply a convention for representing mappings between sets. A property is a value used to denote a characteristic of a class; it can be thought of as a pair of functions, one to set the property value and one to return the property value. A property has a name and only one domain: the class that owns the property. A property can have an override relationship with another property from a different class. The domain of the overridden property must be a superclass of the domain of the overriding property. For example, in WBEM, the Win32_DiskDrive class has numerous properties, such as manufacturer, sectors, system name, size, and so on.

Methods

A method is an operation that describes the behavior of a class. Not all classes have methods. Typically, in object-oriented information models, methods are only added as the model matures. The early versions of the CIM Schema, for example, had very few methods. More are being added over time. A method has a name and only one domain: the class that owns the method. Like a property, a method can have an override relationship with another method from a different class. The domain of the overridden method must be a superclass of the domain of the overriding method.

Note that a class having a method does not guarantee an implementation of the method. To indicate that an implementation is available for the class, the Implemented qualifier is attached to the method.

When a derived class inherits a method, it inherits only the definition; it does not inherit the implementation, and must supply its own. When executing a method, CIMOM starts at the lowest subclass in the class hierarchy and works toward the base class, searching for the Implemented qualifier. For example, a class called Service may have Start and Stop methods. The method would return a Boolean value depending on whether the service was started or stopped.

Associations and References

An association is a mechanism for providing an explicit mapping between classes. In contrast, properties *imply* a mapping between a class and a primitive type, such as a string or a number. CIM assumes that the relationship between classes is less fundamental to the characterization of the object than the mappings to primitive types. The intention of the model is that the schema designer will use a basic set of primitive types to provide information that characterizes the object. Additional information is then provided through the use of associations and extended properties that augment the basic data about the object in arbitrary ways.

In CIM, associations are declared so that the existence of the association is not reflected in the syntax used to declare the object itself. This is an important aspect of the model as it implies that a schema designer can add features to a class through associations without impacting the class itself. This allows schema designers to work independently of each other even though they may be augmenting some common classes.

Inverses

An important notion in associations is that of an *inverse relationship*. Consider the marriage relationship: It involves two roles, namely husband and wife. Assume that a separate association is defined for husband and wife (that is, the schema designer did not recognize a relationship between the two roles). It would then be possible for an object representing a woman to have a husband relationship with a person that does not have the woman as a wife. The anomaly introduced is a reflection of the lack of recognition of the relationship between the husband and wife roles. Clearly, in such a case, the relationship is obvious enough not to be missed; but in practice, it is very easy to miss such correlations and establish schemas in which expected inverse relationships may be separately expressed and therefore susceptible to being established in an invalid way.

CIM decreases the likelihood of invalidly expressed inverse relationships by requiring all associations to be expressed as separate classes in which the various roles of the relationship are expressed as reference properties on the association. In the marriage example, the association would call a class called Marriage with two roles, Husband and Wife, of type Man and Woman, respectively.

Referential Integrity

A system has referential integrity where any of the references (or roles) encountered in associations are guaranteed to refer to valid instances. This can be a major undertaking, as it implies that any time an instance is deleted, all of the associations that might refer to the instance have to be tracked down and updated to reflect the fact that the instance no longer exists. Though this is not required by the CIM standard, a consistent policy is essential for any reasonable implementation.

Indications

In any management environment much management information will be delivered as a result of events in the environment. A certain amount of static data is obviously significant, but the majority of the significant data will likely be in the form of events. Events in CIM are referred to as *indications*. In CIM, events are modeled as classes. The occurrence of the event is reflected by the generation of an instance of the event class. Event instances do not have persistence; in effect, they only exist at the time the event occurs, and special mechanisms must be provided for their detection and consumption.

Events and Architectures

In any management application, how events are handled largely dictates the architecture. A major problem is how the massive flow of events available at the source can be aggregated and filtered to a volume that is both useful and meaningful, yet not be unmanageable. Much event design and processing revolves around issues of filtering and aggregating events as close to the source as possible and to providing efficient logging and event rollup. An effective architecture for handling events is likely to involve multiple layers, caching, and more or less reliable delivery mechanisms, depending on the requirements at hand.

Push versus Pull

Events can be provided in two ways: Events may be *pushed* from a source, in which case the processes running at the source are responsible for initiating the communication that delivers the event; or events may be *pulled* from a source, in which case the process that consumes the event is responsible for polling the event source and determining whether an event has occurred. Both approaches have significant advantages under certain circumstances.

Events and Logs

Instances in event classes in CIM do not have persistence. If the event instances are to be examined over time, it is necessary to deliver the event to some sort of logging mechanism. The log provides a mechanism that can be used to examine the state of the system over time. The types of queries that can be processed against the log will depend on how the log is organized and the type of information captured from the event in the first place. For example, deltas might be captured without also capturing complete state, in which case it would be possible to answer a question such as "what changed yesterday?" It would not be possible to answer a question such as "what did the object look like yesterday?"

Qualifiers

Information about the object model can be divided into two broad categories: information about the objects in the model (represented in the form of properties) and information about the way the objects are provided (represented in the form of qualifiers). Qualifiers are mechanisms for supplying implementation-specific data and hints to the user of the data that explain how the data might be used, provided, or displayed.

There may be cases where you question whether to represent an item of information as a property or a qualifier. In general, qualifiers are values that apply to the class as a whole and define how all instances or properties should be handled. Properties are generally values that vary from one instance to another and do not relate to the way the data is displayed or provided.

Extending the Meta-model

Qualifiers can be thought of as a simple way for a schema designer to extend the meta-model. For example, if a database provides a series of classes in such a way that each class is defined by a single table in the database, it may be desirable to write a generic provider for the class that reads a table and produces the instances of the class. You can introduce a new qualifier that captures the name of the table to be used with the class at hand.

Override

Overriding is the process whereby a property or method provided by a subclass is used as a substitute for a property or method provided by a superclass. For example, the CIM_Battery class has a property EstimatedChargeRemaining. Let's assume a laptop manufacturer has a special and proprietary technique for accurately estimating the value. The manufacturer can provide a subclass with a provided value for EstimatedChargeRemaining that takes advantage of the proprietary technique and overrides the value supplied for the generic implementation of the CIM_Battery class.

Naming and Keys

There are two recognized approaches to providing identifiers for instances in an object-oriented model, namely keys and object identifiers. Object identifiers are arbitrary values that provide a "name" for an instance so that when given the object identifier, the instance can be located efficiently. Object identifiers are contentless in that they have no intrinsic meaning; they are just arbitrary values with no significance outside of the object system itself.

Keys, on the other hand, are designated properties that are required to be unique across all the instances of the class. Because keys are properties, they are generally meaningful in the environment outside of the object system. This meaning is important in an instrumentation scenario in which the objects known to the system must be readily translatable into objects present in the environment being managed, and similarly, objects in the environment must be translatable into objects in the object system. This two-way automated translation is essential for instrumentation, and therefore effectively requires CIM to use keys as the primary mechanism for object identification.

Note, any practical object-oriented database would have to at least support the notion of unique properties or combinations of properties to enable a user to readily identify objects in the system even where the system itself uses object identifiers.

Weak Associations

An object must have a set of properties designated as the keys that will adequately distinguish the instances across the contexts in which queries and other operations are performed. For example a device may require both device identifier and system name as keys to allow the device to be adequately identified in queries that span multiple systems. Because system name is not a property of device, some technique is required for describing the propagation of the system name key to the device. This is accomplished in CIM by the use of weak associations and propagated keys.

In a *weak association,* one of the roles is defined as being weak using the Weak qualifier. The keys of the string side of the relationship are copied across to the weak side and marked with the Propagated qualifier. This qualifier takes as a parameter the name of the key as it appeared in the original class, allowing the property to be renamed if necessary.

The disadvantage of the weak association arrangement is that a great deal has to be understood about the contexts in which the instance will be used across its lifetime. If, at some stage, it is necessary to query the instance in a context broader than that in which it was originally defined, you can only do so at the expense of copying the instance and augmenting the key, thereby changing the name of the instance and effectively making it a different object. You will lose any associations with the original instance and will need to recompute them.

This chapter has covered the basic concepts underlying the Common Information Model (CIM) and the object-oriented model on which it is based. The next chapter will move on to the subject of some of the basic concepts you need to understand in order to design extensions to the Common Information Model. Schema design is rather a large topic and will be tackled in three parts. We will begin with an outline of some of the basic concepts used in designing schemas; this is covered in the next chapter. After looking at some examples of schemas in the form of the systems, devices, and application models covered in Chapters 4 through 8, Chapters 9 and 10 will look at the schema design process (Chapter 9) and how to apply the concepts covered in the rest of the book (Chapter 10).

References

There is a huge literature on object-oriented models, most of it heavily biased towards object-oriented programming rather than object-oriented data modeling. Peter Gray's book on logic, algebra and databases is an excellent source on much of the theory underlying the discussion in this and the later chapters on schemas and modeling. The article by Stamper is a classic on the significance of models and the approach used in this and other chapters on modeling and design has been heavily influenced by Stamper's writing.

DMTF, CIM specification 2.2, June 1999, obtainable from www.dmtf.org

Gray, Peter. 1985. *Logic, Algebra, and Databases*, Ellis Horwood series.

Stamper, Ronald. 1977. "Physical Objects, Human Discourse and Formal Systems." *Architecture and Models in Database Management Systems*, G. M. Nijssen (ed.), North-Holland.

CHAPTER 3

Schema Design Concepts

Modeling

Because modeling is equivalent to systems design in terms of its difficulty and complexity, you must approach it seriously. To be successful as a modeler you must be familiar with the modeling language, have a clear understanding of the tasks involved in modeling, have adequate information about the domain you will be modeling, and have the highest-caliber experts available to validate the models you produce.

What Is a Model?

The most common question an object-oriented designer faces is, "What is an object?" There are number of different answers to this question—each depending on the context. If the context is analysis, the most common answer is: "The objects are the nouns." This answer, however, doesn't help you, because it leaves you asking, "What are the nouns?" The obvious answer is "objects!"

Objects are an abstraction mechanism that provides a language that facilitates the description of a *universe of discourse* (UoD). A UoD must have at least three parts: a set of *types,* a set of *operations* that can be used to manipulate the types, and a set of *instances* of the types. Welcome to Set Theory 101.

The trick is to devise not just a UoD but to devise a *useful* UoD. To be useful, the UoD must have some kind of connection to the real world. There are many useful things to say about how this kind of connection can be established. A large and diverse literature in operational research and the philosophy of science reflect the enormity of this challenge: How do you connect a language to the thing the language describes?

Identifying the nouns is not the difficulty. The difficulty lies in determining how to tie the types and instances of the UoD to the patterns and things in the real world. Although there are no hard and fast answers, some of the work that has been done in this area is very helpful, in particular, the work by Ronald Stamper and his associates at the London School of Economics and the University of Twente in the Netherlands (Stamper 1977). Stamper's concept of formal systems is presented as a view of the "real world." This view has three important aspects:

- The *real world,* where the action is.
- The *formal world,* where everything of interest is recorded and described in a formal language of some kind.
- The procedures performed by people, which link the real world to the formal world. Stamper calls these "operational semantics."

The conceptual schema is a specialized piece of the formal world that helps to tie the formal semantics (the rules that govern behavior in the formal system) to the operational semantics.

In Stamper's world there is no such thing as a simple noun. Rather, a noun is a formally defined object that has an operationally effective procedure that links it to an object in the real world. Analysis consists of the process of establishing a formal system with useful semantics so that the objects contained by the system have a definite, operationally effective procedure. The procedure links objects to the things in the real world that are of interest to the user. In this view, the formal system itself is a relatively minor part of the picture. The most important element is the link between the real and the formal realm.

Object orientation can help link the real and formal world by allowing the analyst to think in terms that are close to the problem (i.e., "What objects does my formal system consist of? How do I link these objects to the things in the real world?"). Don't forget that asking, "What are the objects?" is missing the point. The objects are whatever some responsible individual says they are. If someone is willing to maintain and interpret a formalism of some kind, it's an object.

If it doesn't have (literally) a living connection to the real world, a noun, no matter how obvious or clearly defined, is a dead letter. In terms of formal systems, there is no such thing as the right answer. Many different formal systems can have operationally effective links to the same chunk of the real world. It may be possible for different formal systems to share definitions, though obviously this would be a very problematic process given that the real definition of an object is inherently separate from the system itself. It's not enough to simply compare textual descriptions of objects; as any analyst will tell you, it's essential to actually go out into the world and bang a few heads together to get people to agree on how a thing is to be used and defined.

Another corollary is that no definition can ever exist in isolation. Formal systems are only meaningful in the context of the operations that define the connection of the formal system to the real world. As such, it is nonsense to talk about defining reusable business objects apart from the actual use of the business object in a working application.

One of the major shortcomings of the object-oriented approach is that it assumes the existence of a single set of well-defined objects as the content of the application domain. There is no reason to believe that this is how business application domains are actually structured. Rather than a single set of underlying objects, a business domain typically consists of a set of competing views motivated by and reflecting the dynamics of the organization itself. An individual's perception of product depends largely on what the individual does with product (sells it, consumes it, produces it, taxes it, and so on). Individual perception is not simply a question of different views of the same object; it may be a very real dispute about what the object is. One person may see product as characterized by operating system; another might see product as characterized by environment. The view that prevails may affect the way revenue is carried into the general ledger and, therefore, the relative profitability of different elements of the organization. The analyst faced with such a situation will be left in the unenviable position of having to appeal to a higher authority with all the attendant risks of such an exercise.

Object orientation has also failed to provide adequate mechanisms for dealing with change. Organizations by nature change continually. To the extent that an application is a reflection of the current state of an organization, it too must change to remain useful. Applications should be designed to evolve to meet the changing needs of the business. This means that the construction of the application should be planned as a solution for a class of problems, not for a single problem. Assume that components will be added, deleted, and changed over time. Some guidelines for developing flexible applications include:

- Develop applications separately and then compose them.
- Develop applications so they do not explicitly depend on other applications composed in conjunction.
- Keep in mind that applications might cooperate loosely or closely, and might be tightly bound for frequent fast interaction, or be widely distributed.
- Enable the introduction of new applications into a composition without requiring modification to other applications, and without invalidating persistent objects already created by them.
- Support unanticipated new applications, including those that extend existing applications in unexpected ways.
- Retain within each application the advantages of encapsulation, polymorphism, and inheritance.
- Separate the presentation of data from the representation. Separate data required to control presentation and navigation from the underlying information.
- Employ use cases.

Models as Maps

Models represent conceptual maps. We can use them to indicate the location of information the same way that we use geographical maps to indicate the location of places in physical space. More subtly, we also use maps to understand the relations between things; a map can address questions such as, "How far is it from Redmond to Seattle?" or "Is Redmond next to Seattle?" Relationships between things are the essence of what it is to represent information.

Maps also provide a graphic illustration of the idea of abstraction. Recall that generalization, specialization, and association are all forms of abstraction. Abstraction is a process of omitting details in some systematic way in order to focus attention on some aspect of the domain relevant to the issue at hand. Maps are necessarily an abstraction in that they cannot be as complete as the real surface. The map is not the territory.

Maps come in various types: political, geological, and topological, each of which represents a different abstraction over the same space. The mapmaker follows a well-understood process of measuring using a tool called a theodolite, along with other devices. The mapmaker also follows well-defined conventions for projecting complex surfaces onto a two-dimensional surface. The schema designer has similar conventions for graphically representing information space. These conventions come in the form of schema diagrams such as UML and Venn diagrams, which provide powerful mechanisms for summarizing the topological aspects of the information being dealt with. Venn or UML diagrams literally address issues such as the distance between concepts.

Remember when presenting your schema, if your audience is unfamiliar with the underlying territory, they may not understand the subject matter from your maps alone. It is essential to present pictures or detailed comprehensible narratives as supporting material for the maps if you expect the audience to learn the domain from the material you are presenting. Schema diagrams alone are not sufficient.

Unfortunately, the schema designer has no direct equivalent of the measuring devices available to the mapmaker. He or she has to discover and record the topology of the conceptual space by other means. A fundamental feature of the CIM Schema is the ElementSetting class. Settings are groups of parameters that determine the state of an associated ManagedSystemElement. ElementSettings associate ManagedSystemElements and their Settings (see Figure 3.1). The properties of Settings and ManagedSystemElements both characterize the same objects in the environment. For example, the Win32_BootConfiguration class contains properties that determine the way that the system is

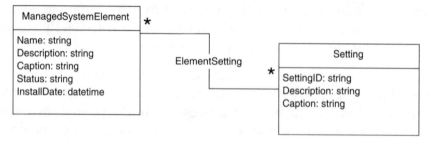

Figure 3.1 Element settings.

initialized, and it has an ElementSettings association to the Computer-
System to which the Settings apply.

The major difficulty with such an arrangement is deciding when to
place a property on the ComputerSystem object and when to place a
property on a subclass of the Setting class. For example:

```
    [Dynamic, Provider ("CIMWin32") , Description (
    "The Win32_BootConfiguration class represents the boot configuration on "
    "a Win32 system.")]
class Win32_BootConfiguration:CIM_Setting
{
    [read, Description (
    "The BootDirectory property indicates the directory location of the "
    "system files required for booting the system.<P>Example: Typically, "
    "this is the root directory.")]
    string BootDirectory;
    [read, Description (
    "The ConfigurationPath property indicates the path to the configuration "
    "files.")]
    [read, Description (
    "The ScratchDirectory property indicates the scratch directory of the "
    "Win32 boot configuration.")]
    string ScratchDirectory;
    [read, Description (
    "The TempDirectory property indicates the directory location where "
    "temporary files are stored.<P>Example: C:\\TEMP")]
    string TempDirectory;
    //other properties left out
};
    [Dynamic, Provider ("CIMWin32") , Description (
    "The Win32_SystemBootConfiguration class represents an association "
    "between a computer system and its boot configuration."),
    Locale (False), UUID ("{8502C507-5FBB-11D2-AAC1-006008C78BC7}") ]
class Win32_SystemBootConfiguration:Win32_SystemSetting
{
    [read, Override ("Element") , Description (
    "The Element reference represents the the computer system.")
```

```
            ]
    Win32_ComputerSystem REF Element;
        [read, Override ("Setting") , Description (
        "The Setting reference represents the boot configuration of the "
        "computer system.")]
    Win32_BootConfiguration REF Setting;
};
        [Description (
        "The Win32_ComputerSystem class represents a computer system operating "
        "in a Win32 environment."), Dynamic, Provider ("CIMWin32")
        , Locale (False), UUID ("{8502C4B0-5FBB-11D2-AAC1-006008C78BC7}") ]
class Win32_ComputerSystem:CIM_UnitaryComputerSystem
{
        [read, Description (
        "The BootROMSupported property determines whether a boot ROM is "
        "supported.<P>Values: TRUE or FALSE. If TRUE, a boot ROM is supported."
        )]
    boolean BootROMSupported;
        [read, Description (
        "The BootupState property indicates the bootup state of the computer "
        "system.<P>Constraints: Must have a value.")]
    string BootupState;
        [Description (
        "The CurrentTimeZone property  indicates the number of minutes the "
        "unitary computer system is offset from Greenwich Mean Time (GMT). The "
        "number is either positive, negative, or zero.") : ToSubClass, Units (
        "Minutes") , Read]
    sint16 CurrentTimeZone;
        [read, Description (
        "The Domain property indicates the domain name of the computer system."
        )]
    boolean InfraredSupported;
        [read, Description (
        "The Manufacturer property indicates the name of the computer "
        "manufacturer.<P>Example: Acme")]
    string Manufacturer;
        [read, Description (
        "The Model property indicates the model name of the computer system."
        "<P>Constraints: Must have a value")]
    string Model;
    //other properties left out
};
```

The example assumes that the value of BootDirectory, ScratchDirectory, and TempDirectory are all changeable. It makes sense to alter these values independently of the state of the system and to set values for these properties independently of the operation of the system. Conversely, it makes no sense to ask for the CurrentTimeZone of the system if the system is not operating, whereas it is quite reasonable to ask for the BootDirectory even if the system is not running or installed. In fact, it is essential to be able to set these values in the absence of a functioning system.

It is possible to have more than one BootConfiguration for a system. For example, a system might have one BootConfiguration used for test and debug and a different configuration used for production. The BootUpState, Manufacturer, and so on are independent of such considerations. A system's manufacturer will not change over the life of the system; a system will not suddenly lose or acquire support for infrared communication.

Essentially Setting values are meant to reflect configuration information that can be manipulated independently of the state or existence of the system itself. The properties of the system are intended to represent the current state of the system.

Issues such as the delineation of configuration and system properties are the substance of the schema designer's conceptual map. It is essential to have a clear account of the rationale behind the division of the schema into classes, the structure of their associations, and the placement of properties. Without such a structure, the formulation of sensible queries is practically impossible, and extending the schema will only lead to increased confusion and complexity.

When it comes to interpreting a model, it helps to ask: What does it mean to populate and use a model, and what distinguishes a useful model from a useless one? Models are social and political documents as well as formal descriptions of a well-defined collection of data. It must be possible to interpret the social model; consider for example:

```
class CIM_Fan:CIM_CoolingDevice
{
    boolean VariableSpeed;
    uint64 DesiredSpeed;
    uint32 SetSpeed([IN] uint64 DesiredSpeed);
};
```

Interpreting this class involves several issues. For one, what is the meaning or effect of VariableSpeed? You could interpret it to mean that if the property is TRUE, it is possible for the fan speed to vary. This is in fact the expected meaning. But it could also mean that the fan speed is variable at that point in time. A third interpretation is that, if the second meaning is true, the fan speed will vary by some amount.

Clearly, the name of the property alone conveys very little; in fact, the name of the property is essentially meaningless. It is an arbitrary label that has no utility other than as a mnemonic. As such, providing the property with an apparently meaningful name should be seen as no more than a device for helping a user who already understands the schema to recall the substance of his or her understanding.

Consider a more complete version of the class:

```
        [Description (
        "Capabilities and management of a Fan CoolingDevice.")]
   class CIM_Fan:CIM_CoolingDevice
   {
        [Description ("Indication of whether the fan supports variable speeds."
        ), read]
      boolean VariableSpeed;
        [Description (
        "DesiredSpeed is the currently requested fan speed, defined in "
        "Revolutions per Minute, when a variable speed fan is supported ("
        "VariableSpeed boolean = TRUE). The current speed is determined via a "
        "sensor (CIM_Tachometer) that is associated with the Fan using the "
        "CIM_AssociatedSensor relationship."), Units (
        "Revolutions per Minute"), read]
      uint64 DesiredSpeed;
        [Description (
        "Requests that the Fan speed be set to the value specified in the "
        "methodìs input parameter. The return value should be 0 if the request "
        "was successfully executed, 1 if the request is not supported and some "
        "other value if an error occurred. "), read,
        write]
      uint32 SetSpeed([IN] uint64 DesiredSpeed);
   };
```

In this case, some documentation is included in the class description along with the simple structure of the class. The bare statement that the VariableSpeed property is an "indication of whether the fan supports variable speeds" is a reasonable clue as to how instances of the class might be expected to behave. But the user is still left with some amount of uncertainty as to the intent of the design itself.

For starters, the DesiredSpeed is expressed as a 64-bit unsigned integer. In other words, the maximum value that can be used for the fan speed is 2^{64}. This is a very large value. Assuming a fan radius of 1 inch, this implies that the tip of the fan is traveling at approximately 15 trillion miles per second. Because 186,000 miles per second (the speed of light in a vacuum) is generally regarded as an upper bound on the speed of physical objects, this is an unnecessarily wide value. The speed of sound is a more reasonable upper bound on the speed of the fan blade. Using a unit of 32 would provide a speed for the tip of the fan in the order of about 3,000 miles per second—still several orders of magnitude too wide a safety margin.

Note that the description of the DesiredSpeed property explicitly states that it is "the currently requested fan speed . . .," not the actual speed. The property is marked as "read," implying that it cannot be set. This is reasonable given that the SetSpeed method is clearly intended to set the value of the DesiredSpeed property. The parameter to the method appears to have exactly the same semantics as the property. It is a request that the desired fan speed be set to the value supplied. However, it carries no expectation that the actual speed of the fan will be set to the value supplied. This raises the question why is the property not simply marked as read/write? One possible explanation is that the schema designer wanted an opportunity to return some result indicating that assignment has failed.

This introduces a host of additional assumptions. Assume, for example, that the fan is currently running at 200 rpm and the DesiredSpeed value is set to 300 rpm. If the fan takes 30 seconds to respond, will this be regarded as an exception worth reporting? Or if the fan immediately responds but periodically fluctuates by 30 percent, is this worth reporting? If it is, how long should the SetSpeed call delay before returning?

Or again consider the division between the SetSpeed method and the DesiredSpeed property. Assume the fan is currently running at 200 rpm and the DesiredSpeed is also 200. SetSpeed is called with a parameter of 300 but the fan does not respond. The method returns an exception. What is the value of DesiredSpeed? It may be 200 on the grounds that the SetSpeed method failed and therefore should be ignored; it could be 300 on the grounds that this was the value requested—it is the current desired speed!

Clearly, these are impossible questions to answer and the prospective user is left wondering how to interpret the class as a whole. The class would be far better defined as:

```
[Description (
"Capabilities and management of a Fan CoolingDevice.")]
class CIM_Fan:CIM_CoolingDevice
{
```

```
    [Description ("The VariableSpeed property indicates whether setting "
    "the DesiredSpeed property can be expected to have any effect. It can "
    "only have an effect if VariableSpeed is true."
    ), read]
boolean VariableSpeed;
    [Description (
    "DesiredSpeed is the currently requested fan speed, defined in "
    "Revolutions per Minute, It is only meaningful when a variable "
    "speed fan is supported (VariableSpeed = TRUE). The fan "
    "Instrumentation is expected to create an event if the fan "
    "diverges from the desired speed. The current speed "
    "is determined via a sensor (CIM_Tachometer) that is associated "
    "with the Fan using the CIM_AssociatedSensor relationship."),
    "Units (Revolutions per Minute"), read, write]
uint32 DesiredSpeed;
};
```

Note here that any deviation from the norm must be handled by the generation of appropriate events. This approach amounts to requiring the fan and its instrumentation to be responsible for determining when an event has occurred.

In practice, it is very unlikely that the user of the class would be able to determine what constitutes unacceptable behavior by the fan. For example it would be possible to register for an event generated when the fan speed (as reported by the associated tachometer) deviated by 10 percent from the DesiredSpeed. But why set the limit at 10 percent? How would one decide what is a reasonable threshold? In reality of course, it would be necessary to understand the heat dissipation and mechanical characteristics of the individual devices. The only individuals competent to establish these parameters would be the engineers who designed the system in the first place. In their absence, the only recourse is trial and error, carefully monitoring the system temperature (assuming it is available in some relevant form) and determining by experimentation what is a reasonable value for desired speed. Obviously, this is a very poor solution as it assumes burning out some number of systems in order to accurately establish the boundary conditions.

Complicating the situation is that some systems might be far more tolerant of fluctuations in fan speed than others. This may be partly a function of the original design (and therefore best understood by the designing engineers), but there may be other relevant factors such as the environment in which the system is deployed. A system deployed in a dirty environment, such as a factory floor, may be far more subject to failure as a result of fluctuations in fan speed. This in turn would lead to the notion that some systems may be far more critical than others.

This rather long and tedious discussion on the subject of fan speeds should make it clear that deliberate management of a system at this level of detail is potentially very expensive. Deciding to do so may come down to which systems are important enough to warrant this level of detail. If a system is expected to stay up 99.999 percent of the time, and a 10 percent fluctuation in fan speed might significantly impact the reliability of the components, this could be a significant concern. The way that the schema is used, interpreted, and instrumented could vary widely depending on the way it is used and to which systems it applies.

Modeling Techniques, Tools, and Methods

Historically, the DMTF CIM community has made extensive use of the UML class diagrams for representing schemas graphically. The Managed Object Format (MOF) has been used for providing a detailed textual representation of schemas that capture information such as property enumerations and comments.

UML is represented both by a set of diagramming conventions and by a meta-model that can be used to capture the data represented by the diagrams. The UML meta-model is large and complex—much more so than the CIM meta-model as it must cover all of the possible diagram types supported by UML. Commonly, tools that support UML support all of the diagram types and, as such, are overkill for the development of CIM Schemas.

In fact, these tools typically have a different purpose. There is no question that the tools supporting UML that have sprung up are primarily intended for the design of programs, not data models. An object in a UML model typically represents a chunk of code with associated state. Objects in a UML model are usually part of a graph of other objects and are reached by graph traversal, not by enumeration. There are no commercially available object-oriented programming environments that provide direct enumeration of the objects of a specific class. Objects typically behave more like types than classes; it is simply not useful to enumerate all the instances of a linked-list class or a dialogue window class, because these are objects that exist only within the scope of a given execution and thus are unlikely to be interesting or meaningful outside of it. When selecting a UML tool, you must consider the fact that most of the tools currently available were not developed with data modeling in mind.

UML class diagrams represent only a small portion of all the diagrams that fall under the UML umbrella. UML defines state transition diagrams, component diagrams, various architecture diagrams, use-case diagrams, and so on. UML must be understood as a set of conventions that cover the whole range of activities required for the specification of a complete application. The primary focus of UML is to provide formalisms for representing all the major aspects of a program—not a data model. The specification of a data model can be seen as one aspect of the specification of a program. Traditionally, data model specification has been provided as a mapping to a database of some kind, usually a relational database. A program design process with UML can be expected to design the objects required to support the program and then devise serializations of the object that allow the objects to be persisted where necessary.

By contrast, CIM is a pure data model. CIM classes will be serialized as they are defined in the model. UML tools should therefore be chosen with caution. Though in many cases, they can be very useful, it is unlikely they will be so "out of the box"; that is, without some thought as to how the model is to be applied to capture the various artifacts of the schema design process.

A major factor to consider when selecting a tool is that there are two representations of CIM Schemas, both of which must be used at various times in schema development. It is essential to have both graphical and textual representations of a schema, just as it is essential to be able to translate from one to the other. Given a model of any size, it is simply impractical to do this translation by hand. Whichever set of tools you use, the tools themselves must support this translation, at least one-way and, preferably, two-way.

The most commonly used tool in the DMTF CIM community is Visio, a reasonable and cost-effective drawing tool. Several Visio templates for UML are available, one from the DMTF Web site. It provides minimal UML class and association definitions. Another UML template available from Visio is a part of the Visio Professional version. It is much more comprehensive and has an interface to the Microsoft Repository. The repository interface is significant, as it provides a bridge to other tools such as Rational Rose or Paradigm Plus.

Visio supports very large diagrams and provides very fine-grained control over the layout and appearance of them. The full CIM 2.1 model includes more than 250 classes and associations and 1,500 properties. It is possible to represent the full model in a single diagram using Visio. The CIM community has introduced the use of color-coded lines, a convention designed to help the reader distinguish association, aggregation, and generalization lines. Figure 3.2 shows a sample CIM Schema fragment that has been rendered in Visio.

The Microsoft WMI SDK supports a MOF compiler that will load schemas into WMI, from where it is possible to extract models into other environments such as Visio and the Microsoft Repository.

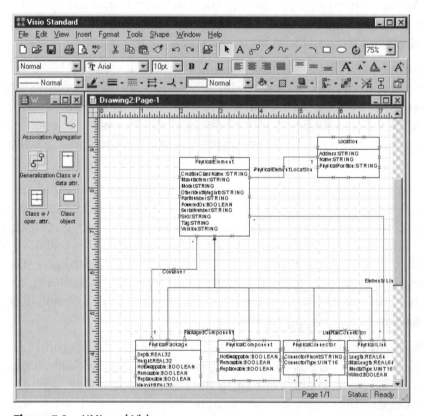

Figure 3.2 UML and Visio.

Design Process

Designs are typically developed so that the artifacts of the design can be revisited and refined through an iterative process. The designer must build an understanding of the problem domain; the developer must determine what is possible with the available technology; and, most important, the customer must define how the system will be accommodated within the framework of existing systems, practices, and personnel. Each of these participants is dependent on the understanding and information brought by the others into the discussion. They approach their respective goals by going through successive rounds of refinement until some workable solution is arrived at.

Remember that you must evaluate tools within the context of the way they will be used. Figure 3.3 gives you a tool-centric view of the development process. There are several salient features here, notably that it is essential to be able to backtrack in the design process. Inevitably, developers discover issues with the schema that the

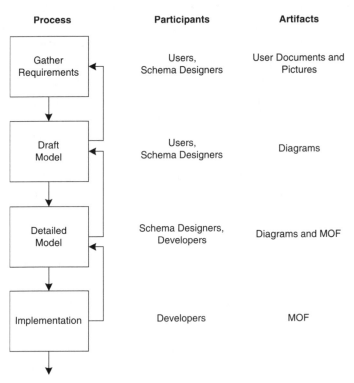

Process	Participants	Artifacts
Gather Requirements	Users, Schema Designers	User Documents and Pictures
Draft Model	Users, Schema Designers	Diagrams
Detailed Model	Schema Designers, Developers	Diagrams and MOF
Implementation	Developers	MOF

Figure 3.3   Design process.

schema designer failed to recognize, for example, that the schema is impractical from an implementation point of view. The developer will recognize such an issue in the artifacts normally dealt with at development time, typically a textual representation of the schema.

The schema designer must assess the impact of the schema change in terms of the artifacts commonly used in schema design, which typically take the form of diagrams. Assuming the user has to be asked to reevaluate the proposal, the proposed change has to be translatable into terms understood by the user. This may take the form of use cases or some ad hoc documentation familiar to the user. All of these transitions must be performed somehow, manually if necessary. Clearly, tool support is highly desirable and can be expected to facilitate the free exchange of information and a more precise evolution of the model.

Relational Models

In 1970, E.F. Codd first proposed the relational model in his seminal paper titled "A relational model for large shared data banks." The relational model provides an explanation of database declarations and queries in terms of predicate calculus. This formal basis and relationship to logic spawned a large and growing literature on various subjects related to relational databases, including database design. Much of this theory is directly applicable to schema design and deserves close attention as a source of useful guidelines and heuristics for the schema designer. The following subsections outline some of the major ideas and results from the relational model and their application to schema design and modeling with an object-oriented model.

General Goals of Relational Design

The relational model is based on the simple idea that data can be represented as tables consisting of columns and rows. The tables can be thought of as predicates that define membership in a set. Consider Table 3.1.

The table itself has a name, Employee, and three columns, Name, Employee Number, and Department Name. The table also has three rows.

Table 3.1 Employee

NAME	EMPLOYEE NUMBER	DEPARTMENT NAME
Joe Bloggs	35623	Toys
Adam Smith	34985	Furniture
Mary Moses	19722	Toys

One way to think of the table is as a three-place function declared somewhat as follows:

```
Boolean Employee(string Name, integer Employee_Number, string Department_name)
```

That is, the table is a function called Employee that returns a Boolean result, which is true if the supplied Name, Employee_Number and Department_Name represent a row in the table; it is false otherwise. So, for example, the value of the expression:

```
Employee("Joe Bloggs", 35623, "Toys")
```

would be true while the value of the expression:

```
Employee("Joe Bloggs", 67432, "Toys")
```

would be false.

This illustrates the connection to predicate calculus, as it allows expressions such as:

```
Employee(X, Y, "Toys")
```

which can be interpreted (by analogy with a language such as Prolog) as designating all the employees in the Toys department. Note, here, that the idea of binding means that the free variables in the expression are successively *bound* to the various rows underlying the predicate, which yield as values for X and Y the various possible values of Names and Employee Numbers for which Employee is true.

A critical aspect of the model is that no two rows in a table can be identical. Logically speaking, two rows that contain identical values for every column are the same row. In practice, this idea has been taken a little further, since it is essential to be able to identify a row in the context of another row in order to represent a relationship. Table 3.2, Department, extends the employee example given in Table 3.1.

The relationship between the Employee table and the Department table is established by the fact that the name of the department the

Table 3.2   Department

DEPARTMENT NAME	DEPARTMENT LOCATION
Furniture	First Floor
Toys	Second Floor

employee works for is embedded in the table representing the employee. The expression:

```
Employee("Joe Bloggs", 67432, X)  and Department(X,Y)
```

can be expected to provide the department Joe Bloggs works for as the bound value of X and the Department Location as the bound value of Y.

Clearly, the use of all the columns of the table to identify the rows would be unworkable in such a situation because it would imply that every table embedded every column of any related table. Some subset of the table columns has to be defined to uniquely identify each of the rows in the table. These columns are referred to as the *table key*, also sometimes known as the *primary key* (for reasons that will become apparent in a moment). The key consists of one or more columns, and the table must be established and maintained in such a way so that there are never two rows in the table with the same key value.

When a primary key has been located in another table to represent a relationship, the key is referred to as a *foreign key*. Foreign keys provide a very flexible mechanism for representing relationships between rows.

It is possible for a table to have more than one key. For example, a person might be identified by employee number or by social security number. These potential keys are referred to as candidate keys. An important part of the design process is identifying all the candidate keys and selecting one of them to use as the primary key.

One of the main contributions of Codd's paper was the identification of a limited set of operators necessary for the manipulation of tables. There are four of them:

Select. The Select operator takes a table and Boolean expression as parameters and returns a table consisting of only those in the original table that satisfy the Boolean condition.

Table 3.3 Employee Department

NAME	EMPLOYEE NUMBER	DEPARTMENT NAME	DEPARTMENT LOCATION
Joe Bloggs	35623	Toys	Second Floor
Adam Smith	34985	Furniture	First Floor
Mary Moses	19722	Toys	Second Floor

Project. The Project operator takes a table and a list of columns. The operator returns a table consisting of only those columns in the list of columns supplied.

Join. The Join operator takes two tables and joins them by matching primary keys and foreign keys in various ways. The Join operator is really a family of operators based on the type of joins being performed. For example, the natural join connects two tables based on matching values in any columns with the same name. The natural join between the Employee and Department tables would result in Table 3.3.

Union. The Union operator takes two tables as parameters and returns a new table that results from appending one table to the end of the other. The two tables supplied must have identical columns, that is, the columns in the table match exactly in both number and type.

Notice that all of the relational operators return a table as a result. This means that all of the operators can be composed, allowing the output of one operator to be used as an input to another. For example, it is quite common to combine Select, Project, and Join in a single query.

Unfortunately the prevailing SQL standard has muddied the waters somewhat because the query language designers chose not to follow the relational operators in structuring the language. SQL expressions have four main clauses and are structured as follows:

```
SELECT <column list>
FROM   <table list>
WHERE  <expression>
UNION  <select-from-where>
```

where SELECT actually corresponds to the relational Project operator, Join is represented variously by elements of the FROM and WHERE clause, and the relational Select operator is represented by the WHERE clause. SQL also supports nested queries that correspond to the composition of functions in Codd's relational algebra. Bear in mind that when applying SQL to object-oriented databases that the SQL language is a bastardization of the original and that much of the theory behind the SQL language is best understood in terms of the original formulation.

Constraints of the Relational Model

A number of constraints can be expressed by the relational model (P. Valduriez and G. Gardarin 1989). These rules underlie the decisions required by the process of designing a relational schema. They are:

R1. Unique key constraint. An attribute may be specified as being a key and therefore unique.

R2. Not null constraint. An attribute may be specified as not null.

R3. Referential dependency. The presence of value v in attribute x of relation X; requires the presence of value v in the primary key y of relation Y, or:

```
for all(x) exists(y) (y = x)
```

R4. Inclusion dependency. This is the same as R3, except that neither attribute is a primary key.

R5. Functional dependency. Implies the existence of a condition such as: supplier name is determined by supplier number.

R6. Multi-valued dependency. Implies the existence of a dependency such that more than one value is dependent on a given primary key value.

R7. General constraints. These correspond to the generalized verification mechanism and represent an arbitrary invariant asserted with respect to the state of the system. For example, the assertion that managers must earn more than the average salary of their direct reports.

R8. Transitional constraints. Some dialects of SQL support the notion of OLD and NEW attributes being visible during an update, thereby allowing constraints such as:

```
VERIFY NEW salary > OLD salary
```

Not all of these constraints are actually implemented by any existing relational database system. The concepts are all easily expressible in terms of the model and must inform any design discussion around a relational model.

In addition to these constraints are the *normal forms*:

1NF. No MV items. First normal form is a matter of definition and amounts to the statement that embedded tables are not allowed. The reason is simple enough; without this constraint, the query language would have to be radically different.

2NF. Everything must be dependent on the key. In second normal form is the simple assertion that every column in a row must be dependent on the key for the row. For example, in the Employee table cited in the previous section, Name is determined by Employee Number in the sense that every time a specific employee number is encountered you can assume that the same employee name will also be found. In this way, employee number is said to determine employee name.

3NF. Everything must be directly dependent on the key. In third normal form, it is possible for something to be determined indirectly by the key. For example, in the table that resulted from joining Employee and Department, Department Location can be seen as dependent on Employee Number, because every Employee Number is associated with a specific Department Location. However, Department Location is actually dependent on Department Name.

4NF. No spurious associations of multivalued dependencies. The classic counter instance to fourth normal form is a table of skills and languages, as shown in Table 3.4.

Assume there is no association between Skill and Language. The table is just a convenient mechanism used for storing both types of information in a single place. The problem with the table is that it lends itself to the interpretation that there is some link between Skill and Language. The table is also inadequate given the possibility of one person having multiple skills or languages. The correct design

Table 3.4 Language Skills

EMPLOYEE NUMBER	SKILL	LANGUAGE
35623	Cook	French
34985	Carpenter	Spanish
19722	Electrician	

Table 3.5   Skill

EMPLOYEE NUMBER	SKILL
35623	Cook
34985	Carpenter
19722	Electrician

Table 3.6   Language

EMPLOYEE NUMBER	LANGUAGE
35623	French
34985	Spanish

for the table (one that conforms to fourth normal form) is to split it into two tables, as shown in Tables 3.5 and 3.6:

Note that Table 3.6 contains no language row for 19722, and it would be a simple matter to represent the idea that 35623 speaks Spanish as well as French, simply by the introduction of another row.

5NF. Derivable relationships must not be stored. The standard example for fifth normal form is a relationship between salesman, product, and company, such that if a salesman sells a product that is supplied by a company, then he also represents that company. The schema is diagrammed in Figure 3.4. Fifth normal form is violated if the represents relationship is stored, not derived from the other two. Note this

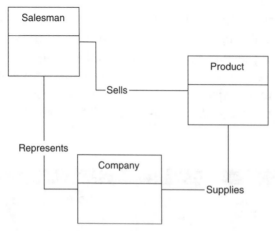

Figure 3.4   Fifth normal form.

is a simplification of fifth normal form but is a reasonable summary of much of its implications for a fuller treatment (Kent 1983).

Object Models

There is a set of rules that constrain the process of designing object models. It roughly corresponds to the relational model's normal forms and the rules outlined by Valduriez and Gardarin (1989).

There are five general rules that you must adhere to when designing structural aspects of a CIM Schema. They are:

D1. Distinct entity rule. All entities must be distinct.

D2. Hierarchy rule. Every member of a subclass must be a legitimate member of all of its superclasses.

D3. Property placement rule. Every property must be a property of its immediate class. It must not be the case that a property is attached to class A but properly speaking is a property of some other class B, regardless of whether B is declared in the schema or not. A less stringent version of this rule allows A to be attached to some other class if B is not declared in the database. Under this interpretation, null may mean inapplicable.

D4. Property derivation rule. No stored property should be derivable from some other stored property.

D5. Referential integrity rule. Inverses must be recognized and declared as being inverses where they are present in the database.

D1 through D5 are the basic rules for the use of the structural aspects of the CIM model. Note that there are no equivalent rules for the use of generalized constraints, other than stating that you should avoid them where possible.

In addition to the five general rules, there are a number of characteristics that can be captured using property constraints. They are:

A1. REQUIRED

A2. Single Valued/Multi Valued

A3. MAX

A4. Range restrictions in the form of types and enumerations

A5. UNIQUE

A6. DISTINCT

These property constraints can be combined with the various property types to yield a wide range of expressible constraints.

It is fairly easy to show that D1 through D5 and A1 through A6 not only cover R1 through R6, but also provide a level of integrity equal to that provided by a database in fifth normal form.

In CIM, you can express transitional and general constraints through a combination of events and custom code, but constraints are not intrinsically supported by the system. This custom code also corresponds to the idea of a policy that contains both a condition—such as a service level agreement—and an action—some operation to perform if the condition is violated.

1NF through 5NF are covered by D1, D3, and D4. The major difference is that the D rules are concerned with the specification and requirements analysis process, whereas the NF rules are predicated on the prior existence of such a process.

It is not possible to proceed with normalization until after the application domain has been expressed in such a way that the items and their dependencies can be derived. If you use CIM in the specification and requirements analysis process, and if you adhere to at least D1, D3, and D4, you can sidestep normalization as a process. Given some minimal assumptions about the process of deriving a physical schema from the logical schema, arrived at the end of the requirements process, the level of integrity provided by the database design will be at least that of a fully normalized database.

The generalized and transitional constraints in the form of events and policies should be seen as the last of a series of constraints that may be applied to the data to be stored in a database. You must observe rules D1 through D5 if you want to achieve a consistent and reasonable database design. D1 to D5, together with A1 through A6, make up the basic repertoire of techniques available to the database designer. Generalized and transitional constraints may be used as a catchall to deal with any cases not covered by these techniques.

Bear in mind that there are two cases, one in which the schema design is to be used with stored data (or repository), the other where the schema design is to be used with instrumentation data. In the case of instrumentation data, the schema designer must focus on representing a stream of data that reflects the current state of the environment. In the case of a repository, the schema designer must represent the current information about the state of the environment; it is not data that directly represents the state itself. Where the data in the repository may be wrong—in the sense that it is not consistent or correct—the data provided by the instrumentation cannot be wrong, for that indicates an undesirable state of affairs that needs to be changed or badly written instrumentation.

Clearly, instrumentation data could also be wrong in that the instrumentation may not be functioning properly, and it may be possible to implement policy on a repository where the policy actions have the effect of altering the environment, thereby indirectly altering the content of the repository. Nonetheless, it is useful to think in terms of instrumentation as subject to policy, and repositories as subject to constraints. The use of the design principles outlined in this section should be qualified in that sense. It is reasonable to use normalization with an instrumentation schema since it may make the data stream easier to understand and appear more organized. However, normalization with instrumentation schemas is not really essential; as long as the schema designer recognizes dependencies between data elements (especially derivable values), exclusive use of third normal form is quite unnecessary. Similarly, policies may be useful in controlling repositories, but they are not a substitute for good schema design and the appropriate application of fundamental principles, such as the separation of interface data and base data.

As far as analysis is concerned, there is a major difference between D1 through D5 and A1 through A6 on the one hand and R1 through R8 and 1NF through 5NF on the other. It is this: The relational rules can only be invoked after an understanding of the application has been established. In particular, normalization—which really is just a technique for expressing aspects of R1 through R8—can only be performed after a set of functional dependencies has been derived. Typically, these functional dependencies are derived from an analysis in terms of the Entity-Relationship model. Relational database design then is an "after the fact" process. If analysis is taken to be the process whereby the analyst establishes an understanding of the application, "relation analysis" becomes a contradiction in terms.

By contrast, the rules D1 through D5 and A1 through A6 are relevant precisely to the process used by the analyst in formulating an understanding of the application. These rules address the major processes of abstraction: classification, generalization, aggregation, and association.

In Chapters 2 and 3 we have covered the concepts necessary for understanding the basics of schema design. This chapter provides an introduction to much of the theory underlying schema design as derived from the relational model and some equivalent ideas relevant to the use of object-oriented models in data analysis and design (as opposed to program design). The next chapter introduces the CIM Core Model which provides a conceptual framework, specific to the management domain that is used to organize the various area specific models such as the system, application, and network models. Chapters 2, 3, and 4 provide the basic tools needed to understand CIM. Chapters 5, 6, 7, and 8 describe how they have been and are being used in the CIM community for developing various management related models.

References

Codd, E.F. 1970. "A relational model for large shared data banks." *Communications of the ACM* 13, 6 (June).

Kent, William. 1983. "A simple guide to five normal forms in relational database theory." *Communications of the ACM* 26:2.

Stamper, Ronald. 1977. "Physical Objects, Human Discourse and Formal Systems." *Architecture and Models in Database Management Systems*, G. M. Nijssen (ed.), North-Holland.

Valduriez, P. and G. Gardarin. 1989. *Analysis and Comparison of Relational Database Systems*. Reading, MA: Addison-Wesley.

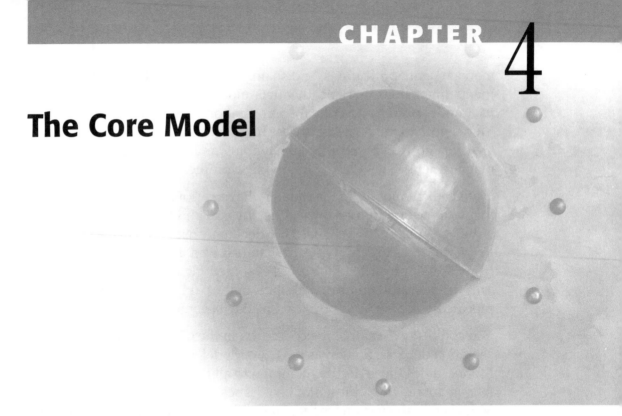

The Core Model

The Core Model is the part of CIM that establishes the major design points or design patterns for representational issues that are not specific to a particular management domain or resource type. The Common Models—systems, devices, applications, or physical—leverage the constructs defined in the Core Model to represent issues in specific management domains or resource types. This chapter will help you understand the motivation for the content of the Core Model and introduce you to the basic constructs used by the Common Models.

In this chapter you will find:

- An introduction to the Core and Common Models, along with an explanation of their position
- Coverage of important design themes shared by all CIM Models
- A discussion of classes to help you understand the design patterns approach to interpreting the CIM Model.

Overview of the Core Model

CIM standardizes the representation of management information for various management tools (for example, instrumentation, operational management applications, and so on.) Such standardization takes on many dimensions. For one, the meta-model for CIM standardizes the techniques used to describe the information. The content of the Core Model goes to the next step by settling several modeling choices that are often hotly debated when developing an information model for management. Consider the following example of a classic debate.

Management models in the industry have various approaches for dealing with the boundary between the physical and the logical world within a complex IT system, so the debate focuses on when a resource in the system is logical (typically, handled by software and/or firmware) or physical in the sense of something one can add or remove. This debate is difficult to settle since, in the past twenty years, we have repeatedly seen what is physical one day become logical tomorrow.

You could say that all of the constructs in the CIM settle various representation debates. So why is the Core Model so unique? Well, the Core Model settles those debates common to all the different domains of management. The representational issues addressed by the Core Model cross the various management domains (network management, application management, desktop management, and so on). Therefore, the definitions in the Core Model are meaningful to the domains addressed by the various common models.

As others have observed, the definitions in the Core Model can be viewed as design patterns that are meaningful across the domains addressed by the various common models (Thompson 1997). As a result, many of the classes within the Core Model are abstract (determined by the abstract qualifier). Figure 4.1 shows how the Core Model relates to the subdivisions in the Common Model.

It is possible (and probable) that additional objects and properties will be defined for the Core Model. But the addition of classes, properties, and associations does not have the same impact as deletions and modifications. Additions do not impact current Common and Extension Models.

Modeling Methodology

Capturing the information for managing complex IT systems is similar to any complex engineering problem in the sense that there are many

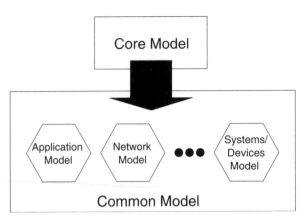

Figure 4.1   Core Model sets patterns for Common Model.

facets involved. To understand this, consider the construction of a building. There are many systems within the building: the structural system, electrical system, plumbing system, heating and air system, and so on. In a well-designed building, each of these systems fits together. However, the contractors or specialists involved in assembling the building focus on their individual systems and want to know about the others only if one system has dependencies in another area. For example, the structural engineer must communicate with the electrician because wiring must go inside the walls.

Within the domain of the CIM, you can think of a personal workstation as a house. Instead of different contractors, you have different administrators, such as the desktop administrator, the network administrator, the storage administrator, the business application administrator, and so on. The desktop administrator manages the workstations, and wants to know about the network administrator's area only if the desktops have a dependency (for example, a network node hosted by a particular workstation).

To truly comprehend the construction of the CIM in general and the Core Model in specific, you need to step back and grasp the idea of the object aspect design pattern (Thompson 1997). This design pattern recognizes that objects in natural classification schemes do not always function as a single type over their lifetime. A house is sometimes a collection of rooms, a set of connected wires, or a set of pipes, and at a particular point in time, it may be easier to learn about a certain aspect of an object without learning others. For example, frequently, you cannot interrogate the physical aspect of an IT resource; rather, you can only discover it through a complex manual procedure. In contrast, the functional aspect of the resource is readily available without requiring information about the physical packaging. For example, a node in a network is easy to detect without knowing whether the node is hosted by a Sun, IBM, Dell, or Cisco box.

There are many similar management situations within the domain of the CIM Model; therefore, the notion of object aspect design pattern is used over and over again. This approach is in direct contrast to others that support multiple inheritance, whereby the various aspects of an object are represented by the inheritance of the different aspects of the object from multiple superclasses. The disadvantages of multiple inheritance are well known; for one, it leads to cross-dependencies in the class structure that make the extension and interpretation of the class hierarchy problematic (Cargill 1992). Therefore, there are numerous associations within the CIM that link various aspects of the resources within a complex IT system.

Figure 4.2 shows how aspects are used within the Core Model and summarizes the major areas, or patterns, addressed by the Core Model. A product represents the unit of acquisition between a pur-

Design Patterns

Design patterns comprise a technique that captures reusable object-oriented designs extracted by experts from recurring situations within object-oriented implementations (Gamma 1995). A design pattern is a systematic way to capture a simple and elegant solution to a specific problem. Essentially, a good design pattern provides a novice object-oriented designer with the insights of an experienced designer so the novice can develop flexible and durable implementations.

The motivation behind the creation of design patterns is not new to information modeling techniques. The development of the Entity-Relationship data model and its many extensions introduced a number of non-object-oriented design patterns for situations experienced modelers encounter over and over again. For example, the introduction of weak and total relationships involved a type of design pattern that experienced modelers found recurring in many information models. In the case of a weak entity, there are implications for the propagation of keys, cardinality of the associations, and the life cycles of the objects involved.

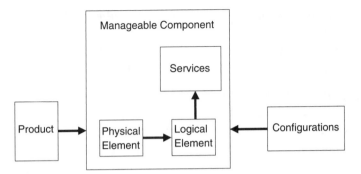

Figure 4.2   Aspects captured by the Core Model.

chaser and a supplier. Manageable components (both logical and physical) are particular aspects of a product. Physical elements have many logical aspects. When these manageable components are added to an IT system, they host aspects for services that can be consumed by other components within the system. The exact nature of the service is dependent on how the manageable components are configured, because many manageable components have various setting combinations.

By leveraging the notion of object aspects, these different perspectives can be represented in the model at the same time. This results in many associations that preclude a complex classification hierarchy, which embeds the wrong data into the classes themselves; for example, having subclasses of the Product class for modems, applications, computer systems, and so on.

NOTE
It is important to interpret this discussion as a design philosophy for the CIM; do not assume it is always followed precisely throughout.

The Core Model

This section details the major parts of the Core Model. The subsections address topical areas of the Core Model so that you can more easily see the design patterns the Core Model provides the Common Models. Each topical area settles one or more of the classic debates that arise when an information model for management is developed. The topical areas (or debates to settle) are:

- *Standard technique for capturing decomposable manageable components.* The CIM_ManagedSystemElement and CIM_System classes are used in combination to represent distinguishable components of a complex IT system that can be decomposed.

- *Standard technique for discerning the physical and logical boundary.* Complex IT systems are composed of physical entities commonly referred to as hardware and logical entities commonly referred to as software. This boundary is, however, constantly changing because hardware capabilities are emulated with software and software capabilities are implemented in hardware. The CIM_LogicalElement and CIM_PhysicalElement classes are, metaphorically, used to put a stake in the ground for the CIM.

- *Standard techniques for describing consumable services.* Management components that exist in a system provide functionality or services for other management components to use. Any given management component can provide none to many different types of service, so services are another aspect of a management component. You need to be able to identify the services and to describe the interfaces to these services. The CIM_Service and CIM_ServiceAccessPoint classes are used to represent this design pattern.

- *Standard techniques for configurations and settings.* Most manageable components have a set of dials and switches that can be used to modify the capability and behavior of the components. Again, these are treated as aspects of manageable components. The CIM_Configuration and CIM_Setting classes are used to capture these details.

- *Standard techniques for a product.* When dealing with the many aspects of a collection of manageable components, it is easy to lose track of how the manageable components were acquired. This aspect of the manageable components addresses what the products are that make up the IT system. The CIM_Product and CIM_FRU classes capture this important aspect.

Manageable Components

A manageable component is the fundamental concept we need to capture in the Core Model. Modeling manageable components is challenging, because there are many valid views of what a meaningful manageable component is, and the most appropriate one depends on

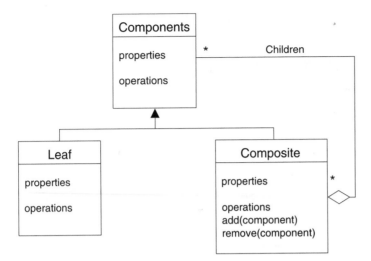

Figure 4.3   Composite design pattern.

the type of management you intend to perform. Manageable components can be atomic or composite, physical or logical, hardware or software, networks or systems, and so on.

Depending on who is asking, the same manageable component can be a very simple, distinguishable item within an IT system or a complex combination of items. The point is, manageable components are actually part-whole hierarchies that one community wants to treat as an indivisible whole and another wants to treat as a combination of many elements. This conflict is addressed in the Core Model by using the Composite design pattern to represent manageable components (Gamma 1995).

The intent of the Composite design pattern is to represent part-whole hierarchies of objects so that it is possible to manipulate individual objects and compositions of these individual objects in a common way. The basic elements of this design pattern are shown in Figure 4.3.

The Component class represents the common behavior of the individual objects and composite objects. The Composite class represents individual components that can be decomposed into children components. The Leaf class represents individual objects that cannot be decomposed. Figure 4.4 shows how the Composite design pattern is exploited in the Core Model to represent manageable components.

The CIM_ManagedSystemElement class plays the role of a component, so it represents the common behavior of atomic and decompos-

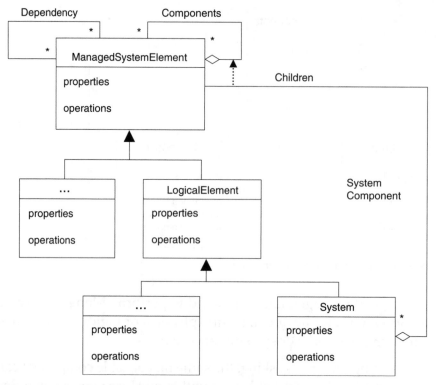

Figure 4.4 Decomposable manageable components.

able manageable components. The CIM_ManagedSystemElement class prescribes these important behaviors:

- *The CIM_ManagedSystemElement class does not prescribe a key.* In contrast to other modeling attempts, the properties of the managed system element (MSE) are not used to define the key or key structures for its subclasses. The temptation to use the MSE to define key or key structure ignores the fact that the range of manageable components requires many different instance identification schemes.

- *The CIM_Component association identifies the CIM_ManagedSystemElement classes into which a particular CIM_ManagedSystemElement can be decomposed.* We will see later that the association that plays the role of the Children association in the Composite design pattern is a subclass of the CIM_Component association.

- *The CIM_Dependency association identifies the CIM_ManagedSystemElement classes on which a particular CIM_ManagedSystemElement class depends to perform or deliver its function or service.* There are a number of distinguishable "flavors" of dependency, notably *existence* and *functional*.

■ *Because the CIM_ManagedSystemElement does not have a key, all the associations defined with this class as a participant are abstract.* For example, the CIM_Dependency and CIM_Components associations are defined on CIM_ManagedSystemElement since these are fundamental relationships for all manageable components. However, it is not really possible to arbitrarily make one CIM_ManagedSystemElement object dependent on or decomposed into another object. This is why the instances of MSE associations are typically subclasses of the associations rather the associations themselves. The value of having MSE associations is that it makes it easy to answer semantic questions such as: Can this managed system element be decomposed into or composed within other elements? The answer is determined by identifying all the associations that can be instantiated for a particular class and determining whether any of them are descendents of the component association.

In the Core Model, the CIM_System class plays the composite role defined in the Composite design pattern. The CIM_ManagedSystemElement class can be decomposed into children manageable components. (Note: There is an anomaly in the Core Model because System is not directly inherited by the ManagedSystemElement class. The LogicalElement class is an intermediate class. However, this anomaly does not impact the use of the design pattern.) The other subclasses of the CIM_ManagedSystemElement class play the role of Leaf classes, which provide the details specific to a particular domain covered by a Common Model.

Two properties are used to identify CIM_System objects: Name and CreationClassName. The Name [CIM_System] property is used to label the CIM_System object. The value of the CreationClassName [CIM_System] property is to act as the name of the CIM class that was used to create an object for a CIM_System class or one of its subclasses. So, if a CIM_System object is created, the value of the CreationClassName property is the string "CIM_System". If a CIM_ApplicationSystem object is created, the value of the CreationClassName property is the string "CIM_ApplicationSystem". This was to done to simplify the use of the model; there is no requirement of a system object of various types to have a unique name for the same namespace.

The CIM_SystemComponent association that relates a CIM_System to the CIM_ManagedSystemElements plays the role of the Children association in the Composite design pattern. Therefore, the CIM_System-Component association identifies the manageable components of a system that are to be considered part of the whole represented by the system. The Core Model allows for any Managed System Element to be part of a whole represented by a system.

Subclassing Considerations

There are many situations within the Common Model in which the part-whole situation captured by the manageable component of the Core Model can be applied. In those situations, the notion of the whole can be a subclass of the System class, and the parts can be subclasses of the ManagedSystemElement class (indirectly via a logical or physical element).

Logical and Physical Split

Many management tasks require you to figure out whether a manageable component is a physical or logical entity. The following two situations make this distinction difficult:

- Today's logical entity may be physical tomorrow; likewise, today's physical entity may be logical tomorrow.
- Multifunction capabilities are combined into a single physical package. (For example, a single PC card can contain memory, a sound card, and a modem.)

Given these two situations, the CIM takes a very narrow, but durable, view of the split between logical and physical elements. Manageable components that are really physical elements (in the sense that they conform to the laws of physics and take up space) are modeled using the CIM_PhysicalElement class. These can be touched and labeled with physical tags. All other manageable components are abstractions used to manage, configure, and coordinate functional aspects, and are represented by the CIM_LogicalElement class. CIM's approach is in stark contrast to other models that would have subclassed CIM_ManagedSystemElement into hardware and software classes. So, the design pattern for the split between the physical and logical worlds establishes the two immediate subclasses of CIM_ManagedSystemElement: CIM_LogicalElement and CIM_PhysicalElement.

The CIM_LogicalElement and CIM_PhysicalElement classes can be contrasted by recognizing that CIM_PhysicalElement objects cannot be realized (in the sense of brought into being). CIM_PhysicalElement can be decomposed, but only into other physical elements. The functional capabilities of a physical element are realized through CIM_LogicalElement classes. The CIM_Realizes association links CIM_PhysicalElement classes with the CIM_LogicalDevice classes (an immediate subclass of the CIM_LogicalElement class) that represent the physical entity's functional capability. The shaded area in Figure 4.5 highlights the parts of the Core Model relevant to the physical and logical relationships in CIM.

Let's look at an example of a physical-logical model. In a PC, there is a multifunction card that has a modem jack and a network port. Given the way the CIM handles the split between logical and physical, the

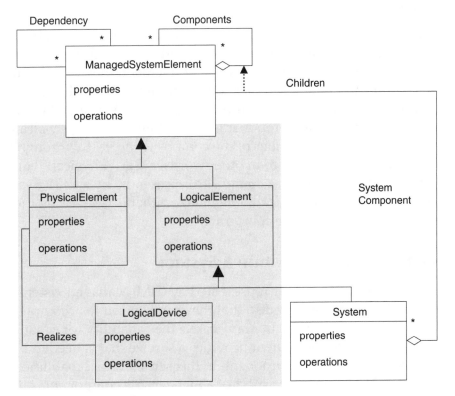

Figure 4.5 Modeling the physical-logical split.

card itself is a physical entity, so either the CIM_PhysicalElement class or a subclass of CIM_PhysicalElement is used. The presence of the modem jack and network port indicates that the card has two purposes: modem and network connection. These are functional capabilities, uses of the card that can be realized by the PC hosting the card. Consequently, the functions are represented as CIM_LogicalDevice or one of its subclasses and linked to the CIM_PhysicalElement object for the card with instances of the CIM_Realizes association.

The Core Model handles the identity of the CIM_LogicalElement and CIM_PhysicalElement differently. For the logical side, the identity is left up to the subclasses because CIM_LogicalElement does not include any key information. On the physical side, the CIM_PhysicalElement class definition does establish a key structure for its subclass. The Tag [CIM_PhysicalElement] holds any arbitrary value, since there are many schemes that can be used to identify physical elements. This allows CIM_PhysicalElement objects to be defined outside the context of a system (the discussion that follows explains why this is important).

Now it is important to backtrack to decomposable manageable components. Because CIM_PhysicalElement and CIM_LogicalElement are subclasses of the CIM_ManagedSystemElement, they can play the role of component in the Composite design pattern. While this is true, and permitted by the model, it is more common to just think of CIM_LogicalElement classes as components and to think of CIM_PhysicalComponent classes as a member of the composite indirectly through the CIM_Realizes association. In other words, a CIM_PhysicalElement object is only part of the a composite represented by a CIM_System object when a CIM_LogicalElement object that is realized by the physical element is part of the composite.

Consumable Capability within a System

Manageable components represented by CIM_ManagedSystemElement objects are deployed so that they can be used to accomplish some business function. In many cases, the capability (or capabilities) of a manageable component provides a service that is needed by another manageable component. In this sense, these capabilities are consumable. So another aspect of a manageable component is its *services*. Figure 4.6 shows the Consumable Services design pattern.

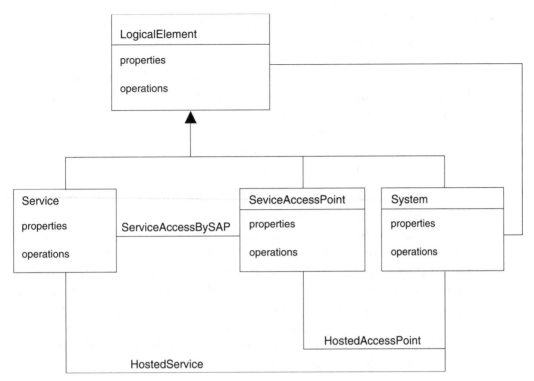

Figure 4.6   Consumable Services design pattern.

The CIM_Service class represents the manageable aspects of the service provided. It does not represent how another manageable component gains access to the consumables of the service. The CIM_ ServiceAccessPoint class represents the way to manage this linkage. Therefore, a CIM_ServiceAccessPoint object can be seen as an entry point in the consumables provided by a particular CIM_Service object. The CIM_ServiceAccessBySAP association represents the linkage between CIM_Service objects and CIM_ServiceAccessPoint objects.

The identity of the CIM_Service and CIM_ServiceAccessPoint object is handled in a similar manner. Both classes use the inherited Name [CIM_ManagedSystemElement] property to label the service or access point. However, the complete identity is based on combining the Name property with the properties propagated from the CIM_System class that is hosting the object. In other words, the identity of services and access points is scoped to the system hosting them. The relevant associations are CIM_HostedService and CIM_HostedAccessPoint. The CIM_Service and CIM_ServiceAccessPoints cannot be hosted by multiple systems.

So far the CIM_Service and CIM_ServiceAccessPoint classes have been described as suspended within the Core Model because two areas remain to be addressed. First, as stated at the beginning of this section, consumable services are one aspect of a manageable component, and we have not discussed their linkage with these manageable components. Second, we have not discussed how the linkage is represented when a consumable service is intended for another manageable component to consume. Let's complete our discussion of consumable service by looking at these two perspectives.

The CIM_DeviceServiceImplemention, CIM_SoftwareFeatureServiceImplementation, CIM_DeviceSAPImplementation, and CIMSoftwareFeatureSAPImplementation association link CIM_Service and CIM_ServiceAccessPoint objects with the manageable components that support them. Each of these associations expresses the fact that either a device or software feature is implementing a particular service or service access point. The Core Model does not support the idea that any CIM_ManagedSystemElement object supports a service, only that CIM_SoftwareFeature and CIM_LogicalDevice objects do. Figure 4.7 illustrates these implementation associations.

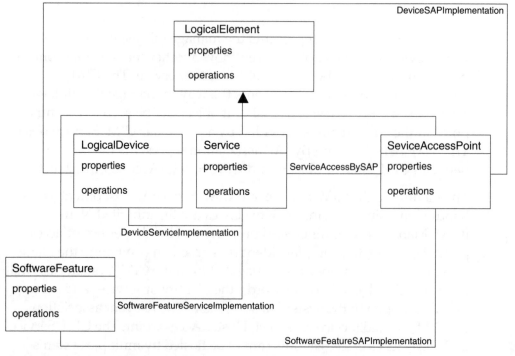

Figure 4.7 Consumable capabilities implementation.

Now we are ready to discuss how the Core Model represents one manageable component using another manageable component. This linkage is considered a dependency to the association used to represent this linkage at subclasses of the CIM_Dependency association. However, the model does not support the notion of a CIM_ManagedSystemElement consuming another CIM_ManagedSystemElement directly. Such dependencies are expressed between CIM_Service and CIM_ServiceAccessPoint objects.

To express that a manageable component (that is, a CIM_ManagedSystemElement) is required or is consuming the services of another manageable component, the consuming component must express the dependencies between one of its services and a service of the supplying manageable component. This situation is captured with the CIM_ServiceService association. The TypeOfDependency property of this association indicates the nature of the dependency.

The existence of a CIM_ServiceService association between two objects indicates that one depends on the other; it does not define the access path. The CIM_ServiceSAPDependency association identifies the service access point of the supplying service that the consuming service uses.

Finally, since a service access point is implemented either by devices or software features, service access points can have dependencies on other services. This dependency is expressed using the CIM_SAP-SAPDependency. Figure 4.8 summarizes these different types of dependencies.

Configurations

When manageable components are deployed, switches or dials may be set or changed to modify their behavior or the behavior of the services they support. The CIM_Setting class is used to capture a set of properties that represent these settings. The Core Model does not specify how a particular CIM_ElementSetting object is identified. The subclasses of CIM_ElementSetting must specify the key and the actual setting parameters.

The CIM_ElementSetting association is used to connect CIM_ManagedSystemElement objects with a particular set of settings. CIM_ElementSetting is a very generic association, as it allows a particular CIM_ManagedSystemElement to be associated with multiple

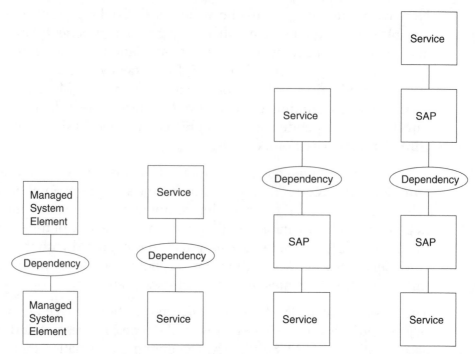

Figure 4.8 Different ways to express logical dependencies.

CIM_Setting objects at the same time. Therefore, the CIM_ElementSetting association presents a set of possible settings rather then one particular setting. Another important item to notice about the CIM_ElementSetting is that the cardinality specified, which states that a CIM_Setting must be related to at least one CIM_ManagedSystemElement, prevents the CIM_Setting object from dangling.

In addition to being organized by CIM_ManagedSystemElement objects, CIM_Setting objects can also be grouped or organized by CIM_Configuration objects. The CIM_Configuration class is used to collect a related set of CIM_Setting objects so that a particular CIM_ManagedSystemElement can express a dependency on a particular set of settings. In other words, you can represent that a particular manageable component must have a certain set of settings when it is a member of a particular system. The CIM_SettingContext association identifies the CIM_Setting objects that are part of a CIM_Configuration object. The CIM_ManagedSystemElement object that depends on a configuration is located using the CIM_ElementConfiguration association. CIM_Configuration classes are concrete so they can be instan-

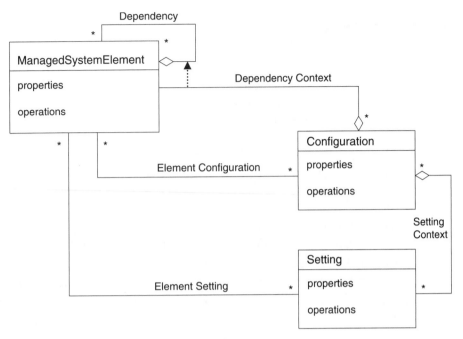

Figure 4.9 Setting/Configuration model.

tiated. Figure 4.9 summarizes the setting/configuration aspect of the Core Model.

Products

After a manageable component has been deployed and recombined in a complex IT system, it is easy to forget how the component was acquired. This is why the Core Model has the CIM_Product class. The CIM_Product class represents a unit of acquisition. Acquisition implies an agreement between a supplier and the consumer, which may affect licensing, support, and warranty. The CIM_Product class is intended to cover any form of acquisition, including deployment of internally generated applications, even though no actual purchase is involved.

The CIM_Product class can contain two types of manageable components. The CIMProductSoftwareFeature association makes it possible to include CIM_SoftwareFeature objects, and the CIMProductPhysicalElement makes it possible to include physical pieces of hardware. Because CIM_Product sometimes gets very complex, the CIM_ProductParentChild association can be used to include another product object.

Common Operations

Following are some common operations, given in the form of questions, that can be performed on the constructs in the Core Model. This list is not intended to be comprehensive, but only to serve as a means to test your understanding of the material presented in this chapter.

Is a particular managed system element a part of another whole?

Answer: Yes, if it is a target of a System Component association.

How can you identify the physical elements that make up a system?

Answer: There are two answers to this question. The preferred way is to enumerate all the CIM_LogicalDevice objects in the CIM_System using the CIM_SystemComponent association. The physical elements in the system are then those associated with the logical device using the CIM_Realizes association. The other way is to enumerate the CIM_PhysicalElement object directly with the CIM_SystemComponent association.

Summary

The Core Model is the part of DMTF's Common Information Model (CIM) that establishes the major design points or design patterns for representational issues that are not specific to a particular management domain or resource type. The major topics covered by the Core Model are: how manageable components are represented, how the Core Model handles the split between physical and logical resources is handled, how consumable services are modeled, how configuration properties are specified for manageable components, and how products are modeled. The Common Models that address specific management domains, such as systems and applications, use the approaches outlined in the Core Model to deal with their domain. For example, the Common Model for applications uses the CIM_Product class to represent a software product.

The Core Model provides the basic structure or framework for the definitions in the Common Model. This fact has motivated the CIM TDC to maintain the stability of the Core Model, because modifications (such as deletes to the Core Model) would result in a major representational change to all the definitions in the Common Models. Therefore, we do not anticipate disruptive changes to the Core Model.

The chapters that follow will discuss design patterns associated with specific management domains like systems or applications.

References

DMTF Application Management Work Group. 1997. "Application Model White Paper," V2.0, DMTF Web site.

DMTF Committee. 1998. "Common Information Model (CIM) Specification," V2.0, DMTF Web site.

Cargill, Tom. 1992. "C++ Programming Style," Massachusetts: Addison-Wesley.

Gamma, Erich, et. al. 1995. "Design Patterns: Elements of Reusable Object-Oriented Software," Massachusetts: Addison-Wesley.

Thompson, J.P., and Sweitzer, J.W. 1997. "Successful Practices in Developing a Complex Information Model," 16th International Conference on Conceptual Modeling. Proceedings in *Computer Science*, Vol. 1331. pp. 376-93. New York: Springer-Verlag.

System and Device Models

The System and Device Common Models of the CIM Schema detail the many classes for describing and managing general-purpose and dedicated computer systems. These models describe hardware components that make up computer systems and the base classes for entities associated with them (for example, operating systems, jobs, and file systems).

After reading this chapter, you should understand:

- Critical design themes and objects in the System and Device Models
- Use and instantiation of the models for managing systems and devices in an enterprise
- Criteria for appropriate subclassing of the models

Purpose of the System and Device Models

The goal of the CIM System Model is to describe general system concepts and specific computer system objects. The general concepts provide context and semantics for all systems and are available for subclassing in this and other models, such as the Application and Network Models. The System Model focuses on computer systems, their BIOSs, operating systems, processes, threads, jobs, file systems, files, and more.

The CIM Device Model attempts to describe and abstract the configuration and operation of hardware. It focuses on describing the multitude of devices, from low-level sensors to sophisticated printers and video monitors. The Device Model describes general relationships, such as redundancy for sparing and load balancing, and the association of devices to their supporting software and the physical environment.

As we mentioned in Chapter 4, "The Core Model," systems (the subclasses and instances of CIM_System) aggregate and host a wide assortment of managed entities. A system is identified as a single object in the enterprise that must be uniquely named. For example, to identify all the servers, workstations, and nodes of an enterprise, you must be able to locate and name the individual CIM_ComputerSystem objects.

One type of component aggregated by a system is the class of CIM_LogicalDevices. The CIM_SystemDevice association in the Core Model highlights this relationship and explains that devices exist within the scope of a system. As mentioned in Chapter 4, devices are *weak* to a system—meaning that the devices are named relative to the system that aggregates them. A C: drive in an enterprise is certainly not a unique entity, but the C: drive on the computer system whose name is Finance001 may indeed be unique.

CIM_LogicalDevices describe the functional aspects of hardware (such as a modem's configuration), as well as the controller and bus characteristics behind the operation of the hardware. For example, the Device Model defines entities such as SCSI (Small Computer Systems Interface), PCI (Peripheral Component Interconnect), and video controllers. Devices participate in implementing and providing the CIM_Services and CIM_ServiceAccessPoints that are hosted on a system.

The tie between systems (the aggregation) and devices (entities that are aggregated and operate together to create a functioning system) is very strong. When one is discussed, the other is naturally mentioned and completes the discussion.

System Methodology and Design Patterns

The following three key concepts are important for understanding systems as defined in the CIM Schemas:

- Systems act as aggregation entities.
- Systems host services (that is, provide functionality) and the mechanisms for accessing services.
- Systems are top-level objects for scoping and naming purposes.

To address the aggregation aspects of a system, the CIM_SystemComponent association is defined in the Core Model. This association is subclassed in the CIM_SystemDevice relationship, relating devices to the systems that contain them. This relationship also links the naming of the devices to these systems. (Details and figures describing these concepts were presented in Chapter 4.)

You might ask why devices are tied to the very high-level CIM_System class, as opposed to a lower-level, more concrete class like CIM_ComputerSystem. The answer is that there are many kinds of systems and many kinds of devices. Typically, devices are related to computer systems. However, a tape library is not a computer system; but it is a kind of CIM_System (a CIM_StorageLibrary) and aggregates devices. So, having the device relationship at a high level in the model is very useful.

Subclasses of CIM_SystemComponent associate and aggregate other entities with CIM_Systems. For example, operating and file systems are linked to their host computer systems using the CIM_InstalledOS and CIM_HostedFileSystem relationships, respectively. As for devices, operating and file systems are named relative to the CIM_ComputerSystem (a subclass of CIM_System) that hosts them.

Not all associations to CIM_System are aggregations. Many other relationships, such as CIM_Dependency, are defined. For example, CIM_Services and CIM_JobDestinations (queues) are hosted on systems. They are not integral to the systems (that is, they are not aggregated as parts of the system), but are dependent on the system, running within the operating system or requiring the devices aggregated by the system.

Relationships involving systems are not unidirectional, with entities dependent only on the system; a CIM_ComputerSystem may also be dependent on other entities. The CIM_RunningOS association describes the concept that a computer system is dependent on an executing operating system in order to function.

The subclasses of CIM_System are defined with particular semantics, such that the list of objects that are "reasonably" aggregated or hosted are straightforward. The CIM System Model focuses on two subclasses: CIM_ComputerSystem and CIM_StorageLibrary. Storage libraries are defined as cartridge (or tape) libraries that aggregate media transfer devices (such as pickers and changers), access devices (such as doors and library ports), and media readers (such as tape drives). Computer systems perform general or dedicated compute activities and aggregate one or more operating systems and multiple devices, such as an initial load device, keyboard, monitor, and power supplies (see Figure 5.1).

CIM_ComputerSystem has three subclasses. They describe:

- Individual computing nodes (CIM_UnitaryComputerSystem)
- Virtual systems (CIM_VirtualComputerSystem)
- Clusters (CIM_Cluster)

Note that some of the same devices (for example, doors or tape drives) may be aggregated into both CIM_StorageLibraries and CIM_Com-

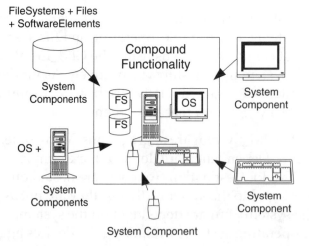

Figure 5.1 Aggregating a computer system's components.

puterSystems. The differences between these systems are their semantics (storage libraries certainly don't perform compute activities) and the complete list of objects that are reasonably aggregated or hosted. In fact, a CIM_StorageLibrary may have a CIM_ComputerSystem as one of its CIM_SystemComponents, but the storage library would not have an operating system.

You may wonder why the System Model subclasses only computer systems and storage libraries, where routers or network-attached disk storage systems are modeled, and whether these are new subclasses of CIM_System. Actually, routers and disk storage systems are instances of CIM_ComputerSystem, where the Dedicated property of the class indicates their purpose. Such systems really do fit the semantics of a CIM_ComputerSystem. They aggregate devices and (at least) "mini" operating systems and provide compute capabilities to carry out their functions. On the other hand, we expect additional system subclasses to be defined over time. The list of CIM_System subclasses is by no means complete.

A review of the System Model reveals that many other system elements are also defined there. Elements such as operating systems, processes, threads, jobs, and files are examples. (Note: These concepts were placed in the System Model because of their close relationship to computer systems, the main focus of the model.)

System Names

The CIM_System object and its subclasses are critical components in describing and managing an enterprise's computing environment. In the CIM Schema, they are top-level objects, meaning that they are required to provide naming information for other components, such as services and devices.

Computer systems in an enterprise can be discovered using various management protocols and techniques. Some of these techniques include IP address ping, checking for resident Desktop Management Interface (DMI) instrumentation, and querying a directory. Because different discovery mechanisms are based on various independent technologies, it is possible that one "real-world" system might be discovered multiple times. This duplication, illustrated in Figure 5.2, may

CIM Object Manager 1	CIM Object Manager 2
Namespace default includes an instance of CIM_UnitaryComputerSystem with Name = ABC	Namespace other includes an instance of CIM_UnitaryComputerSystem with Name = 10.10.10.1

Named using
DMI Instrumentation

Named using
IP Address
Identification

Real-world system

Figure 5.2 Discovering and naming systems.

result in more than one object instance being created for the single real-world system.

Practically, it seems impossible to come up with a single *mandatory* algorithm to create a system name and have such an algorithm uniformly applied. Enterprise environments and naming schemes abound. An enterprise and/or its management software must decide how systems are identified and named. Ideally, the same naming scheme would apply to systems identified in an enterprise-level directory, as well as to smaller CIM-based repositories. For example, naming of nodes may be based on network domain and operating system-specific computer names. One issue with this scheme is that users can change their computer's name, but the underlying entity that is represented by that CIM_ComputerSystem object remains the same.

The DMTF *CIM System Model White Paper* describes a naming schema, which is summarized here. It instructs a discovery engine to use an ordered set of rules to determine a system's name. The first possible match defines the contents of the CIM_System's Name property for the discovered system. The mechanism, or rule, used to define the Name property is described in the NameFormat string property, which is also a property of the CIM_System class. The naming heuristic (summarized in the bullets below) is not necessarily the "right answer" for an enterprise, but it does serve to indicate the complexity involved in defining consistent and unique system names.

- If the system supplies a single IP hostname or single IP permanent address, Name should be set in dot notation to the fully qualified IP hostname or the address. The value for the NameFormat property should be *IP*.

- If the system supplies many hostnames or permanent IP addresses, Name should equal a whitespace-separated list of the fully qualified hostnames or addresses in dot notation. The order is arbitrary. The value for NameFormat should be *IP*.

- If the system provides a unique hardware ID, such as a CPU serial number, and gets a dynamic, protocol-assigned IP address, Name should be the value of the hardware ID. The value for NameFormat should be *HID*.

- If the system provides a single network interface and gets a dynamic, protocol-assigned IP address, Name should equal the hardware address of the network interface. The value for NameFormat should be *HWA*. This value should also be used when a dial-up connection is used and the network interface (although present) is inactive.

- If the system provides a dial-up connection only, and a unique value for the system's primary owner exists or an enterprise-wide unique operating system license is available, Name should be set to the Primary Owner string or license number. The value for NameFormat should be *DIAL*.

- If the system represents a network in itself, Name should equal the network address. The value for NameFormat should be *NWA*.

- If the system provides a logical name by which it is known for dedicated access mechanisms, Name should contain this string. The extension model in which this subclass of System is defined describes the value for NameFormat.

- Systems that provide network access through any mechanism other than IP are not covered by the naming heuristic. It is suggested that similar network addressing or logical names be used to define the Name value. The NameFormat should indicate the network type. The currently defined values include *X25, IPX, ISDN, DCC, ICD, E.164, SNA,* and *OID/OSI*.

Device Methodology and Design Patterns

To understand CIM_LogicalDevices, keep these four key concepts in mind:

- Devices are abstract and can be realized in hardware.
- Typically, there are multiple different aspects to a device.
- Configuration information (assigned system resources) and details on supporting software are needed to manage a device.
- Connections and associations between devices are crucial to their operation.

CIM_LogicalDevice represents the management and configuration aspects of hardware. The logical device is *not* the hardware itself; this is a very difficult distinction to make and maintain. For example, you may want to say that an adapter card or a chip on a motherboard "is" the CIM_NetworkAdapter, but this would not be correct.

Devices (the subclasses and instances of CIM_LogicalDevice) abstract hardware and are "realized" by that same hardware. ("Realized" is enclosed in quotation marks because this is the definition of the CIM_Realizes relationship; see Figure 5.3.) Hardware is represented in the Physical Model, while the functional and configuration aspects of a device are instantiated in the Device Model. The two representations are linked using the CIM_Realizes association.

Relating the physical and logical aspects of hardware is accomplished using the CIM_Realizes association; relating different logical aspects of a *single* device is accomplished using CIM_DeviceIdentity. The latter

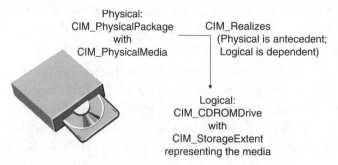

Figure 5.3   Physical and logical aspects of a device.

explains that two device instances really represent the same object, but different aspects of it. The association's semantics are similar to those conveyed by multiple inheritance (which is not supported by the CIM Schema). CIM_DeviceIdentity links together two CIM_LogicalDevices, and is a subclass of the CIM_LogicalIdentity relationship, as defined in the Core Model.

Where would you use the CIM_DeviceIdentity relationship? One scenario is to represent a device as both a bus entity and a functional entity. For example, a device could be both a USB (Universal Serial Bus) device, as well as a CIM_Keyboard. The properties of CIM_USBDevice describe the class, subclass and protocol codes of the bus interface, along with other protocol-specific data. The properties of CIM_Keyboard describe configuration and status information related to the device functionality (for example, whether the device IsLocked is a property of the CIM_Keyboard class). These two aspects of the device would be linked by instantiating a CIM_DeviceIdentity relationship between them. Another scenario is one in which a device plays multiple functional roles that cannot be distinguished by their hardware realization alone. For example, a Fibre Channel adapter might have aspects of both a CIM_NetworkAdapter and a CIM_SCSIController. In this case, both network adapter and SCSI controller device instances would be created and associated using the CIM_DeviceIdentity relationship.

To operate in a system, devices need resources assigned to them, and some sort of supporting software, such as a device driver, to configure and utilize them. This is depicted in Figure 5.4.

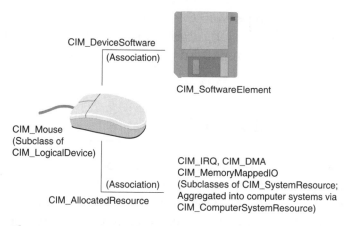

Figure 5.4 Device software and resources.

We'll address software first. The CIM_DeviceSoftware association ties a device to a CIM_SoftwareElement (defined in the Application Model) and details the functionality provided by the software. A property of the association, Purpose, indicates whether the software is driver code, application software, instrumentation code, or BIOS (to name a few of the enumerated values). Another property indicates whether the software is loaded on the device (for example in read-only memory) and/or upgradeable on the device (if in programmable or flash memory).

Turning to system resources, the CIM_SystemResource superclass describes objects such as IRQs, DMA channels, and memory and port I/O resources. A resource is a component of a computer system and is named relative to its aggregating system. The association that describes this semantic is CIM_ComputerSystemResource. Once resources are named and their configuration described in their class objects (CIM_IRQ, CIM_DMA, or CIM_MemoryMappedIO), it is necessary to understand the devices to which they are assigned. This is defined using the CIM_AllocatedResource association, which describes that a device is dependent on its assigned resources and creates an explicit association tying these entities together.

The last design pattern of the Device Model deals with the wide variety of communication connections and dependencies that may exist between devices. This topic is so extensive, and sometimes so closely tied to the individual device classes, that we devote the next section to describing it.

When reviewing the Device Model, note that it is easy to become overwhelmed by its volume. To prevent this happening, remember that the content deals with low-level configuration details for many different devices and utilizes the design patterns we discussed in this section, nothing more.

Device Connections and Associations

Connections and associations between devices abound in the real world. A printer may be connected to a parallel port; a USB device may be connected to a port on a USB hub. These are examples of the CIM_DeviceConnection association. Typically, when devices communicate, they first negotiate their speed (bandwidth) and data width.

This information is part of the class definition of CIM_DeviceConnection, the NegotiatedSpeed and NegotiatedDataWidth properties.

A subclass of CIM_DeviceConnection is CIM_ControlledBy; it describes that a particular connection is between a CIM_Controller and its "downstream" device. Controllers are devices with a single protocol stack whose primary purpose is to communicate with, control, and reset connected devices. There are many subclasses of CIM_Controller, addressing SCSI, PCI, USB, serial, parallel, and video controllers.

The CIM_ControlledBy association adds properties to those inherited from CIM_DeviceConnection. These properties deal with the number of hard and soft resets of the downstream device, and whether the controller is currently the "active" one communicating to the device. This property is needed when multiple controllers can communicate with a single device (SCSI is one example where this scenario might occur).

SCSI introduces the topic of storage. When dealing with storage, you are concerned with disks, tapes, cartridges, and memory. These entities typically participate in layering relationships. One storage entity can be based on (possibly) many other storage objects, perhaps to build up RAID redundancy. These relationships are conveyed using the CIM_BasedOn association. Figure 5.5 shows a simple example of the use of this association, as well as the CIM_Realizes and CIM_ControlledBy relationships.

At first glance, this media storage example may not seem so simple. But take a minute to examine it. Physical packages describe the hardware—conceivably an adapter card that realizes the SCSI controller and a disk package that realizes the media and the media access hardware. The physical packages in turn realize devices—the SCSI controller, storage media, and a media access device. The latter is the disk drive or "player." What is being "played" is indicated by association, using the CIM_MediaPresent relationship.

If you are wondering why the media is separated from its player, when the physical package can't be taken apart, then you have missed the point about separating the logical and physical worlds. The logical properties of the two entities, media access device and the media itself, are very different and so are modeled as separate objects in the device hierarchy.

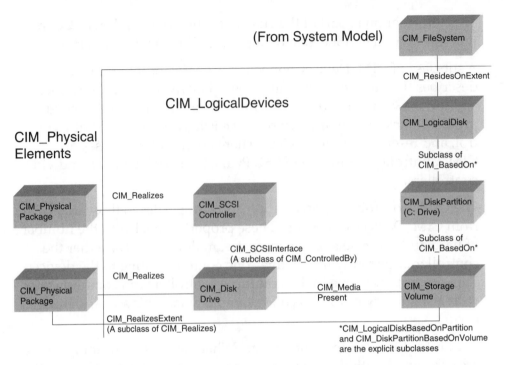

Figure 5.5   Modeling a C: drive and its storage media.

Once the low-level devices are modeled in Figure 5.5, their relationships and layering are described using the CIM_SCSIInterface and CIM_BasedOn relationships. Disk partitions are built on low-level storage volumes. Then a logical disk (the C: drive) is layered on the partition. Finally, the file system resides on the C: drive. This is indicated using the CIM_ResidesOnExtent association.

You may argue that we don't need to describe the file system, since its existence is inferred from the data stored in the partition and logical disk objects. But this is not true for all hardware environments; and again, the properties of storage are very different from the properties of a CIM_FileSystem. Hence, CIM defines and instantiates unique classes for file systems.

Now we can return to the discussion of associations in the Device Model. Redundancy was discussed briefly in the preceding paragraphs; this is a key concept of the Device Model, and, in fact, of any management schema. Redundancy comes in three flavors:

Sparing. Embodies failover and is modeled by the CIM_SpareGroup.

Extra capacity. Includes load balancing and is indicated by the CIM_ExtraCapacityGroup.

Storage-related redundancy. Includes RAID and is modeled by the CIM_StorageRedundancyGroup.

Associations, such as CIM_RedundancyComponent (and its sub-classes), describe which entities participate in a redundancy group, as well as specific details related to failover and load balancing of the entities.

The concepts of sparing and storage-related redundancy (mirroring, striping, parity checking, and so on) are fairly well understood. But what is the meaning of an *extra capacity group*? This group describes that all the redundancy components are active, and together supply "capacity" beyond what is required. An example is the insertion of additional power supplies into a system to provide headroom and perhaps to participate in load balancing.

Sometimes questions arise as to why CIM_RedundancyGroup is a subclass of CIM_LogicalElement and not of CIM_CollectionOfMSEs (also defined in the Core Model). The answer is fairly simple. CIM_CollectionOfMSEs describes a "bag" of objects with no status or ability to be managed. CIM_RedundancyGroup describes a manageable entity, with an install date (for example, when RAID redundancy was established) and a status. The Status property is inherited from CIM_ManagedSystemElement and may indicate "Error." Additional information could be supplied in the RedundancyStatus property to indicate "Redundancy Lost."

The remainder of the device-related associations explain that a device's function is specific to, and in support of, another device. For example, AssociatedMemory indicates that an instance of CIM_Memory is not general-purpose, but tied to the device(s) referenced by the association. As other examples, AssociatedSensor or AssociatedBattery describe the devices dependent on a particular sensor or battery backup.

A Sample Computer System and Its Devices

To help you understand the System and Device Models, we will walk through an example that features a three-node application failover

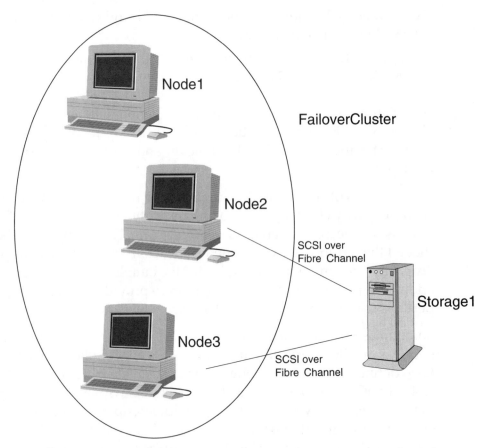

Figure 5.6 Sample configuration.

cluster, where two of the nodes utilize storage provided by a dedicated subsystem. The nodes in the cluster are composed of numerous devices. The sample configuration is shown in Figure 5.6. (Note: Throughout the remainder of this chapter, we will reference the example introduced here.)

The following is a brief overview of the CIM objects that make up the sample configuration:

CIM_Cluster and the association, ParticipatingCS. Describes a single entity representing the cluster and which computer systems participate in the cluster.

CIM_ClusteringService. Represents the failover functionality provided by the clustered systems.

CIM_UnitaryComputerSystem. Describes the nodes and the dedicated storage system.

CIM_ComputerSystemPackage. Associates the CIM_UnitaryComputerSystems to their physical packaging.

CIM_InstalledOS and CIM_RunningOS associations. Conveys operating system-specific information for the nodes and the storage system.

Various subclasses of CIM_LogicalDevice and the association, CIM_SystemDevice. Represents memory, processors, keyboards, Fibre Channel adapters, SCSI controllers, storage volumes (published by the storage system and accessed by the nodes), and numerous other devices. The association, CIM_SystemDevice, describes how the devices are aggregated into the CIM_UnitaryComputerSystems.

CIM_SystemResource and its associations, CIM_ComputerSystemResource and CIM_AllocatedResource. Describes the IRQs, DMA channels, memory and port resources of a computer system, and how these resources are allocated to devices.

CIM_FileSystem and CIM_LogicalFile. Represents file systems residing on the node's storage, along with the files existing within the file systems.

CIM_SpareGroup with its association, ActsAsSpare. Describes that storage volumes are available to the nodes as spares.

This list is long, but it is not exhaustive. The discussion could go in many different directions as additional management information is instantiated. For example, the operating systems on the nodes have executing processes and threads (described as instances of CIM_Process and CIM_Thread, respectively). CIM_Jobs are being executed; perhaps print jobs are being sent to a printer's queue. And, the nodes have CIM_BIOSElements for booting.

On the device side, CIM_PowerSupply and CIM_TemperatureSensor are likely components of the nodes. Certainly, a CIM_EthernetAdapter is present, supporting the interconnect between the nodes of the cluster. All these components have associated DeviceSoftware. Also, a "blinking light" CIM_AlarmDevice may be installed on the storage cabinet. A network printer might be available to the nodes, which would have associated print queues, services, and access mechanisms.

All these entities have corresponding objects in the Device Model and could be instantiated.

We encourage you to review the System and Device MOFs (Managed Object Format files) on the DMTF Web site (www.dmtf.org) to familiarize yourself with all the objects, properties and associations that have been defined.

Classes, Associations, and Attributes

The following subsections describe the CIM Schema as it relates to the sample systems and devices in Figure 5.6. We provide UML diagrams of the pertinent CIM classes and their associations, along with some discussion and interpretation of these diagrams. Our goal is to identify and define the salient objects of the sample configuration.

CIM Systems

Figure 5.7 shows the high-level system and computer system objects from a combination of the Core and System Models.

After examining Figures 5.6 and 5.7, it would be reasonable to assume that a CIM_Cluster is instantiated to represent the failover cluster. In this example, the keys of this cluster instance are defined simply as:

- CreationClassName = "CIM_Cluster"
- Name = "FailoverCluster"

In reality, the object's key (the combination of CreationClassName and Name) must be unique in the enterprise. In this example, another Name value (other than FailoverCluster) might be defined which is more unique. One alternative is "Engineering Failover Cluster 20.20.20.2".

Besides the key properties (which are inherited from CIM_System), many other properties of the CIM_Cluster object are used to characterize it. These include owner contact information, the roles that the object plays (for example, "Finance failover cluster"), the interconnect mechanism for heartbeats and other cluster communications (probably Ethernet using today's technologies), and the type of the cluster (set to 2, Failover). ClusterState is another property, describing

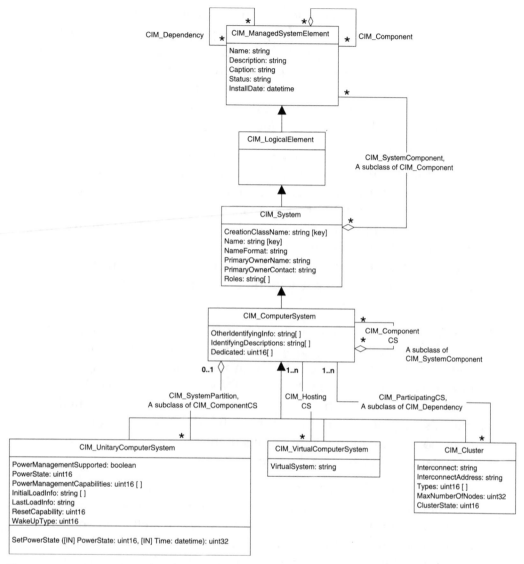

Figure 5.7. System UML diagram.

whether the cluster is online, offline, degraded, or unavailable. This is a very high-level status for the cluster, as a whole. And there are more properties!

When you look at the CIM_Cluster object in more detail, you see a Dedicated property, inherited from CIM_ComputerSystem. From examining the UML alone, you can't determine this property's semantics. (The MOF describes these semantics.) The Dedicated property describes the function of the computer system—distinguishing between computer systems for general-purpose use versus systems "dedicated to" storage, printing, or network processing (for example). Note that that the Dedicated property does not describe access rights. (The latter is the job of the User Model, to be released post-CIM V2.2.) In the example's cluster object, the Dedicated property is set to 0 (meaning that the system is "Not Dedicated").

A cluster in the CIM System MOF is defined as being made up of individual systems creating a functional "whole to increase the performance, resources and/or RAS (reliability, availability, and serviceability) of the component" systems. (This quotation comes from the CIM_Cluster object description in the System MOF.) With that in mind, how do we describe these component systems? That is the purpose of the CIM_ParticipatingCS association. It explains that the cluster is dependent on its participating computer systems in order to exist.

The CIM Schema defines various properties for the CIM_ParticipatingCS association. These properties detail the state and role of the computer system in the cluster. Information such as joining the cluster or paused is conveyed in the StateOfNode property; RoleOfNode indicates whether the participating computers are peers, associated as primary/secondary, or another of the defined values. This sort of data does not belong in the node objects themselves or in the cluster, but in the relationship between the two.

Why does the CIM_ParticipatingCS relationship run to CIM_ComputerSystem and not CIM_UnitaryComputerSystem (that is, a node)? This allows flexibility for future technologies. When a cluster can be built out of other clusters that are really virtual systems, hosted on nodes, the System Model will be able to describe this. If this seems unbelievable, here are the objects to be instantiated:

- Top-level cluster is a CIM_Cluster.
- It is built on lower-level CIM_Clusters, each associated to the top-level cluster by instances of the CIM_ParticipatingCS association.
- The lower-level clusters are in turn built on virtual systems. The virtual systems are instances of CIM_VirtualComputerSystem, and their participation in the lower-level clusters is indicated using CIM_PartiticipatingCS.

- The virtual systems are hosted on nodes. The nodes are instances of CIM_UnitaryComputerSystem, and the act of hosting a virtual system is described using CIM_HostingCS.

Imagine describing these relationships and data in DMI or SNMP!

We need a few more instances to complete the system side of the sample configuration. These are the instances of the storage system and the nodes that participate in the cluster. To start, we need four instances of CIM_UnitaryComputerSystem, where CreationClassName is set to CIM_UnitaryComputerSystem and the Name properties are Node1, Node2, Node3, and Storage1 respectively. (Again, note that this is a simplistic and unrealistic naming scheme.)

What do the properties of CIM_UnitaryComputerSystem describe? Primarily, they characterize the power state and other power management aspects of the node, including whether power and reset switches are currently enabled (indicated by the ResetCapability property). Also, they describe initial load information and why the system booted. The latter is defined in the WakeUpType property and highlights whether the system booted due to power being restored, the power switch being depressed, modem ring, or other events. This type of information is especially useful for security purposes.

As we described for cluster systems, the nodes and storage system of the sample configuration contain many properties. These include status, owner contact, and role information, inherited from CIM_System. Also, the Dedicated property is inherited by CIM_UnitaryComputerSystem. For the example's storage system, Dedicated should be set to 3, Storage. For all the node systems, it is initialized as 0, Not Dedicated.

Before leaving the topic of high-level objects in the System Model, we should mention the CIM_ComponentCS association. CIM_ComponentCS describes that one computer may be a part (component) of another. This is different from clusters being built on other systems or virtual systems hosted on a computer system. The latter are dependencies, not whole-part relationships.

It is difficult to visualize how a virtual system is a part of its host platform, or how the individual nodes of a cluster "are" the cluster. However, it is reasonable to view these relationships as dependencies. The virtual system is dependent on its host. The cluster is dependent on its participating nodes. On the other hand, something like an I2O (Intelligent I/O) subsystem, embedded in a node, is really a computer system (with an operating system, managed devices including a processor, hosted services, and more). This embedded system is truly a part of the node and takes power from the node—a semantic described by CIM_ComponentCS.

CIM Cluster and Boot Services

Services and the access points (mechanisms) to utilize them are hosted on cluster systems and nodes. The System Model defines two types of services: CIM_ClusteringService and CIM_BootService.

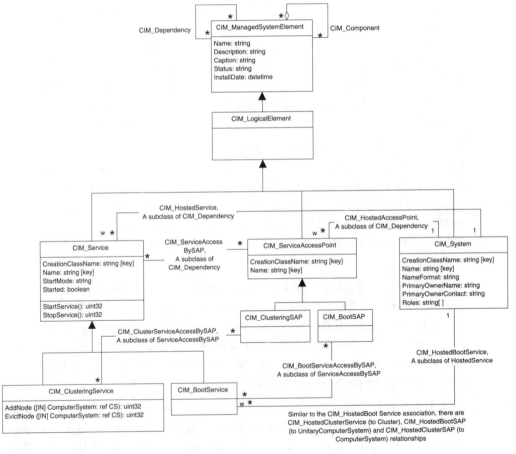

Figure 5.8 Services in the System Model.

Clustering services represent the functionality of the failover services in the sample configuration. However, the model is not yet complete in this area, and specific failover methods and information are not included in the object definitions. (This work is targeted for release post-CIM V2.2.)

- *CIM_ClusteringService is a superclass for failover, load balancing, and other similar services hosted on a cluster.* At this time, its sole purpose is to define methods to add and evict systems from the cluster. The service's access points are hosted on the individual computer systems that are added, removed, or otherwise involved in the clustering.

- *CIM_BootService represents functionality such as PXE (Preboot Execution Environment), BootP, and other network load services for a system.* Boot services are hosted in systems, since booting from a "network system" is possible. But their access points are hosted on nodes (CIM_UnitaryComputerSystems) since these are the entities that "boot."

Figure 5.8 is a UML diagram of these concepts. And keep in mind, the service and access point objects need further definition.

Operating Systems, File Systems, and Files

Computer systems are more than hardware, devices, and boot services. They require software in order to provide compute capabilities. To describe the software environment, a computer system aggregates and provides scoping for one or more operating systems, which are either formally released products (such as Windows 2000 Server) or firmware and proprietary software loaded into nonvolatile storage (such as OpenDOS).

The CIM_OperatingSystem object represents software or firmware that makes a computer system's hardware usable. It implements and/or manages the system resources, file systems, processes, user interfaces, and services that are available on the system. Properties of the class include information related to operating system type (for example, Linux) and version, last boot time, maximum number of licenses, memory information (such as amount of visible physical memory or amount of virtual memory), and whether the operating system is distributed (a Boolean value). The CIM_OperatingSystem properties also define methods to reboot and shut down the operating system.

CIM_InstalledOS association defines the operating systems that are aggregated by a computer system. When more than one operating system is available on a system, the one that is currently booted can be indicated using the CIM_RunningOS dependency association.

CIM's operating system objects and associations are shown in Figure 5.9, along with those for file systems.

CIM_FileSystem represents a file store and the underlying services to access that store. The System Model defines both local and remotely accessed file systems. The perspective from which to discuss *local* versus *remote* is that of the networking infrastructure required by the computer system using the file system. For example, if access of the file system requires network services (perhaps using the Network File System (NFS) protocol), then the file system is remote. If only basic device driver and file system services are used (for example, if "open and read 10 bytes from file foo" causes the local SCSI driver to retrieve 10 bytes), then the file system is local. Physically, the foo file may be on disks in an external SCSI enclosure, but this is physical only. (Remember the logical and physical distinction described earlier.) To the operating system and its file system, there are no intervening and supporting network services, just local driver access of files.

Currently, the only example of a remote file system in the CIM Schema is a Network File System (NFS). The CIM_NFS object and its associations describe the client-side configuration information for NFS file access. NFS functions by allowing the *export* of directories from a local file system and their *mount* by a remote system. Mounted directories are accessed as though they were local. The remote directories are grafted into the local file store. The System Model describes relationships of export and mount using associations of the same names. The CIM_Export association has one property, ExportedDirectoryName.

Data modeled in the CIM_NFS class reflects the client system's configuration of its NFS services. For example, the class properties capture information related to mount failure retries, read and write buffer sizes, and whether attribute caching is on. Additional remote file systems, as well as generalizing the concepts of export and mount, will be defined in the System Model, post-CIM V2.2.

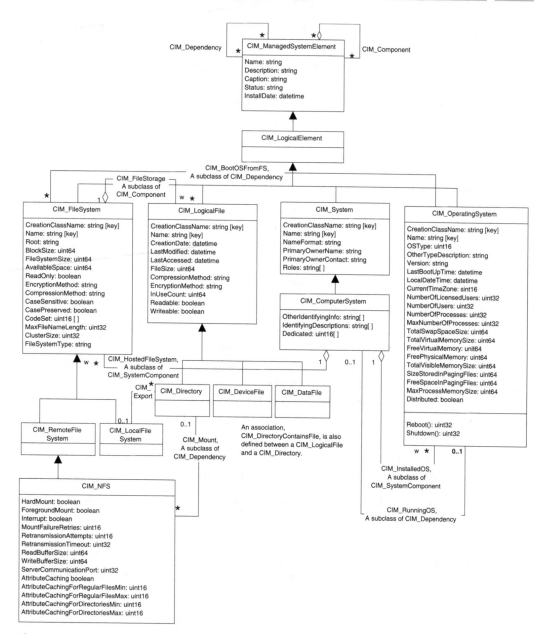

Figure 5.9. Operating and file system objects.

Moving beyond the file system to the files themselves, these are modeled using the CIM_LogicalFile object and its subclasses. CIM defines three subclasses: CIM_Directory, CIM_DataFile, and CIM_DeviceFile. (It should be noted that data files include executables.) The semantics of data files and directories follow normal conventions.

You may ask, why aren't executable files a subclass of CIM_DataFile? The answer is that it is difficult to define what an executable file is. For example, is a Java byte code file an executable or simply a data file? In the end, it is executed. Instead of arguing these difficult distinctions, the CIM System and Device Working Group decided to model the relationship between data files and executing CIM_Processes. The association that ties these executables and data files together is CIM_ProcessExecutable.

Returning to the discussion of CIM_LogicalFile subclasses, CIM defines one additional class. CIM_DeviceFile represents the access of a device using a byte stream I/O model. UNIX is one example of an operating system where this type of device access occurs. The device associated with and accessed via the CIM_DeviceFile is specified using the CIM_DeviceAccessByFile relationship.

Now that we have defined files and file systems, we need to examine how they are identified and named. Files are *scoped by*, or *weak to*, file systems; it does not make sense to talk about files outside the context of the file system that dictates their naming and access services. File systems, in turn, are weak with respect to the computer systems and operating systems in which they execute. The scoping relationships for files and file systems are defined by the CIM_FileStorage and CIM_Hosted-FileSystem component associations, respectively. The CIM_BootOS-FromFS relationship captures the idea that an operating system boots from a file system. Figure 5.9 shows all of these file system associations.

We can reasonably assume that file systems reside on some kind of storage (a disk partition, RAID extent, RAM Disk, and so on). The CIM_ResidesOnExtent dependency association makes the file system/storage relationship explicit. It ties together a CIM_FileSystem and a CIM_StorageExtent instance (where CIM_StorageExtent is a subclass of CIM_LogicalDevice).

Our discussion has now transitioned to the device level. Therefore, it is wise to move back to the Device Model, to elaborate on its concepts and object designs.

CIM Devices

As discussed in Chapter 4, the CIM_LogicalDevice object generically represents status, power on hours, and error information. The object's definition includes power management capabilities and methods, as well as methods to reset and enable/disable the device.

Since it is possible to identify (and therefore name) devices using multiple mechanisms, the properties OtherIdentifyingInfo and IdentifyingDescriptions were added to CIM_LogicalDevice. An example of the use of these properties occurs when you have a Fibre Channel adapter in a personal computer. In this case, you may set the DeviceID (one of the object's key properties) to its plug-and-play identification. The adapter's World Wide Name and device driver's hardware identification are stored in the first two entries of the OtherIdentifyingInfo array. The associated array, IdentifyingDescriptions, would contain string entries explaining the data in OtherIdentifyingInfo. In this case, the values, "Fibre Channel World Wide Name" and "Device Driver ID," could be used. Figure 5.10 shows the high-level device objects of the Core Model.

Many of the device associations that we have previously discussed are shown in Figure 5.10, including CIM_DeviceConnection, CIM_DeviceSoftware, and CIM_DeviceIdentity. The CIM_Realizes and CIM_SystemDevice associations are important for understanding a device's physical representation, as well as its containment and naming schemes. Remember that the CIM_SystemDevice aggregation defines the scoping of a device by a CIM_System. As a result, the device's name is based on a compound key structure that includes the aggregating system's name properties:

- Host system's CreationClassName and Name properties
- Device's CreationClassName and DeviceID properties

For example, a C: drive in one of the nodes of the sample configuration might be named SystemCreationClassName="CIM_UnitaryComputerSystem", SystemName="Node1", CreationClassName="CIM_MediaAccessDevice", DeviceID="C:".

A device's statistical information represents another important aspect of management data. General statistical data is located in subclasses of the CIM_StatisticalInformation object (defined in the Core Model). One subclass (CIM_DeviceErrorCounts) tracks the number of critical, major, minor, and warning errors that have occurred for a device, and provides a method to reset those error counts. An instance of CIM_

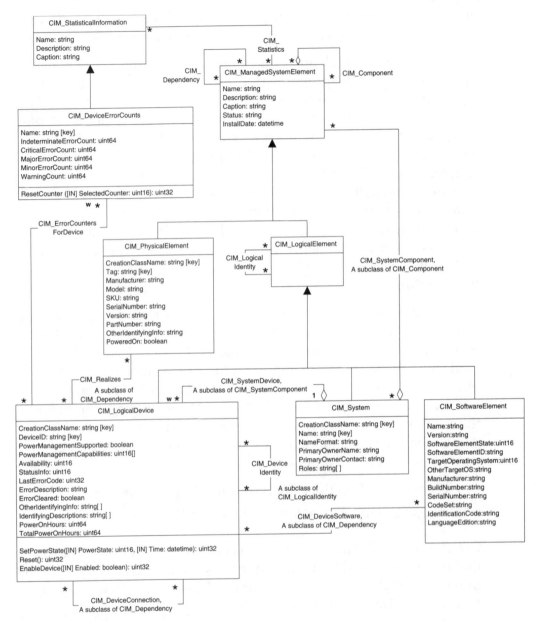

Figure 5.10 UML diagram of device objects.

DeviceErrorCounts is associated with and named relative to the device whose statistics are reported. The CIM_ErrorCountersForDevice association defines this relationship between the statistical data and the device.

Modeling Storage

The sample configuration in Figure 5.6 includes disk storage, disk drives, and SCSI controllers (in the nodes and storage subsystem), user input devices such as mice, keyboards and monitors, processors, memory, Fibre Channel adapters (for storage access in two of the nodes), and Ethernet adapters (for cluster and data communication). In this and following sections, we overview each of these device types, beginning with storage.

Storage media are abstracted as subclasses and instances of CIM_StorageExtents, while the entities that access (read and/or write) the media are kinds of CIM_MediaAccessDevices. Both removable and nonremovable types of storage are modeled. CIM Device and Physical Models describe disks, CD-ROMs, tapes, and other media players and storage entities. Figure 5.11 illustrates many of the storage-related objects in the Device Model, although we do not show all subclasses.

CIM_StorageExtent describes the logical characteristics of any type of storage space, including media and memory. (Note that the CIM_Memory object is a subclass of CIM_StorageExtent.) If you examine the properties of the storage objects, you will find information related to device capacity, block size (structure), and access mechanisms. Access mechanisms are concerned with distinguishing:

- Read, read/write, or write-once access (defined by the Access property)
- Requirements for sequential versus random access (described using the SequentialAccess Boolean)
- Support for variable- or fixed-length blocks (defined by the DataOrganization property)

Storage can be assembled in many different ways to create larger logical entities, or partitioned into multiple smaller ones. As mentioned previously, the CIM_BasedOn association or one of its subclasses describes the hierarchical (or layered) relationship between storage extents. The following classes and "based on" relationships would be instantiated in the sample configuration:

- *Within the storage enclosure, four instances of CIM_StorageExtent are defined.* These represent the logical abstractions of four physical disks.

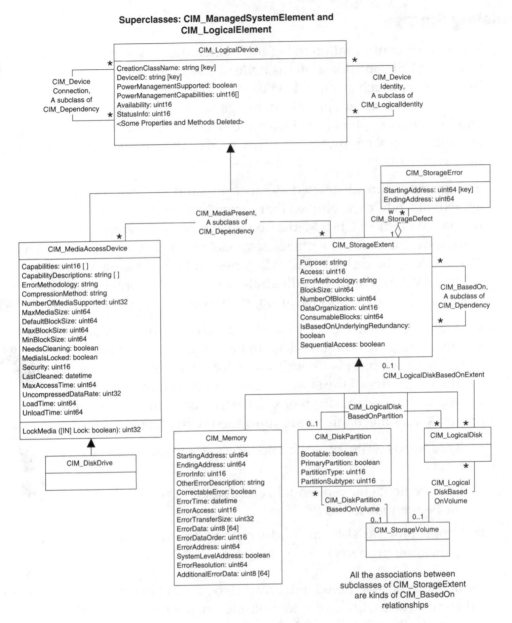

Figure 5.11 Storage device objects.

■ *By twos, the low-level storage extents are grouped to form stripe sets for performance.* The result of the striping is that two CIM_StorageVolumes are published by the enclosure—one for each connected node. Figure 5.12 depicts this storage configuration.

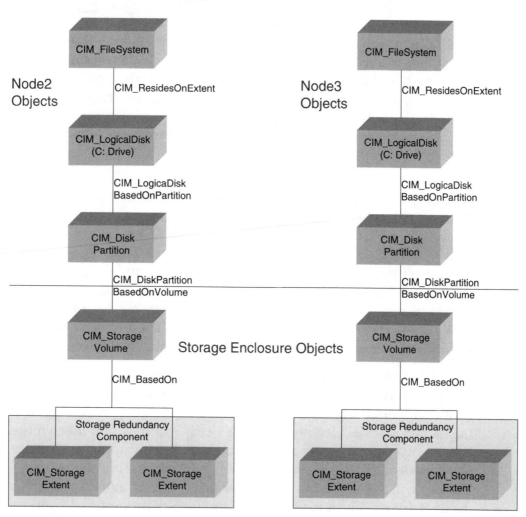

Figure 5.12 Storage extents in the sample configuration.

- *For each instance of CIM_StorageVolume published by the enclosure, there are two CIM_BasedOn relationships.* These explain that the volumes are built on lower-level storage extents. Given that striping is defined across these lower-level extents, each volume's Boolean property, BasedOnUnderlyingRedundancy, should be set to true. This property is inherited from CIM_StorageExtent and indicates that redundancy data is associated with the underlying extents. (Redundancy information is defined using the CIM_Redundancy-Group object and its subclasses.)

- *Within the nodes, a CIM_DiskPartition is based on an instance of CIM_StorageVolume.* The CIM_DiskPartitionBasedOnVolume association (a subclass of CIM_BasedOn) describes this layering. The properties of CIM_DiskPartition convey information on the partition's type (primary, extended, or logical) and the structure put down in preparation for the file system. For example, the Partition-SubType property is used to indicate the creation of NTFS, Linux, or a wide variety of other partitions.

- *On top of the CIM_DiskPartitions are CIM_LogicalDisks, perhaps the D: drives for each node.* Instances of the CIM_LogicalDiskBasedOnPartition association (a subclass of CIM_BasedOn) describe this node/drive relationship.

Several key concepts are still missing from the example. We need instances of CIM_DiskDrive to access the physical media in the storage enclosures. And instances of CIM_SCSIController describe the use of SCSI device drivers and the SCSI protocol to communicate with the storage enclosure, and access the published storage volumes.

CIM_DiskDrive is a subclass of CIM_MediaAccessDevice. It inherits many properties describing block sizes for data access, number of media supported, compression schemes when reading or writing to the media, whether cleaning of the device is required, and much more. You may wonder whether all these properties really apply to all types of access devices. The answer is no. For example, the NeedsCleaning Boolean will always be false for a disk drive. You cannot disassemble the disk drive to clean it. Despite the fact that all properties do not apply, there is much similarity between media players. So, the CIM System and Device Working Group decided to define a single class describing generic media access.

It is interesting to note the entries in the Capabilities property enumeration for CIM_MediaAccessDevice. Since this property is an array, multiple capabilities can be simultaneously defined for a device. The enumerated values include:

- Sequential and random access
- Supports writing
- Supports encryption and compression
- Supports removable media

- Manual or automatic cleaning
- SMART (Self-Monitoring and Alert Reporting Technology) notification
- Supports dual-sided media
- Predismount eject not required (when supporting removable media)

You can assume that new methods, properties, and associations will be defined in future releases of the Device Model to configure and obtain operational details for these capabilities.

Now that we have definitions for storage extents and their access devices, we must make the relationship between them explicit. This is the semantic behind the CIM_MediaPresent association. It describes that a particular storage media is being read or written by a particular media player. The association also defines whether the media are removable from the access device. This information is conveyed by the association's FixedMedia Boolean property.

Before concluding our discussion of storage, we feel a brief aside regarding the CIM_StorageError class, shown in Figure 5.11, is necessary. CIM_StorageError describes that "bad blocks" are mapped out of disk, bypassed on a tape, removed from active memory usage, and so on. These objects are defined and named relative to the storage that they map. The association that creates this relative referencing is CIM_StorageDefect.

Modeling Controllers and Network Adapters

Previously, we mentioned SCSI controllers and Fibre Channel adapters. Now it's time we examined the modeling of these devices.

Controllers abstract hardware that has a single, explicit protocol stack and that exists primarily for communication with downstream devices. Examples include serial, parallel, video, PCI, USB, and SCSI controllers. Controller communication is for data access, reset, and configuration of the downstream entities. Protocol details are typically defined in subclasses of the CIM_ControlledBy association. For example, CIM_SerialInterface describes the number of stop bits, parity, and flow control for communication with the serial controller. CIM_SCSI-Interface describes the number of time-outs and retries to the downstream device, initiator and target ID information, target LUN, whether a SCSI reservation is in place, and much more. The data (such as target LUN) varies for each entity that is controlled. From the perspective of the downstream device, if it communicates with several controllers, then multiple LUNs and multiple copies of other interface data will be defined. The only reasonable location for this information is in an association between the controller and the controlled objects.

But, why spend time discussing SCSI controllers when there is no SCSI hardware in the communication path to the storage subsystem in the sample configuration? A Fibre Channel adapter is used instead to access the storage volumes, communicating via a SCSI protocol. This is resolved in the model by allowing the instantiation of both a CIM_FibreChannelAdapter and a CIM_SCSIController object. The two objects are then tied together as different aspects of the same underlying entity, using the CIM_DeviceIdentity relationship.

CIM_FibreChannelAdapter represents the networking aspects of the hardware, not its capability to control downstream devices using the SCSI protocol. The latter is the functionality described by the CIM_SCSIController object, which is why both objects are instantiated and then linked via CIM_DeviceIdentity. CIM_FibreChannelAdapter is a subclass of CIM_NetworkAdapter. Other subclasses include Ethernet and Token Ring adapters.

A network adapter describes the possibility for multiple higher-level protocols to be supported and for peer devices to communicate. Distinguishing between a bus (where the protocol exists and must be followed explicitly) and a network (where peers communicate with much more flexibility) is the difference between a controller and a network adapter.

What is important at the controller level are downstream devices. What is important for the network adapter is to provide CIM_ProtocolEndpoints, and hence connectivity. Protocol endpoints tie the Device Model to the CIM Network Model, where these objects are defined. They are types of CIM_ServiceAccessPoints that are implemented on CIM_NetworkAdapters. Protocol endpoints describe connectivity, or the potential for connectivity, between networked peers.

Figure 5.13 depicts the CIM_Controller and CIM_NetworkAdapter classes and several of the subclasses pertinent to this discussion.

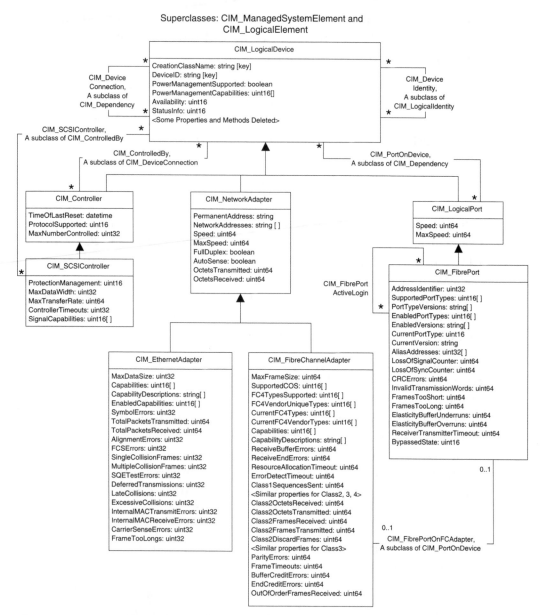

Figure 5.13 Controller and network adapter objects.

In Figure 5.13, Fibre Channel adapters have explicit port devices associated with them, but Ethernet adapters do not. The reason for this difference is that the Fibre Channel ports are individually managed, logical entities, with different properties from the adapters. CIM_FibreChannelPort contains Layer 1 protocol data and participates in logging in to establish connections. In the case of the Ethernet adapter, the port's data (the connector and Layer 1 information) is not logically distinguished from the adapter.

It is tempting to argue the preceding statement by raising the case of multiport Ethernet adapters. But this argument fails. In the case of a four-port adapter, there would be one physical card and four instances of the CIM_EthernetAdapter class. This is modeled as individual instances of the adapter because each port and its backing hardware behaves and is managed as though it were an independent adapter, running independent protocols and operating at unique addresses.

But what if an adapter could use one of multiple connectors? For example, what if an Ethernet adapter could use either a BNC or an RJ45 connector to communicate? In the end, there would still be a single adapter using a single port. The physical card would have multiple connectors defined. The association, CIM_AdapterActiveConnection, could be used to relate the CIM_NetworkAdapter to the CIM_PhysicalConnector through which bits are flowing.

If you look closely at the properties of the Ethernet and Fibre Channel adapter classes you will see that statistics are embedded as properties of the classes. Why isn't this statistical data modeled in a subclass of CIM_StatisticalInformation? The answer is that data critical to understanding the operation of the hardware is in the class itself. However, some statistics for the Fibre Channel adapter and its port can be found in subclasses of CIM_StatisticalInformation; for example, the Device Model does define CIM_FCAdapterEventCounters and CIM_FibrePortEventCounters classes. In these cases, the object's data would not typically be retrieved as part of the device's status and operation. So, the data is placed in a subclass of CIM_StatisticalInformation, instead of locating the data in the object itself.

To close out our discussion of devices, take a look at Figure 5.14, which presents the UML diagram for the remaining "hardware" objects in the sample configuration. The figure shows object definitions for processors, monitors, keyboards, and mice.

This section has touched on only a subset of the Device Model's classes. There are many devices in the world and many that could be called out in the sample configuration. But hopefully, you have gained an understanding of how devices are modeled and can apply what

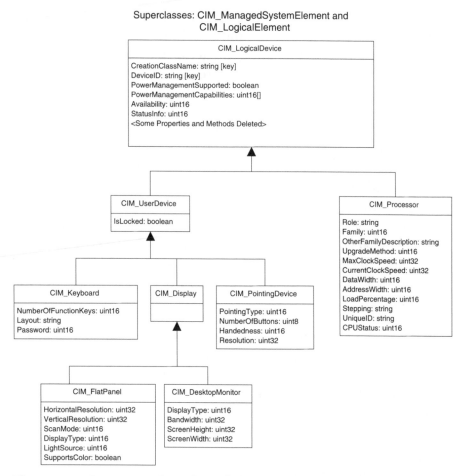

Superclasses: CIM_ManagedSystemElement and
CIM_LogicalElement

Figure 5.14 Processor and user input devices.

you have learned when you review the other entities defined in the
Device Model.

Redundancy

We have raised the topic of redundancy several times, but we'll discuss it more fully here. (Remember that the CIM Schema describes
three types of redundancy—sparing, extra capacity, and storage-
related.) Sparing will be described as part of the sample configuration.

We need to answer the question, what would be instantiated if the
storage subsystem had additional volumes that were available as
spares—for use in case of media failure, loss of power to a section of

the enclosure or other error conditions? This type of information would be very valuable for failover. Figure 5.15 illustrates the concept of a spare group, aggregating the items that are spared, with associations to the entities that act as spares.

Based on Figure 5.15, the following classes would be instantiated:

- *CIM_SpareGroup to represent the collection of spared entities.* The two volumes currently published by the storage subsystem (accessed by Node2 and Node3) would be aggregated into the group using the CIM_RedundancyComponent association.

- *CIM_ActsAsSpare to represent one or more entities that are available for failover or sparing.* Any unused storage volumes or even low-level storage extents could be associated with the CIM_SpareGroup using the CIM_ActsAsSpare relationship. This association's Hot-Standby Boolean indicates availability of the entities for rapid failover.

It is possible to model much more redundancy than just spares. Subclasses of CIM_RedundancyGroup describe load balancing and storage mirroring, striping, and other data redundancies such as parity information. It does not seem necessary to delve into these various details now. The flexibility and power of the CIM Schema should be clear.

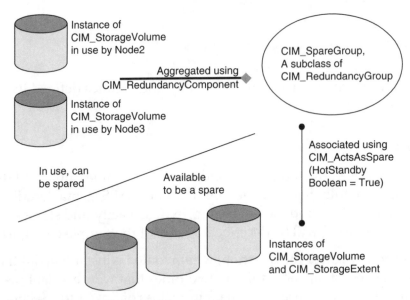

Figure 5.15 Storage available as "hot" spares.

Subtyping and Extending the Models

When is a computer system really a CIM_System and not a device or another object? For example, consider a network printer. Is it a kind of CIM_ComputerSystem or a kind of CIM_LogicalDevice? This is a trick question. The answer is, it is both. A network printer is a kind of CIM_UnitaryComputerSystem whose Dedicated property is set to 11 (Print) and that aggregates CIM_Printer and CIM_EthernetAdapter devices, at a minimum.

A CIM_ComputerSystem should be capable of executing a program and providing compute capabilities. Therefore, it requires both hardware and an operating system in which to launch the program, even if that operating system is specialized firmware. The firmware still works to control resources, execute code, and so on.

Conceptually, defining a system as an aggregation that operates as a functional whole could be applied on many levels. For example, consider the subcomponents of a computer. This definition might be extended to permit the modeling of a sound system (a sound card + firmware and drivers + speakers) or an ISDN subsystem, as derivatives of CIM_ComputerSystem. However, the subclassing and instantiation of CIM_System is limited to entities hosting compound functionality and services, and having significance in the enterprise.

"Significance in the enterprise" is usually associated with some sort of accessibility or network connection. Given that access or connectivity exists, systems typically have one or more unique identifiers, such as their network addresses, in the context of the managed environment. This is not true for a sound system within a computer system. And the ability to host compound functionality is certainly not provided by either a sound system or an ISDN subsystem.

The concept of a device as an abstraction of hardware seems much easier to convey than the concept of systems. Nevertheless, questions still arise as to whether an entity or property is physical (that is, restricted by the laws of physics) or logical (dealing with the various states or configurations of a device). Be careful to analyze concepts with respect to this logical/physical split and subclass them from the appropriate locations in the CIM object hierarchy. Any entities that are abstractions of hardware are candidates for subclassing from

CIM_LogicalDevice, even if not all the properties defined for CIM_LogicalDevice apply.

A prime example of where questions arise is in the area of storage. Because CIM_StorageExtents abstract hardware (physical media), they are subclassed from CIM_LogicalDevice. But not all the properties of CIM_LogicalDevice are applicable—for example, consider the properties related to power management. This does not change the fact that these devices are realized in physical elements, have a status and an install date, can be online/offline, and have other device-related aspects. Therefore, storage elements are modeled as subclasses of CIM_LogicalDevice.

Past and Future of the System and Device Models

The CIM System and Device Models (as well as the Core and Physical Models) are produced by a single Working Group (wg-sysdev) within the DMTF. The objects, properties, and associations in the models are mapped from:

- DMI MIFs (Management Information Format files, many available from the www.dmtf.org Web site)

- SNMP MIBs (Management Information Bases, many available from the www.ietf.org Web site)

- Other IETF (Internet Engineering Task Force) efforts such as the Internet Printing Protocol (IPP)

- Personal and company experience of the Working Group members

When CIM data can be mapped to/from another standard, information on the correspondence between the standards is indicated in the MappingString qualifier. MappingString data is defined as an array of strings of a particular format that describe the instrumentation source for a CIM construct. MappingString qualifiers can apply to CIM classes, properties, associations, references, or methods. For example, the IRQNumber property of CIM_IRQ can be mapped from the DMI attribute "MIF.DMTF | IRQ | 001.1". On the other hand, the PrinterStatus property of CIM_Printer can be obtained from the SNMP attribute "MIB.IETF | Printer-MIB.hrPrinterStatus."

Since computer-related hardware continues to evolve at an ever increasing rate, the CIM System and Device Models will continue to evolve to track these advances. Some of the work for future releases of CIM is directed at:

- More complete modeling of clusters and cluster services
- Support for tape and cartridge media management
- Generalizing the export and mount associations defined for NFS
- Modeling of home network devices—cameras, video phones, and so on
- Support for storage-related copy, backup, and restore
- Describing system and device diagnostics and event logs

The goal is to create a set of interrelated information models that describe the entire managed environment, from hardware to systems, from low-level sensors to software. With this set of information models, the managed environment can be characterized using consistent syntaxes and semantics.

Physical Aspects of Systems and Devices

This chapter overviewed the key concepts and objects of the CIM System and Device Models. It described a wide variety of logical entities and the relationships between them. However, to manage "real-world" entities, you must also understand their physical realization. The next chapter, "The Physical Model," describes the objects used to "realize" devices and to represent the packaging of a system.

References

System and Device Working Group. 1999. Common Information Model (CIM) Schemas. Version 2.2. DMTF.

System and Device Working Group. 1999. "CIM System White Paper." Version 2.2 in review. Available Fall 1999. DMTF.

The Physical Model

The Physical Common Model of the CIM Schema describes objects that can be tagged with a label, occupy space, and are subject to the laws of physics. These objects include chassis and docking stations, chips, physical media, connectors, and cables. Relationships between these objects (mostly dealing with containment and location) are defined as associations in the model.

After reading this chapter, you should understand:

- Critical design themes and objects of the Physical Model
- Use and instantiation of the model for describing the physical environment
- Criteria for appropriate subclassing of the model

Goals of the Physical Model

The main goal of the CIM Physical Model is to describe general packaging, enclosure, component and cabling information for inventory and asset management. Also, the model allows the location (physical positioning) of an entity, and the description of its ability to contain or connect to other elements. The latter allows you to describe how the physical element *could* be configured versus how it is currently installed and cabled. Location data is important for repair purposes such as finding and replacing damaged elements.

Subclasses of CIM_PhysicalElement are defined in the Physical Model. (CIM_PhysicalElement itself is defined in the Core Model, as discussed in Chapter 4.) These subclasses have general applicability across problem domains. For example, there is almost no difference between a chassis that functions as a network router and one that is a printer. Both contain other "packages," such as power supplies, and may have slots to add cards, contain memory chips, and possess other physical similarities. On the logical or functional side, however, there is a huge difference in the devices, services, and elements that are modeled.

Whereas the CIM_LogicalDevice object abstracts the status and configuration of hardware, the subclasses of CIM_PhysicalElement represent the physical aspects of this hardware and the enclosures (for example, racks or chassis) that contain it.

Methodology and Design Patterns

The following three concepts are essential for understanding the elements that the CIM Physical Model defines:

- The physical environment is concerned with describing what physically exists and where it is located.

- Modeling begins by describing high-level enclosures and packaging components (subclasses of CIM_PhysicalPackage).

- Information to support repair and to define capacity motivates object definition.

Answering the questions of "what" and "where" requires knowledge of the racks, chassis, and other enclosures in the enterprise environment. Describing these entities is the purpose of the CIM_Physical-Frame subclass of CIM_PhysicalPackage. Once you establish the existence of a frame, you can answer the "where" question, by recording its location. The CIM_Location class provides information related

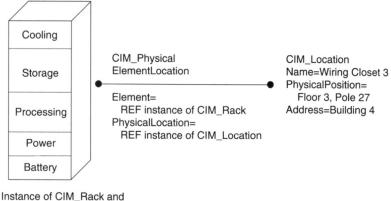

Instance of CIM_Rack and
5 Instances of CIM_Chassis
(Subclasses of CIM_PhysicalFrame
chassis are associated to the rack
using CIM_ChassisInRack)

Figure 6.1 Frames and locations.

to physical position. Locations are associated with elements in the same vicinity using the CIM_PhysicalElementLocation relationship. Figure 6.1 illustrates frame and location concepts.

Given that the racks, chassis, and frames are known, the elements contained within them can be described. Here is a brief list of the types of components that are modeled:

- Motherboards, instances of CIM_Card
- Adapter cards, instances of CIM_Card
- Chips, instances of CIM_Chip
- Memory, instances of CIM_PhysicalMemory
- Tape cartridges, instances of CIM_PhysicalTape
- General connectors, instances of CIM_PhysicalConnector
- Slots, instances of CIM_Slot
- Cabling, instances of CIM_PhysicalLink

Figure 6.2 depicts the physical object hierarchy (without listing any properties) for these entities.

All containment relationships are subclasses or instances of the CIM_Container aggregation association. To avoid *object explosion*, the container relationship includes a string property, LocationWithinCon-

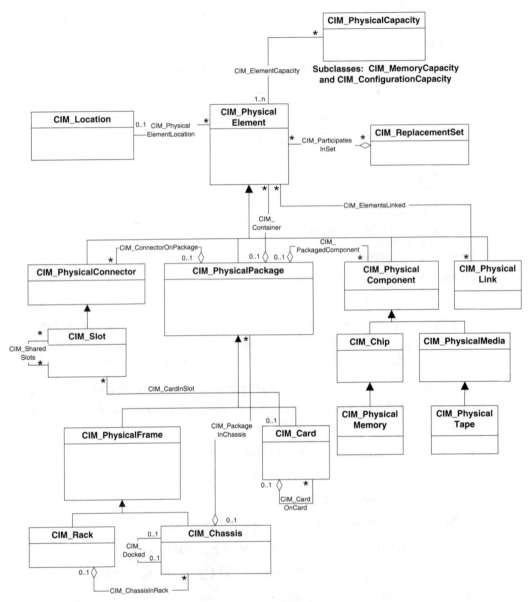

Figure 6.2 Object hierarchy for physical elements.

tainer, to describe relative positioning. What does object explosion have to do with this property? Without LocationWithinContainer, you would need both a CIM_Location object and its association to a physical element (CIM_PhysicalElementLocation) to describe locality. Why create these instances when the container association can describe this information just as effectively?

The CIM_ReplacementSet and CIM_PhysicalCapacity objects were added to the Physical Model to support hardware repair and replacement, and to provide data about capacity. Replacement sets group objects that should be removed and reinstalled together. CIM_PhysicalCapacity and its subclasses describe the capability of the hardware to hold or connect to a minimum and a maximum number of entities. Later, this concept is more fully explored in relation to an example enclosure.

Naming Physical Elements

When the CIM System and Device Working Group defined the key structure for CIM_PhysicalElement, they considered the nature of the element itself. The fact that the object would continue to exist and be identifiable (whether contained in a package or sitting on a desk) dictated how physical elements were named.

As a concrete example, consider a CPU chip. Initially, a modeler may be tempted to name this entity relative to its containing chassis. But if the chip were part of a spare inventory, sitting in a lab cabinet, this would lead to problems. The chip exists whether in a cabinet or operating in a chassis, so it must be named consistently in both these scenarios.

Therefore, the key structure of CIM_PhysicalElement is based on the following properties:

Creation Class Name. To limit the scope over which tags must be unique

Tag. An arbitrary string to identify the element. It could contain asset "tag" information, a serial number, or be based on another naming scheme as defined by an enterprise.

This naming scheme is inherited to all physical elements.

Common Questions

The previous sections highlighted the key concepts of the Physical Model, but did not address all the questions that may arise when reviewing the schema. This section answers three of the most common questions that often cause confusion.

Question 1: There are a variety of associations defined in the Physical Model that seem to be out of place or duplicates of concepts in other parts of the CIM Schema. Why are they included?

Answer 1: Several categories of associations define specific semantics for physical elements. These associations do not duplicate, but clarify, the semantics in other models. Three categories of associations are defined in the Physical Model:

- *Explicit CIM_Realizes subclasses that define the link between physical media and storage extents.* CIM_RealizesExtent is one example. These associations are included in the Physical Model to reduce the scope of the references in CIM_Realizes and to restrict the cardinalities. Storage extents should not be realized in just any subclass of CIM_PhysicalElement, but only by types of physical components (physical memory for CIM_Memory storage elements and physical media for other types of storage extents). In addition, the definition of the storage extents often dictates and restricts the cardinality of the relationships. Instead of being many-to-many associations, they become relationships of at most one physical component to many storage entities. These semantics are defined by the CIM_Realizes subclasses in the Physical Model.

- *System packaging associations such as CIM_ComputerSystemPackage and CIM_LibraryPackage.* The system packaging relationships are semantically similar to CIM_Realizes. They tie a computer system or storage library instance to the enclosures and frames that house its physical elements. This information must be defined in independent associations, since CIM_Realizes is restricted to associating a CIM_LogicalDevice with a CIM_PhysicalElement.

- *Associations defining the operation of a device in the context of an enclosure.* Often, a temperature sensor monitors a physical frame's general operational characteristics, not specific devices within the frame. This semantic is defined using the CIM_PackageTempSensor association. Similarly, an entire enclosure may be cooled by a device, or have an associated alarm element (defined using the CIM_PackageCooling and CIM_PackageAlarm relationships, respectively). The same information (as is conveyed by these "package" associations) could be defined by instantiating many CIM_AssociatedSensor, CIM_AssociatedCooling, or CIM_AssociatedAlarm relationships. The latter associations reference a temperature sensor or a cooling or alarm device on the one hand, and

CIM_LogicalDevices on the other. Unfortunately, these device-level associations would be required by all the CIM_LogicalDevices realized by entities in the enclosure. This leads to an object explosion. The explicit association to the physical frame is much easier and more straightforward. Note that if an entire enclosure is *not* monitored, cooled, or alarmed, but only a subset of the devices that are realized in the enclosure, then the individual CIM_AssociatedSensor, Cooling, and Alarm relationships must be used.

Question 2: Why is cabling and very low-level component information modeled?

Answer 2: Every chip or cable in a computer system should not be instantiated and inventoried using the Physical Model. There is little value in knowing that a SCSI parallel cable runs to a SCSI drive bay in a computer chassis. That the cable is present can be inferred from the fact that SCSI communications are occurring. There is nothing to manage about this cable. It just exists. That said, there are scenarios where the cabling that runs between buildings on a campus should be modeled as corporate assets. Critical hardware components such as the processors and physical memory of a computer system, or the physical tapes in a tape library, may be valued hardware assets and important to management applications. In these cases, you should instantiate the cabling and physical components of a package.

Question 3: How is the Physical Model instrumented?

Answer 3: Using today's technologies, this is a very difficult task. Typically, physical data is input at manufacturing or at the installation of the physical element at a customer's site. This information is often manually created or copied from a database based on the manufacturing order, then it is statically stored. Mechanisms to automate and maintain this information are being investigated for future implementation.

A Sample Enclosure

To help you to better understand the Physical Model, this section presents an example enclosure. The enclosure is a rack, with a computer system's processing chassis and a storage chassis mounted in it, and is graphically depicted in Figure 6.3.

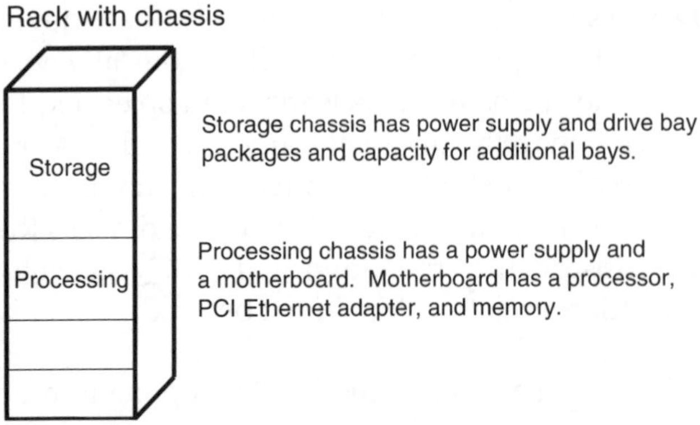

Rack with chassis

Storage chassis has power supply and drive bay
packages and capacity for additional bays.

Processing chassis has a power supply and
a motherboard. Motherboard has a processor,
PCI Ethernet adapter, and memory.

Figure 6.3 Sample physical configuration.

Using this example, we will describe several components of the two
chassis—power supplies, the motherboard in the processing chassis,
the motherboard's processor and a PCI-based Ethernet adapter, and
disk drive locations in the storage chassis. (We assume that several of
the drive locations in the storage chassis are empty.) Obviously, we
have not provided an exhaustive list of physical elements, only a representative one.

Classes, Associations, and Attributes

The following subsections describe the CIM Schema as it relates to the
sample enclosure shown in Figure 6.3. We have provided UML diagrams of the pertinent CIM classes and their associations, along with
some discussion and interpretation of these diagrams. Our goal is to
identify and define the salient objects of the example.

CIM Physical Packages and Locations

Figure 6.4 shows the high-level physical element, package, and location objects from the Physical Model. The properties of CIM_Physical-
Package describe object identification (many of these properties are
inherited from CIM_PhysicalElement) and hardware-oriented data
such as height, weight, and whether the entity is replaceable, removable, and/or hot-swappable.

Information such as height and weight are not mandatory for managing a physical element, but they are very useful when replacing a

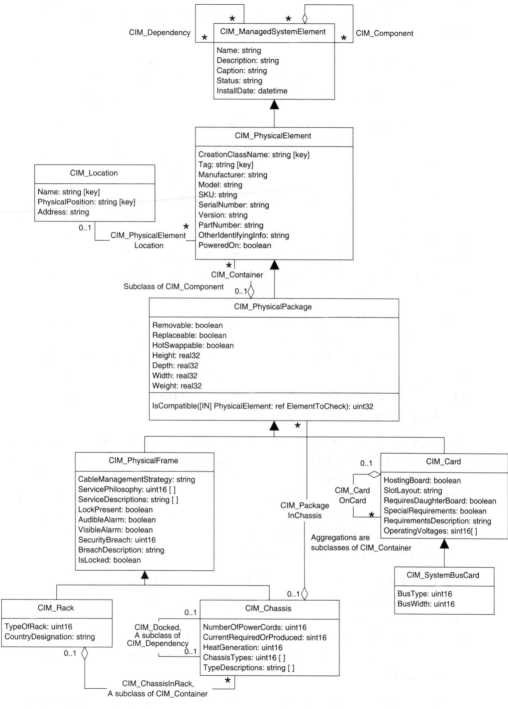

Figure 6.4   Physical package and location objects.

physical package. For example, knowing that a package weighs 200 pounds should tell you that the replacement task will require more than one person.

Packages are the containers for other physical elements and are likely to be labeled or tagged. In some scenarios, they may be the only physical elements instantiated and tracked from an asset perspective.

In many cases, when adding new hardware to a package, you will want to perform a compatibility check. It would be good to know (for example) that a particular power supply should not be inserted into a package due to a potential for overheating. The IsCompatible method of CIM_PhysicalPackage defines a means to perform such a check, especially when the number of elements that can be added to a package is small. Conversely, when the number of elements that can be added is potentially limitless, this method may address only the most likely entities and therefore may be unable to indicate compatibility for everything else.

Subclasses of CIM_PhysicalPackage define frames, racks, chassis, cards, and more. No extraordinary concepts are introduced by these objects. Their properties are oriented toward describing the entity itself (such as the TypeOfRack property on CIM_Rack, or CurrentRequiredOrProduced on CIM_Chassis) or to provide general management, maintenance, and repair information.

You will need a little more detail regarding cards. The Physical Model defines the CIM_CardOnCard association to capture the semantics of daughtercards, and the plugging of a card into a motherboard. The CIM_CardInSlot association locates adapters in slots, which are in turn contained on a motherboard. (The latter relationship is described by creating instances of the CIM_ConnectorOnPackage association between the motherboard and the slots.)

In any scenario where the CIM_Slot object is not defined, only the CIM_CardOnCard association can be used to convey location information for an adapter. (CIM_CardInSlot can not be used since the Slot reference would not exist.) When the CIM_Slot object is defined, the CIM_CardOnCard and CardInSlot associations convey redundant information.

Motherboards are simply instances of CIM_Card (that is, they are only represented in the physical environment). To distinguish a motherboard from an adapter, you set the card's HostingBoard Boolean property to true. No logical entity represents a motherboard, but there are a multitude of devices that could be realized from it.

When we apply the model shown in Figure 6.4 to the sample configuration, the following objects are instantiated. (Remember that this figure illustrates the class definitions that give syntax and semantics to an instance's data. The figure does not indicate which instances are actually created.)

- *An instance of CIM_Rack defines the outermost physical frame.* In this configuration, the TypeOfRack property is set to 1, indicating a "Standard 19 Inch" rack.

- *Two instances of CIM_Chassis describe the processing and the storage chassis.* To define the packaging format, the ChassisType property is used. This array is set to 17 and 23 for the processing chassis (indicating that this is the "Main System Chassis" and a "Rack Mount Chassis"). For the storage chassis, the values are 22 and 23 (describing the element as a "Storage Chassis" and a "Rack Mount Chassis").

- *Two instances of CIM_ChassisInRack define the chassis as contained by the rack enclosure.* The BottomU properties of these instances define where the chassis begin in the rack. (For those of you unfamiliar with rack configuration, a U represents 1.75 inches of height.)

- *Two instances of CIM_PhysicalPackage represent the power supplies in each chassis.* These instances are then associated to CIM_PowerSupply logical devices using the CIM_Realizes relationship. The association to a logical device provides details on the use of the package.

- *Five instances of CIM_PhysicalPackage represent five disk drives and their media in the storage chassis.* Again, CIM_Realizes associations would be instantiated to tie the physical packages to their logical devices.

- *Seven instances of CIM_PackageInChassis describe the location of the power supply and disk drive instances in the processing and storage chassis.*

- *One instance of CIM_Card identifies the motherboard of the processing chassis.* For this instance, we set the HostingBoard Boolean property to true.

- *One instance of CIM_SystemBusCard identifies the PCI Ethernet adapter.* We assume it is a 32-bit PCI adapter. In this case, the value 43 (PCI) is written to the BusType property of CIM_SystemBusCard and the value 32 is written to BusWidth.

- *For the Ethernet adapter, if a CIM_Slot object is available for association, the adapter is defined to be "in" the slot using the CIM_CardInSlot association.* If a slot object is not defined, the adapter can be associated with the motherboard using the CIM_CardOnCard relationship. The MountOrSlotDescription property of CIM_CardOnCard conveys explicit slot positioning for the adapter. Additional location data can be placed in the LocationWithinContainer property, inherited from CIM_Container.

- *One instance of CIM_Location describes where the rack is located, in which building, on which floor, and so on.*

- *One instance of CIM_PhysicalElementLocation associates location information with the rack, to enable finding the rack for repair or inventory purposes.*

Physical Capacity

The CIM_PhysicalCapacity object and its subclasses define minimum and maximum capacities for a variety of physical objects. The physical element whose configuration is described is identified using the CIM_ElementCapacity association. The pertinent classes are shown in Figure 6.5.

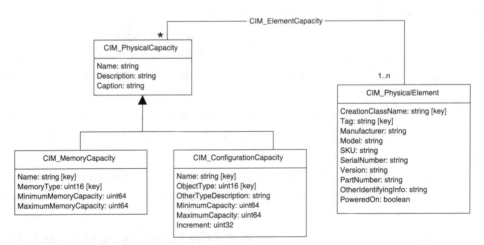

Figure 6.5 Physical capacity UML diagram.

It is obvious, even from the class name, that the CIM_MemoryCapacity subclass defines only minimum and maximum memory configurations, where the MemoryType property distinguishes the different kinds of memory that may be installed on a physical element. Alternately, the CIM_ConfigurationCapacity class describes minimums and maximums for a variety of different objects. The ObjectType property identifies the type of entity whose configuration is defined. Since the memory and configuration capacity classes are so similar, you may wonder why one is not subclassed from the other. The answer is that the key properties of these objects are quite different; these differences cannot be supported if the objects are subclassed.

Can the CIM_PhysicalCapacity objects be used for capacity planning? The answer is no, except in some very limited applications. These objects simply represent minimum and maximum, raw capacities. In addition, trade-offs that may be required to add a physical element are also not modeled. For example, to add a tape drive to an enclosure, you may need to the remove some half-height disk drives. The current Physical Model does not describe all combinations and permutations of configuring an enclosure.

The use of the CIM_PhysicalCapacity classes is best described by example. For the sample configuration, the following instances would be created:

- *One instance of CIM_ConfigurationCapacity defines the ability of the storage chassis to hold CIM_MediaAccessDevices (Drives).* In this case, the ObjectType property is set to 7, indicating that drives are being described. For discussion purposes, anywhere from 0 to 10 drives can be added to the chassis. The class properties would be set as follows: MinimumCapacity = 0, MaximumCapacity = 10, Increment = 1.

- *One instance of CIM_MemoryCapacity defines that up to 640Mbytes of DRAM can be placed on the motherboard.* To describe this configuration, the following data would be placed in the class properties: MemoryType = 2 (DRAM), MinimumConfiguration = 10Mbytes (for example, required for booting), and MaximumConfiguration = 640Mbytes.

- *Two instances of the CIM_ElementCapacity association exist.* They tie the CIM_ConfigurationCapacity instance to the storage chassis and the CIM_MemoryCapacity instance to the motherboard.

Physical Components

CIM_PhysicalComponents represent low-level hardware, such as chips and physical media. These entities are associated with their containing packages (frames, adapter cards, etc.) using the CIM_PackagedComponent relationship. Figure 6.6 illustrates the component-level objects in the Physical Model.

A quick review of the objects and their properties does not reveal any new design patterns. We define reasonable data for a chip (such as form factor) or media (such as capacity and whether a label is attached).

Applying the model shown in Figure 6.6 to the sample configuration, the following instances would be created:

- One instance of CIM_Chip represents the motherboard's processor.
- One instance of CIM_PhysicalMemory represents the motherboard's current memory (its speed, current data width, and other properties).
- One instance of CIM_PackagedComponent associates the processor with the motherboard package.
- One instance of CIM_MemoryOnCard, a subclass of CIM_PackagedComponent, associates the memory with the motherboard.

Subtyping and Extending the Model

Most extensions to the CIM Schema deal with the logical side of the model, as opposed to the physical. New classes in the Physical Model should define new types of hardware, or new containment and dependency relationships. Take care when you examine properties and classes to guarantee that their semantics truly deal with the physical, touchable world and not logical function.

Past and Future of the Physical Model

The CIM Physical Model is a product of the System and Device Working Group (wg-sysdev) within the DMTF. The objects, properties, and associations in the models address the requirements of hardware con-

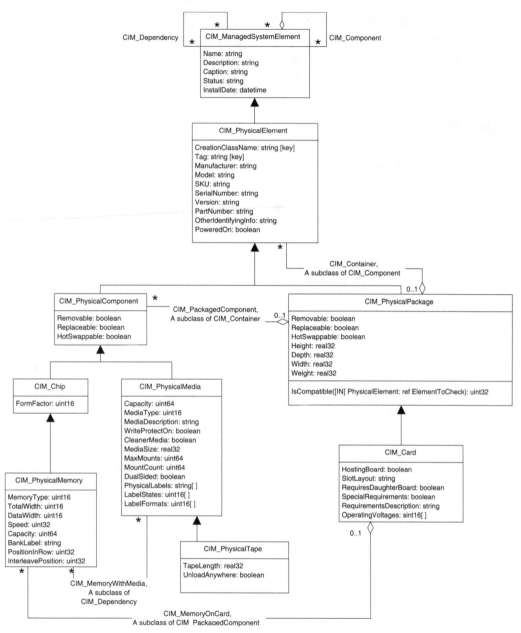

Figure 6.6   Physical component objects.

figuration (i.e., "rack builder") applications and the needs of the team members to identify and locate hardware. Many aspects of the model are derived from (and mapped to) similar concepts in the Directory Enabled Networks (DEN) Specification.

Future extensions of the CIM Physical Model will address capacity planning and requirements to support hot-swappable hardware. Of course, logical aspects of these concepts will also be modeled in the CIM System and Device Models.

References

System and Device Working Group. 1999. Common Information Model (CIM) Schemas. Version 2.2. DMTF.

Strassner, J., and S. Judd. 1998. "Directory Enabled Networks, Information Model and Base Schema." Version 3.0c1. DEN Consortium.

Common Model
for Applications

T he Common Model for Applications extends the constructs defined in the Core Model to provide ways to represent issues associated with managing applications or parts of applications in a distributed environment. This chapter will help you to understand the content of the Common Model for Application, by explaining the following:

- How the model uses the concept of an application life cycle to differentiate important aspects of managing an application.

- How the basic building blocks—files, installation scripts, shared components, and others—are represented.

- How dependencies on operating systems services are described to make it possible to automate many installation scenarios.

- How critical dependencies of one application on another are captured so that complex distributed applications can be properly configured.

Managing Distributed Applications

As you become more familiar with the CIM and issues surrounding the management of complex IT systems, it will become clear that deployed or about to be deployed distributed applications comprise one of the most difficult areas. The advanced technologies used by these exciting applications often introduce enormous complexities that impede their successful deployment and operation. The CIM Common Model for Application Management is an information model designed to describe a set of details that is commonly required to manage software products and applications.

The Common Model for application management can and should be used in different ways throughout the process of moving an application out of the development organization into operational environments. Some common ways the model can be used include:

- *An application developer with or without a tool can use the model to describe management details about an application.* An application/software provider produces an instance of the model that describes the manageable aspects of their product. The manageable aspects include details such as the installable or deployable units, the files these units are composed of, the memory required to properly execute the software, and so on.

- *An operating system can use the model to represent installed components.* In the case of operating systems, utilities that install software or maintain local databases of installed software can process the information model so that users do not need to type the details in.

- *A software change management tool typically knows the files that are produced from a build and can automatically record this information in the CIM Application Management Model format.* Management tools can consume instances of the information model so that their users do not have to type in the details. For example, a software distribution tool can learn what needs to be done when the software is distributed to various operating system platforms. Thus, the information model can be used by a wide variety of tools.

- *By packaging an instance of the Application Management Information Model with an application or with some software, operating systems utilities and/or management tools can consume the model in order to learn about the software.*

Application Fundamentals

Before getting into the details, let's start by establishing a common understanding as to what we mean by an application and what the application life cycle is. These two areas must be well defined before embarking on a discussion of the details of the Applications Model.

What is an application? This is a difficult question because the answer depends on who is asking. The good news is that each person's perspective eventually leads to a fundamental aspect of an application. That is: An application is a related set of files. But this is the lowest-level view of an application, and the challenge of a model that represents an application is to surround the notion of a related set of files with higher-order constructs that are meaningful. To that end, the Common Model for Applications starts by abstracting the low-level notion of a related set of files into a software element.

Software elements represent a collection of one or more files and associated details that are individually managed on a particular platform; they are the components that are installed or uninstalled into a computer environment. Software elements tend to be defined at the level of granularity meaningful to applications developers. For example, an applications developer might say: "If you want the Web server feature of our product on your Solaris system, you'll have to install software elements 1, 4, and 6." Since this level of detail is often complex, and thus a burden to the user, the Application Model provides a means to abstract related collections of software elements into software features.

Software features are components of an application that are intended to be meaningful to a consumer or user of the application. To be meaningful, software features have to reflect a particular function or role that a component of an application plays, such as a trading client, quote server, or bidding gateway. For many reasons, one of which is the emergence of software suites, CIM provides ways to abstract a related set of software features into the notion of a software product.

Software products comprise the unit of acquisition between the consumer of an application and the provider. *Acquisition* implies an agreement between the consumer and supplier that includes terms of licensing, support, or a warrantee. Commonly, this agreement is thought of as being between vendors, but for in-house-developed applications, the agreement can exist between organizational entities such as divisions, business units, or departments.

There is one other way software features can be grouped. Because software products are typically bought and then combined to support some business process or business system within a company, software features can be collected into the notion of an application system. *Application systems* are collections of software features from one or more software products that are used in combination to fulfill a particular business function.

The basic objective of the Common Model for Applications is to describe the structure of software according to its life cycle components.

Application Life Cycle

What is the application life cycle? The application life cycle is a collection of critical points or states that occur in the process of transitioning application from a development environment to an operational environment. The states are important because management details like require disk space or file list can and do vary at each stage.

The application life cycle concept is applied to the lowest-level component of an application: the software element. The life cycle captures information about a software element in the following four states:

Deployable. Includes details for distributing the software element and transforming it to the next state.

Installable. Includes details for installing the software element and transforming it to the next state.

Executable. Includes details for starting the software element, and transforming it to the next state.

Running. Includes details for monitoring the software element and operating it on a started element.

To conceptualize how the details vary state to state, think about the related set of files for a software element, like an executable program. In a common environment like Microsoft's Windows, when a software element is in its installable state the file list will include a setup.exe file. When the setup.exe file is launched, the software element moves into the executable state, and the file folder containing the executable setup.exe explodes into many more files. In its exploded form, the program is not executable. Advance management functions like self-healing require management tools to understand the details in various states.

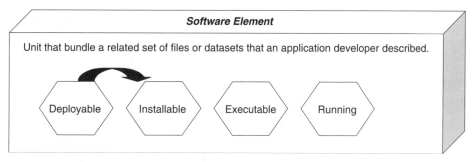

Figure 7.1   Application Model building blocks.

Application life-cycle concepts can be used to describe applications with various structures ranging from a standalone desktop application to a sophisticated, multiplatform distributed, Internet-based application. As you read the details about the Common Model in the next section, keep Figure 7.1 in mind. It shows how components of an application and the notion of an application life cycle are related.

The Common Model

From a CIM Core Model perspective, most of the classes defined in the Common Model for applications are subclasses of CIM_LogicalElement. Next we will explore how the model deals with situations commonly faced by users or producers of application management details. Each section covers a major topic related to creating or interpreting the Common Model.

Simple Application

If you strip the CIM Application Model down to its essence, the notion of a software element remains. A software element is an installable package or part of an application that can be added or removed from a hosting system or environment. As such, a software element is considered the finest grain application part you can represent with the CIM Application Model. In this section, we will assume that such a part is the application itself, so we can learn about the basic mechanics of the CIM_SoftwareElement class. In latter sections we will learn about other classes that organize software elements into high-order concepts like software features.

When creating a CIM_SoftwareElement object, you must answer the following questions:

- How is the software element going to be labeled or typed?
  - For example, if a software element object is being created for an installable package of database routines, the software element object can be typed as a database routine by providing the Database Routine value for the Name [CIM_SoftwareElement] property. At the same time, a value should be supplied for the version (Version [CIM_SoftwareElement] property) and for the unique identifier (SoftwareElementID [CIM_SoftwareElement] property).
- What operating system is the target of this software element?
  - As in installable package, the software element object must declare the hosting environment or operating system it expects by setting the appropriate value for the TargetOperatingSystem [CIM_SoftwareElement] property.
- What application life cycle state is being installed by this software element?
  - Since the CIM Application Model is structured around the notion of an application life cycle, a software element object must identify its life cycle state by setting the SoftwareElementState [CIM_SoftwareElement] property to the appropriate value.

The combination of these five properties (Name, Version, SoftwareElementID, TargetOperatingSystem, SoftwareElementState) form the key of the CIM_SoftwareElement class, so a software element object represents a particular installable package in a particular application life cycle state for a particular platform. As a result, if you want to represent the database routine element in all four of the application life cycle states, you would need to create four software element objects. The keys for these objects would be the same except for the value of the SoftwareElementState [CIM_SoftwareElement] property. If the database routine can be hosted by three different operating systems, three software element objects will exist for each state.

Now that you have a basic understanding of how the CIM_Software-Element class works, we will look at ways to add more detailed information. The next several sections cover how file lists are created, how directory structures are specified, and how install scripts or routines are specified.

File Lists for Software Elements

The most basic data about a software element is the file information. The file information for a software element is a set of file specifications rather than an actual list of system files. The reason the actual system files are not represented in the Application Model is there are management application scenarios like software distribution that use file information before the software element actually exists on a computer system. Therefore, it is not possible to know the disk device name and/or the high level directory name before the software element is placed onto a particular computer system. A CIM_FileSpecification class specifies this system-independent notion of a file for a software element. An instance of this class is specifying a file that is expected to be on a computer system when the software element exists in that environment.

Since CIM_FileSpecification is specifying an expected condition within an environment, it is a subclass of the CIM_Check class. CIM_File-Specification is a subclass of CIM_Check because when a software element exist in a particular environment, the files for the element are expected to be in the environment. The association that relates file specifications to a particular software element is the CIM_SoftwareElementChecks association (inherited by CIM_FileSpecification from CIM_Check). The identity of a CIM_FileSpecification object is based on the keys defined for the CIM_Check object.

The CIM_Check can also specify "not true" conditions in one of two contexts: conditions for the current state and condition required to go to the next state. Therefore, it is important to follow the rules when specifying the files of a software element.

1. The Phase [CIM_SoftwareElementChecks] property must be set to in-state.

2. The CheckMode [CIM_Check] property must indicate condition is expected (that is, be set to true).

The CIM_FileSpecification class contains properties you would expect like file name (Name property), file size (FileSize property), and creation timestamp (CreateTimeStamp property). Other properties like Checksum and MD5Checksum provide a reliable combination of properties for a software signature that can be used to accurately test for the existence of a file.

File List with Directory Structures

We have not yet covered the way files are organized into directories, for which you use the CIM_DirectorySpecification class. The CIM_DirectorySpecification class captures the major directory structure of a software element. Like the CIM_FileSpecification class, CIM_DirectorySpecification class is also a CIM_Check. The file(s) that belong in a particular directory are specified with the CIM_DirectorySpecificationFile association.

This CIM_DirectorySpecification class organizes the files of a software element into manageable units that can be relocated on a computer system. They are relocated since the DirectoryPath property [CIM_DirectorySpecification] that captures the name of a directory is actually a default or recommended path name. The value of the DirectoryPath property can be used by a software distribution or installer tool to suggest a high-level directory name to a user. If a user elects to change the default, this value can replace the current value of the DirectoryPath property. Such a change does not change the identity of a CIM_DirectorySpecification object is the key of this object is based on CIM_Check.

The DirectoryType property characterizes the type of directory being described. Examples include: Product base directory, Product log directory, Shared library directory, and Shared include directory.

Installation Routines

Useful installation routines or scripts that will actually install a software element can be defined using CIM. CIM_ExecuteProgram class specifies installation routes. Instances of CIM_ExecuteProgram identify the program or programs that, when run, will install the software element.

The CIM_ExecuteProgram class is not directly associated with the CIM_SoftwareElement because it is a subclass of the CIM_Action class. The CIM_Action class captures operations that can either transition a software element into the next state or remove an existing software element.

CIM_Action objects are associated with CIM_SoftwareElementActions associations. So, a CIM_SoftwareElement object can reference many CIM_Action objects with the CIM_SoftwareElementActions association. In order to locate the installation routine, one is only interested in the CIM_Action objects that are specified as next-state actions by the Direction [CIM_Action] property. When there is only one CIM_Action object for a particular software element object, the installation routine is a single program or script.

In many cases, the installation routine is actually a series of programs or scripts that must execute in a specific order. This situation is recognizable when there are multiple CIM_Action(s) for a given software element object in the next-state action category. In this case, the CIM_ActionSequence association (used to order the actions for a particular software element into a continuous sequence) determines the execution order. This means that when there is more than one CIM_Action object for the same direction, they must all be ordered using the CIM_ActionSequence association.

In order to start the installation routine sequence, you must locate the first CIM_Action object in the sequence. This is the one and only one action object that does not have an instance of the CIM_ActionSequence association referencing it in the 'next' role.

The last important detail is illustrated in Figure 7.2. In order to locate the installation routine for a particular state of a software element, one must look at the previous state. So, as shown in the figure, if one wants to locate the installation routines for a software element in the executable state, one must query the next-state actions for the software element object in the previous state (i.e., installable state).

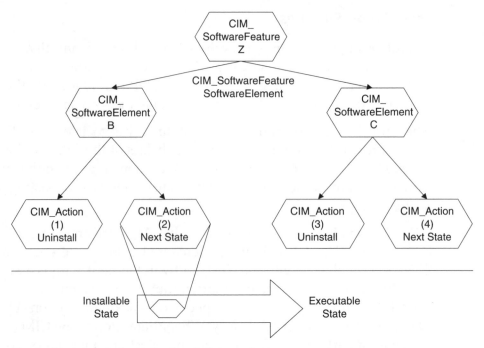

Figure 7.2 How to locate an installation routine.

Many applications also define uninstall routines. These are handled in a manner similar to install routines using the Direction [CIM_Action] property to locate the uninstall action rather than the next-state actions. Table 7.1 summarizes categories of action sequences supported by CIM.

User/Administrator Friendly Application Parts

When you are developing an easy to install application, it is not appropriate to reveal the details of a software element to a user or an administrator. Software elements are the *internals* or *packaging structure* of an application. You would not want desktop technicians/network administrators to see the list of software elements installed on their computers. The CIM Application Model defines another class to describe the function of an application rather than its internal packaging structure—the CIM_SoftwareFeature class. CIM_SoftwareFeature class hides internals so the person installing software sees only a software feature that represents a functional component of an application (for example, database, word processor, Web-based trading, and so on).

Table 7.1 Categories of Action Sequences

STATE	DIRECTION	DESCRIPTION
Deployable	Next-State	The next-state actions for a software element in a deployable state perform the unpackage task to create a software element in the installable state.
	Uninstall	The uninstall actions for a software element in the deployable state remove the software element in the deployable state.
Installable	Next-State	The next-state actions for a software element in an installable state perform the install task to create a software element in the executable state.
	Uninstall	The uninstall actions for a software element in an installable state remove the software element in that state.
Executable	Next-State	Start the software element.
	Uninstall	Uninstall the executable state.
Runnable	Next-State	Stop or terminate the running software element.
	Uninstall	Not used for a software element in a runnable state.

CIM_SoftwareFeature classes are instantiated in the context of the CIM_Product class defined in the Core Model. The CIM_Product class defines a unit of acquisition for software features delivered in the context of a product. Since features are delivered through products, CIM_SoftwareFeature classes are always defined in the context of a CIM_Product class using the CIM_ProductSoftwareFeature association. We know software features must be specified in the context of a product because the CIM_ProductSoftwareFeature association specifies the CIM_SoftwareFeature participant as weak with respect to CIM_Product. The identity of a software feature is based on the keys of the CIM Product class that are propagated and the value of the Name [CIM_SoftwareFeature] property. The Name property defines the label by which the software feature object is known to the outside world since it is intended as a human-readable label that uniquely identifies the element in the context of its product's namespace.

In addition to providing a more user-friendly handle for an application part, the separation of functionality into a SoftwareFeature and packaging details into a CIM_SoftwareElements makes it possible to specify shared parts. So, the model allows configurations like the one shown in the following figure:

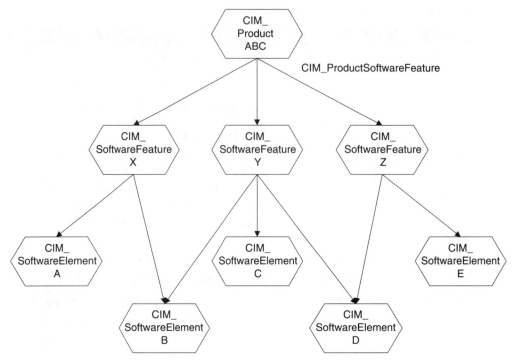

Figure 7.3. Shared components.

In Figure 7.3, the B and the D software elements are used by multiple software features. Software element B gets installed when either software feature X or Y is installed. Software element D is installed when either software feature Y or Z is installed. So, the model allows shared packages to be defined within an application.

We now know that CIM_SoftwareElement objects are what actually get installed on a computer system, and we know the Application Model is designed so the administrator of application selects and installs software features. The disparity can be reconciled in the following way: When an administrator installs a software feature, the install engine actually installs the software elements of the feature. So, based on Figure 7.3, installing software feature Y implies installing software elements B, C, and D.

Multiplatform Applications

Because modern applications have parts that run on different platforms or operating systems, the CIM Application Model has constructs to address multiplatform applications. In all but the simplest of cases, the details of a part for one operating system are different from another operating system. Therefore, when a software feature can be hosted by multiple operating systems, you must create a unique set of software elements for each hosting environment. Capturing platform information at the software element level rather than the software feature has the advantage of making it easy to hide platform details from administrators dealing with software features.

When a software feature can exist on multiple platforms or operating systems (for example, a client component of a three-tiered client/server application might run on Solaris, Windows NT, and Windows 95), a software feature is a collection of all the software elements for the different platforms. In this case, an application using the model must cluster the software elements by the value of the TargetOperatingSystem property when the application user is concerned with a particular platform. For example, when installing a client component on Windows NT, only the software element objects with a TargetOperatingSystem property for NT are of interest.

We can see what the application must deal with by looking at Figure 7.4 and asking the question: How many platforms can software feature X and software feature Z run on? Software Feature X can run on two platforms: Windows 2000 and OS/390. Software Feature Z can run on one platform: Solaris. In order to properly install software feature X into an OS/390 system, you must install both software elements B and C.

Describing Operating System Dependencies

The CIM Application Model is capable of describing the set of dependencies a software feature has on the environment hosting it. Dependency information is important for tools that install a software feature in a new environment as well as tools for analyzing the impact of specific changes to the environment on an application by its hosts. The dependencies a software feature has on its hosting environment are the conditions the software feature expects to be true of that environment. These conditions are described using the CIM_Check class.

The CIM_SoftwareElement objects associated with a particular CIM_SoftwareFeature object are the part actually placed into an environment. Therefore, the CIM_Check classes are associated with the

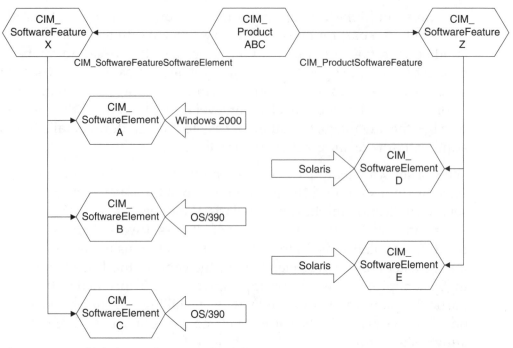

Figure 7.4   Multiplatform software configuration.

CIM_SoftwareElement using the CIM_SoftwareElementChecks association. So, the dependencies a software feature has on a particular environment are the combined dependencies of the software elements referenced by the software feature.

Since it typically does not make sense to describe dependency conditions out of context of a software element, CIM_Check classes are *weak* with respect to CIM_SoftwareElements, so the keys of the software element are propagated to the CIM_Check object. The CheckID property is used to distinguish checks within a particular scope.

The checks associated with a particular software element are organized into one of two groups using the Phase property of the CIM_ SoftwareElementChecks association. Conditions that will be satisfied when a software element is in a particular environment are known as *in-state conditions*. Conditions that must be satisfied to move the current software element to its next state are known as *next-state conditions*.

The CheckMode property indicates whether the condition can be expected to exist or not exist in the environment. When the value is

True, the condition is expected to exist (for example, you expect a file to be on a system). When the value is False, the condition is not expected to exist (for example, you do not expect a file to be on a system).

The environment that in-state and next-state conditions characterize is defined by an instance of a CIM_ComputerSystem. A CIM_Computer-System object represents the environment in which CIM_SoftwareElements are already installed or in which CIM_SoftwareElements will be installed. For the case in which a software element is already installed, the CIM_InstalledSoftwareElement association is used to identify the CIM_ComputerSystem object that represents the "environment." When a software elements is being distributed and installed on a different computer system, the CIM_ ComputerSystem object for the system hosting the targeted environment is used.

The Application Model does not require all the aspects to be consistent. For example, if there is a next-state check for a particular file on a software element in a deployable state, there does not have to be an in-state check for the same file on the software element in the executable state. Although one might argue that these inconsistencies could be confusing, it is safer and easier for applications to deal with checks only in their defined context.

Table 7.2 summarizes the dependencies that can be defined in the current models. Details about each of these are in the following section.

OS Version Dependency

The CIM_OSVersionCheck class specifies the versions of the OS that can support the OS version dependency software element. When such a dependency is specified, the assumption is that the application takes advantage of some services or APIs that are specific to that version of the environment.

The details of OS version check are compared with the details of a CIM_OperatingSystem object referenced by InstalledOS association for the CIM_ComputerSystem object that describes the environment. As long as there is at least one CIM_OperatingSystem object that satisfies the details discussed below, dependency is met. In other words, all the operating systems on the relevant computer system do not need to satisfy the condition.

Table 7.2   Dependencies in Current Models

CONDITION	IN-STATE INTERPRETATION	NEXT-STATE INTERPRETATION
Memory Requirements	Minimum amount of memory required to transition into the *current* state.	Minimum amount of memory required to transition into the *next* state.
Disk Space	Minimum amount of disk space being consumed by the software element in this state.	Minimum amount of disk space required to transition into the *next* state.
Swap Space	Minimum amount of swap space consumed by the software element in this state.	Minimum amount of swap space required to transition into the *next* state.
Architecture	The architecture required by a software element in the current state.	The architecture required by the software element to transition into the *next* state.
Files	A file that is expected to exist or not exist when a software element is in the *current* state.	A file this is expected to exist or not exist before a software element transitions into the *next* state.
Directories	A directory that is expected to exist or not exist when a software element is in the *current* state.	A directory this is expected to exist or not exist before a software element transitions into the *next* state.
OS Version	The version or ranges of versions a software element requires in its *current* state.	The version or ranges of versions a software element elements requires before it transitions into the *next* state.

Before comparing using the details of this check class, it is important to verify that the operating system type is the same. You can verify that OS type is the same by ensuring the value of the TargetOperatingSystem [CIM_SoftwareElement] property is equal to the value of OSType [CIM_OperatingSystem] property.

The CIM_OSVersionCheck class specifies a range of releases for an OS using the values of the MinimumVersion and MaximumVersion properties. The range allows the situations in Table 7.3 to be covered.

Remember, the value of a version is encoded either as

```
<major>.<minor>.<revision> or <major>.<minor><letter revision>
```

so the comparison operation need to be more than a simple string comparison.

Table 7.3 Ways to Specify Software Version Information

DESIRED CONDITION	HOW TO SPECIFY	VERSION PROPERTY FOUND IN A CIM_OPERATINGSYSTEM
Specific OS	MinimumVersion and MaximumVersion must have the same value	The Version property value must equal the value of either the MinimumVersion or MaximumVersion property.
This version or higher	MinimumVersion contains the minimum and MaximumVersion is null	The Version property value must be greater than or equal to the value of the Minimum-Version property. No comparison with the value of MaximumVersion property is valid.
No higher this than version	The MaximumVersion contains the maximum and the Minimum version is null	The Version property value must be less than or equal to the value of the Maximum-Version property. No comparison with the value of MinimumVersion property is valid.
Range	The MinimumVersion and MaximumVersion both contain a value with the value of MinimumVersion being before the value of MaximumVersion.	The Version property value must be greater than or equal to the value of the Minimum-Version property and less than or equal to the MaximumVersion property.

Architecture Dependencies

One of the dependencies an application component can have on its hosting environment is the machine architecture or instruction set understood by that environment. The CIM_ArchitectureCheck class specifies the hardware platform on which a software element can run. The ArchitectureType property identifies a particular type of architecture or architecture family required to properly execute a particular software element. The intent is to capture the details about the machine instructions exploited by the executables of the software element.

The value of the ArchitectureType [CIM_ArchitectureCheck] property is compared with the Family property found on a CIM_Processor object referenced by a CIM_ComputerSystemProcessor association for the CIM_ComputerSystem object that describes the environment. For the check to be satisfied, you must have at least one CIM_Processor object that has a matching Family property.

Minimal Memory Dependencies

The MemorySize property of the CIM_MemoryCheck class specifies a condition for the minimum amount of memory that must be available on a system. The value of the MemorySize property of an CIM_MemoryCheck object is compared with the value of the Free-PhysicalMemory property of the CIM_OperatingSystem object referenced by an CIM_InstalledOS association for the CIM_Computer-System object that describes the environment. When the value of FreePhysicalMemory property of a CIM_OperatingSystem object is greater than or equal to the value specified in MemorySize, the condition is satisfied.

Be careful not to compare the two values without consulting the UNITS qualifier value for each. Obviously, a simple comparison is fine if the units are the same. Otherwise, the values must be converted to common units before comparing.

Minimal Disk Space Dependency

The AvailableDiskSpace property of the CIM_DiskSpaceCheck class specifies the minimum amount of disk space that must be available on the system. The value of AvailableDiskSpace is compared with the value of the AvailableSpace property of a CIM_FileSystem object associated with the CIM_ComputerSystem object that describes the environment. When the value of AvailableSpace property is greater than or equal to the value specified in AvailableDiskSpace, the condition is satisfied. This value comparison must verify that the units for the two properties are the same.

Minimal Swap Space Dependency

The SwapSpaceSize property of the CIM_SwapSpaceCheck class specifies the amount of swap space that must be available on the system. When the value of the TotalSwapSpaceSize property of CIM_OperatingSystem object referenced by InstalledOS association for the CIM_ComputerSystem object describing the environment is greater than or equal to the value specified in SwapSpacesize, the condition is satisfied. You must make sure the units are the same for the two properties.

Dependencies on Other Applications

The previous section dealt with specific dependencies a software element has on it hosting environment. In addition to having dependencies on its hosting environment, a software element can depend on the existence of another application in the environment. The CIM Application Model captures dependencies between applications in the following ways:

1. Dependency between software element objects.
2. Dependency between services (one software feature depends on the service of another software feature).

Software Element Dependencies

One of the challenges with capturing dependencies between applications or application components is that you need access to the correct information. When the details of a software element object you depend on are readily available and stable, the most straightforward way to express an interapplication dependency is to use the CIM_SoftwareElementVersionCheck class.

Suppose that software element A is dependent on a software element B. Software element A would defined a CIM_SoftwareElementVersionCheck for software element B. In order to verify the dependency, the CIM_InstalledSoftwareElement association is used to locate the software element already installed on the targeted CIM_ComputerSystem objects. As long as there is at least one CIM_SoftwareElement that satisfies the details of the condition, the check is satisfied. In other words, not all the software elements on the relevant computer system are needed to satisfy the condition.

The following properties in the CIM_SoftwareElementVersionCheck are used to evaluate the dependency:

- The SoftwareElementName property labels the software element being checked.
- The LowerSoftwareElementVersion property is the minimum version of a software element being checked.
- The UpperSoftwareElementVersion property is the maximum version of a software element being checked.

- The SoftwareElementState property is the state of the software element being checked.

- The TargetOperatingSystem property is the target operating system of the software element being checked.

In general, these element version check properties are compared with the key properties of the software element object installed on the targeted computer system. The following should help you understand how this comparison works:

- The CIM_SoftwareElementVersionCheck declares a dependency on a type of software element object. The Name [CIM_SoftwareElement] and Version [CIM_SoftwareElement] properties specify the dependency. The CIM_SoftwareElementVersionCheck class does not reference the SoftwareElementID [CIM_SoftwareElement] since this property is used for instances of a particular type of software element object.

- The CIM_SoftwareElementVersionCheck class can specify dependency on a particular version of a software element, on a range of versions of a software element, or on an open-ended range of "no sooner" or "no later than." These dependencies are represented in a way very similar to the CIM_OSVersionCheck. The upper and lower bounds are specified with the LowerSoftwareElementVersion [CIM_SoftwareElementVersionCheck] and UpperSoftwareElementVersion [CIM_SoftwareElementVersionCheck] properties.

Since there are many different types of CIM_Check objects, you should pay close attention to two aspects of the CIM_SoftwareVersionCheck class when looking for these dependencies. First, ensure that Phase [CIM_SoftwareElementCheck] property indicates an in-state check. Second, the CheckMode [CIM_Check] property must indicate that the condition is expected to be true.

Earlier, we stated that CIM_SoftwareElementVersionCheck class was a good way to express dependencies between applications when details about the dependent software element are known. You may find the information you need for software elements within a software feature and software elements between software features that are part of the same product. It is more difficult to use this technique for software elements in different products because details may not be readily available.

Dependencies on Services

Another way to express dependencies between applications is to describe dependencies between services. As we will see in the following discussion, CIM_SoftwareFeature class can implement services for others to use. These services can have dependencies on other services in the environment. Other software features implement those services. So, this mechanism for specifying dependencies between applications is the same as declaring: Software feature x has a service that depends on another service, and it does not matter how that service is implemented.

Figure 7.5 outlines the service dependency approach. We will define the cross-application dependency from the perspective of the software feature object labeled X (in the shaded area). The services supported by any CIM_SoftwareFeature are identified using the CIM_SoftwareFeatureServiceImplementation association. In Figure 7.5 CIM_Service object C is a service implemented by the software feature X.

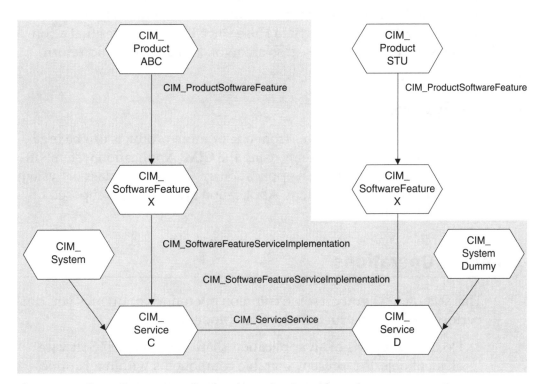

Figure 7.5   Illustrating cross-application dependencies with services.

We express the fact that service object C depends on another service using an instance of the CIM_ServiceService association. In the figure, there is such an instance between service object C and service object. Since CIM_Service classes are scoped by CIM_System classes, we need to create a dummy system object.

Following are two important observations:

1. We now have a cross-application dependency because service object D is not implemented by a software feature in software product object ABC.

2. The shaded area represents model items required prior to installing the software feature. In others words, the CIM_Product and CIM_SoftwareFeature object shown in the upper right corner of the figure are unnecessary. In fact, they would not exist until service object D actually existed in an environment.

Incompatibilities

In general, CIM_Checks can also be used to identify conditions with which a software element is incompatible. You should set the Check-Mode [CIM_Check] property to False since False indicates that a condition is not expected to exist, so an invoke() method would return "false".

Business Systems

Optionally, software features from one or more products can be organized into application systems using the CIM_ApplicationSystemSoftwareFeature association. An application system is a subclass of System known as Application System. Application systems are composed of Software Features.

Common Operations

This section tests you on some common operations or queries you can perform on the constructs in the Core Model.

1. Do different parts of an application share components? Software element objects represent sharable components within an application so you can determine the shared components by finding the

software element objects that are referenced by more than one instance of the CIM_SoftwareFeatureSoftwareElement association.

2. How do you determine the life cycle state for a particular software feature? The life cycle state is based on the value of the Software-ElementState [CIM_SoftwareElement] property.

3. On what platforms can a software feature run? This information is captured in the software element object that a particular software feature is composed into. If we assume that by "run" we can assume the question is asking on what platforms a software feature can exist in an executable state, then we'd answer the question by locating all the software elements for the software feature in the executable state (based on the value to the SoftwareElementState property) and take the union of the values found in the TargetOperatingSystem property. Each unique value represents a platform the software feature runs on.

4. When a software feature has multiple software elements, should you install them in any particular order? The answer depends on whether or not dependencies have been defined between the software elements using the CIM_SoftwareElementVersionCheck class. When a dependency exists, you must install the software element that is depended upon first.

5. What information do you need to specify in the model to completely define the compatibility of a software element in a particular operating system? To ensure a software element is compatible with a particular environment, you should look at the following three areas:

- The TargetOperatingSystem [CIM_SoftwareElement] property specifies the operating system environment.

- The CIM_OSVersionCheck contains the details for making sure the target operating system is a compatible version.

- The CIM_ArchitectureCheck specifies the details needed to ensure binary compatibility.

Summary

Figure 7.6 summarizes the major classes used in the Common Model for Applications, which builds on the Core Model. In order to grasp the Common Model for Applications, you must understand the roles

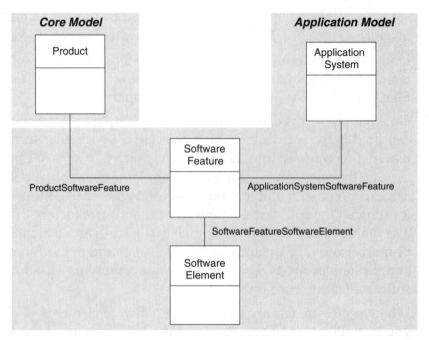

Figure 7.6 Base classes for application management.

of the different building blocks, the notion of an application life cycle, how checks are used to define expected conditions within an environment, and how actions are used for install and uninstall routines.

References

DMTF Application Management Working Group. 1998. "CIM Application Management Version 2.0 White Paper." DMTF(www.dmtf.org).

CHAPTER 8

Emerging Models

Although much of the development of the Common Information Model (CIM) is complete there are still many other areas in development that augment the model covered in the previous chapters. New models build on the work that has already been done and extend the model into new management domains like databases, networks, users, application performance, and support. The DMTF is continuing to address other areas of distributed management and will form additional working groups as the need arises.

Expansion of the Common Model of CIM will be an ongoing process to standardize CIM classes and their properties in order to create more interoperability between management systems. The CIM domains will need to accommodate new technologies as well. As the world becomes more interconnected with mobile phones, pagers, and automobile navigation devices, we will need to instrument these systems for manageability. Home networks are another area of great expansion, and such technologies will all become an integrated piece of our ever-expanding global network. Technology only becomes more complex in its push for ease of use. System integration and increased connectivity will create new and yet unimagined components and systems to be modeled and managed.

Before we can move into new areas we must model the current systems and how they are managed. This chapter presents some of the key models under development today within the DMTF. Working groups are leading the modeling efforts, made up of member companies of the DMTF with expertise in the particular area being model. Often the work requires joint sessions of multiple working groups to negotiate the boundaries and associations of the management models. Some of the decisions are arbitrary (as whether something is model in one part of the schema versus another) but interactions of the committees will ensure that the models fit together well.

This chapter will present five models in various stages of completion (they may be completed by the time this book is published). We hope to make you aware of current models in development and provide insight into the thinking behind them. You should always check the schemas and specifications available on the DMTF Web site at www.dmtf.org. These models are constantly being improved and enhanced.

Networks: Beyond the Desktop

Characterizing and controlling network elements and services is inherently complex. You must organize information to enable different people and applications to use it. The Directory Enabled Networks (DEN) initiative (which includes the current CIM work and extends it to integrate with directory services) will be used as a starting point to ensure seamless integration with directory services. The Network Working Group will define detailed schemata and a comprehensive information model that models LANs, MANs, WANs, system area networks, storage network elements, and network services.

The Network Working Group will also identify the network-centric elements and services involved in LANs, MANs, WANs, System Area Networks, and Storage Networks that will be defined by the Systems and Devices working group. It will also identify the network-centric services involved in LANs, MANs, WANs, System Area Networks, and Storage Networks for definition by the User Definition working group and create the specific extensions to the service framework as required to support naming, resolution, and discovery.

The Working Group will also define the associations that enable clients (e.g., users, applications, and host machines) to be bound to services that are available on the network. This will be based on the definition of a policy framework that associates the needs of the user with network mechanisms. In addition they will describe the relationships between different types of network elements and services.

The ongoing work of this group will need to address the structural, behavioral, and functional models of network elements and services. They will also need to model network states (e.g., current, desired, alternative, failed etc.). Modeling of the logical and physical network topology including the flow of data and its control will be done.

Cross group work will be done in a number of areas including working with the User Definition working group on profiles that define the association between user and network policies. In addition they will identify security-related requirements as input to the DMTF Technical Committee.

Network services include data transmission such as forwarding, routing, switching, naming, resolution and discovery. The Network Working Group will define the following four fundamental knowledge domains:

1. *Physical connectivity*. A model of the physical connections between components.

2. *Logical connectivity*. An idealized view of the network.

3. *Physical containment*. A model of the location and spatial relationships of components.

4. *Logical containment*. The intersection of network elements and services with business organizations.

These four knowledge domains enable the application to learn and navigate a physical or a logical network topology (for example, virtual subnet configuration) using objects that are independent of the underlying network media, access protocols, and physical hardware. The Network Working Group will focus on defining the relationships and associations between devices and network services and other CIM objects to facilitate, enhance, and define how different objects interact with each other. They will also collaborate with other DMTF and industry working groups. It is imperative that the Network Working Group work closely with other groups to ensure common definitions of schemata and the underlying information model.

User and Security: Roles of Man and Machine

The CIM User and Security Working Group is defining objects and access methods required for *principals*, where principals include users, groups, consumers, and organizations. Where possible, the working group is using the existing body of work. The User and Security Working Group assumes its models will operate and manage objects in a heterogeneous enterprise environment. The group will also define the mapping of CIM to current directory models.

The group will model users including the definition of corporate, residential, and organizational users. It will also include groups, representing collections of related users and their associated roles. The model will also address legal entities, organizations, consumers, cost centers, custodians, naming and management domains, accounts, addresses, aliases user policies (for example, "pays for gold level of service"), and user profiles.

The User and Security Working Group will address issues related to schema mapping to and from CIM as it relates to current directory technologies. They will identify and develop security-related constructs (classes, metaschema extensions, and so on). They will also define classes of relationships to users, groups, and other major classes (ownership of resources, usage of resources, participation in a group, and so on).

The group plans to describe how the CIM maps to directory models, naming, syntax, matching rules, and so on, to provide consistency for future CIM working groups.

Policy and Service Level Agreements (SLAs): Controlling the Enterprise

Policy and SLAs is an effort to define a schema for service level agreements and the associated dependencies on the CIM Model. Dependencies will include support for policies upon which service level agreements depend, which in turn will require support for queries, rules, and expressions (conditional statements), not yet part of the CIM Model. Schema definition deliverables are expected to fall after the release of CIM 2.2 due to dependencies on other aspects of the CIM Model including:

- Directory enabled networks (DEN)
- Quality of service
- Policy and the IETF

The SLA Working Group has developed the core policy objects that document the current status of the policy model. The model is relatively simple, and includes some very basic policy objects:

- *PolicyGroup.* Aggregates PolicyRules for administrative purposes
- *PolicyRule.* Aggregates PolicyConditions and PolicyActions
- *PolicyCondition.* Expresses the criteria which must be evaluated to "true", in order for the associated PolicyAction(s) to apply
- *PolicyAction.* Describes the action to be taken when the associated PolicyCondition evaluates to "true"

The model also documents several objects that are subclasses derived from PolicyCondition and PolicyAction, in order to capture specific condition and action semantics, including PolicyValidityPeriod, a more general-purpose condition expression and method action, and a mechanism for vendor specific escapes, called VendorPolicyCondition and VendorPolicyAction.

The SLA Working Group is working on policy extensions to the CIM Model and is mapping the model to an LDAP directory representation. They have the proposed the LDAP representation as an Internet draft to the Policy Frameworks Working Group of the IETF. The DMTF will have ownership of the information model from which the LDAP representation for networking policy is derived. However, both the DMTF and the IETF have separate change control over their own documents. IETF and DMTF liaisons must work to keep both representations in synch and translatable to the other.

The Policy Schema Internet draft should be stable soon. Members of the SLA Working Group, many of whom also participate in the IETF Policy Frameworks Working Group, will then take feedback on the LDAP representation of the policy model, and use it to update the

DMTF CIM policy extensions. They hope to reach stability on the DMTF CIM policy model shortly after IETF stabilizes the LDAP representation of the same model.

The Policy Frameworks Working Group of the IETF is also planning to map the application of the Core Policy Schema to QoS management. This work will proceed as soon as the Core Policy Objects Schema draft is advanced through the IETF last call process. We expect work to progress in the DMTF Networks Working Group in the area of QoS management in networks. Similar work will be done for QoS management in the Applications and Systems/Devices Working Groups, and the Policy Working Group will continue to help coordinate work across the policy disciplines. They will need to map QoS policy work to an LDAP representation and submit it to the IETF Policy Frameworks Working Group (similar to the process we followed for the Core Policy objects). We also expect the SLA Working Group to document how to represent *service level agreements* and *service level objectives*, and to associate them with policy objects currently being defined.

The IETF Policy Frameworks Working Group is also working on documenting architecture for implementing network policy. This architecture work is exclusively in the domain of the IETF. We expect the Policy Schema Internet draft to progress in the Policy Frameworks Working Group. The charter of the DMTF SLA Working Group does not include work to document system or network architecture.

Database: Managing the Data Warehouse

The Database Working Group will produce a model defining information required to manage databases, the interaction between a database and its environment, and the relationship between database instances throughout the enterprise. Initially the working group will model relational database systems and, at some point in the future, expand the model to include object and legacy database systems.

The model will contain entities common to all relational database systems and provide the basis for vendor-specific extensions. The goal of the model is not to define a replacement for existing database management tools. Instead, its aim is to supply accurate information for database management tools to consume by means of the Common Model.

The database information modeled will include database users, groups, roles, database objects (tables, indexes, views, procedures, and so on), data sources, transformations, and distributions. The model will also include aspects of the physical data storage, database transactions, database security and accessibility, database performance and volume metrics, database backup, and replication information.

The model will purposefully avoid supplying functionality such as issuing ad hoc database queries, creating, modifying, or removing database objects, or initiating database administrative tasks, such as starting a backup. Vendors who wish to implement such operations through a CIM Model will have to supply their own extension to the Common Database Model that the Database Working Group develops.

The Database Working Group will relate the Common Database Model to the other CIM common schemas. For example, the representation of a database's physical data storage should relate to the Systems/Devices Schema. Likewise, database users should relate to the CIM User Schema.

The working group will also define standard methods to populate the model, including mappings from SNMP MIBs that have already been defined for database systems, and working with database vendors to encourage extensions to the Database Model for their particular products.

Distributed Application Performance (DAP): Monitoring the Applications

The DAP group is an outgrowth of the Application Response Monitoring Working Group (responsible for developing the ARM APIs for distributed application performance monitoring). DAP is a DMTF Working Group that is defining a common model for the runtime behavior of distributed applications. The model will contain a unifying model for a unit of work. Examples of a unit of work are business transactions, batch jobs, database calls, and conceivably even low-level operations like I/O.

DAP group even plans to investigate extending the Core Schema, if necessary, to model run-time performance and incorporate quality of

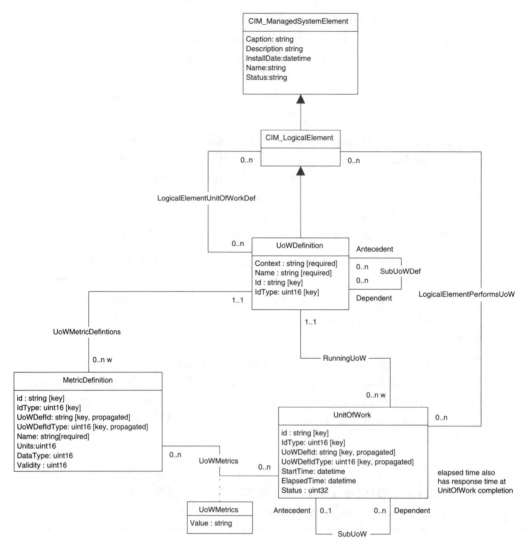

Figure 8.1 Distributed Application Performance Model in progress.

service objects. In addition, they will create associations between the DAP Models and to the common schemas of the other management domains such as the Systems/Devices, Network, Applications, Service, Support, and User Models.

The group also hopes to evolve standard methods to populate the model, independent of operating system or performance agent availability. The DAP Working Group assumes that the Distributed Application Performance Model will operate and manage objects in a heterogeneous/enterprise environment.

Support: Bugs and Fixes

The CIM Support Working Group is defining objects and access methods necessary for support information to be shared between service requesters and providers. It is a basic assumption of the working group that its models will operate and manage objects in a heterogeneous/enterprise environment. The information will model problems, resolutions, agreements, and support collateral. This working group is building on to the existing work that has been done in the Solution Exchange Standard (SES) and the Service Incident Standard (SIS) that has been developed in conjunction with the Customer support Consortium. This information is intended to be used in helpdesk systems as well as to exchange information between various support centers.

Problem information includes the description of the original problem, diagnostic and cause information, and relationship to specific supported products. Resolution information includes the description of the proposed resolution, its relative cost and scope, and any products used to remedy the situation.

The model also covers agreement descriptions, which are used by a support business model to determine the *type of service* (ToS) expected and service terms and conditions. It will also cover support collateral information which includes adequate identification of the requestor (or user) and provider, costs, and billing information.

The information described in the Support Working Group can be used as solution knowledge to be exchanged between a knowledge creator and consumer. Or, it can be incorporated in a request for service (service incident), which is then jointly managed by the service requestor and the chosen service provider. This working group will address definitions and models required for computer systems to describe their service needs and their current problem to a service provider, as well as helpdesks and management applications to electronically receive service requests and to escalate them intelligently to other helpdesks and management applications. This automation will facilitate the sharing of the solution knowledge obtained through the support process.

Summary

In this chapter we have reviewed several of the models that are being developed within the DMTF. It is anticipated that this work will continue to expand to include other domains such as telecommunications. As it is the intention for this work to be always up-to-date, we recommend the reader review the current schema posted on the DMTF Web site.

The CIM was built by its creators with the intention that it would be extended. The models intend to cover all of the aspects that are truly common between all managed systems and elements. Now that you have a better understanding of CIM and the models that have been developed we will cover in the next chapters how to design your own models and build extensions to the existing schema.

Steps in Schema Design

The CIM Schema is only a portion of the overall management application environment. Management applications are typically very complex and require other software components, such as transaction processing monitors, complex distributed interfaces, and specialized event delivery and communication structures. A complete system requires a variety of additional elements such as documentation, training courses, distribution and deployment systems, and support staff. The schema designer must consider all these factors.

As a designer, it is a good idea to consciously follow a development methodology. Be clear about what you expect at each stage of the development process. Schema design can be a very long and protracted undertaking, one that requires careful planning and long-term commitment of qualified people and other resources.

The body of this chapter outlines an approach to schema design. Note that that though this sequence may work as a methodology, it is really intended as a definition of the tasks involved in the schema development life cycle. Any large-scale schema design effort should be headed by experienced schema designers. If the project is small, you may decide to hire that expertise in the form of consultants. But given a sufficiently large project, you will need a full-time schema design staff.

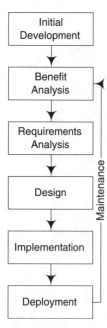

Figure 9.1 Schema life cycle.

Application Development Cycle

The following sections outline a process that takes a management application from initial development to deployment. Schema design is a major component of this development cycle; and since we'll be implementing CIM, that implies the use of schemas as the main organizing element in the development of the application. Though a variety of approaches have been taken in application development, those of an iterative nature have been emphasized in the object-oriented movement.

The life cycle illustrated in Figure 9.1 is typical of those in the schema design process.

The functions covered by each phase are described as follows:

Benefit analysis. Essential to any successful application development effort is a clear understanding of why the application is being developed in the first place. Everyone involved in the project must understand how the application will help to achieve the goals and objectives of the organization. Objectives may include systems administration, network inventory, and configuration planning, which will have to be aligned with the high-level objectives of the organization.

Requirements analysis. The purpose of this phase is to identify and study a management problem that warrants a computerized solution. Solution requirements are decomposed and organized. Detailed requirements are specified in a document generally referred to as a requirements specification. The process of determining the requirements may be very long and involved. The requirements themselves will reflect the structure and concerns of the organization being served; for example, the decision to provide physical inventory must be justified in terms of the cost of gathering the inventory. Requirements gathering also means delicately balancing between the technical necessities associated with identifying the bounds of the project and the political exigencies associated with meeting the needs of different segments of the organization being served.

Design. During the design phase, the artifacts necessary to define how the requirements will be met are produced. Artifacts may be documents, prototypes, or other formalized expressions of the structure of the proposed solution. The design may involve a functional specification, but it will be primarily expressed as a schema that is either unpopulated or partially populated using static data (that is, data not derived directly from the live environment). The design phase itself typically involves iterations as the structure of the schema is refined.

Implementation. In the implementation phase, the infrastructure necessary for populating the schema is established. There are a number of possibilities for accomplishing this. In a typical data architecture there are schemas at various levels, ranging from live production data to derived data used for offline analysis. Each level is likely to have different schema requirements and different implementation constraints. For example, the *N*-tier applications that are primarily concerned with instrumentation and control are likely to be associated with very detailed volatile schemas of restricted scope. The schema used in the Operational Cache is necessarily of a broader scope, and can be expected to encompass enterprise-level structures—if not the enterprise itself. Finally, the Data Warehouse offers the prospect of schemas that cover the entire enterprise across time.

Deployment. In the deployment phase, systems are installed and retired. The successful deployment rate of systems management applications is notoriously poor (most in the late 1990s failed). CIM is specifically intended to address this issue, by providing a standard schema that is designed and widely accepted as a basis for schema development and deployment efforts. Successful installation, however, depends on training and the establishment of stable and predictable usage patterns.

This five-phase model is not necessarily comprehensive, but it does reflect a typical application development approach. Furthermore, the phases are rarely performed in a particular sequence. Instead, the process is iterative: work done at any phase may reveal deficiencies that prompt a return to a previous phase. Moreover, developers of different application components may be working in different phases at the same time.

Somewhere in the development life cycle, designers cross the threshold from problem to solution. This usually occurs in the design phase, but sometimes earlier. It is important to keep track of problem elements (requirements), as opposed to solution elements (implementation), so that appropriate elements can be described and verified by appropriate personnel (e.g., users, programmers, database designers, etc.). It is a fatal mistake to expect developers to evaluate requirements or end users to evaluate implementations.

Once the system has been installed, it is put into active use (sometimes called "in production"). At that point, the system is monitored for performance and problems, often resulting in new requirements. The identification of new requirements causes the system to be put into a *maintenance cycle* in which the life cycle is repeated: new requirements are analyzed, designed, implemented, and installed. These maintenance cycles are the source of the majority of software costs, not the initial application development.

When you develop an application system, you should employ some kind of formal process to perform each development phase and to manage the overall application life cycle. Such a process can help to ensure the accuracy, completeness, and quality of your system. Within the process, you can use any of several techniques to develop and maintain specific application components. These techniques are termed *methodologies*.

Development Methodologies

Within the application life cycle, various methodologies can be used to develop specific components, such as programs and databases. The methodology chosen must be appropriate for the type of component being built; it must integrate the development of separate components within the application. In the following sections we describe common methodologies for program and database development.

Program Development

A common methodology used for program development is structured analysis and design, which uses a mixture of data-driven and process-driven techniques for transforming business requirements into an implemented system. Various representation techniques are used to describe requirements, data analysis, and task hierarchies. One drawback of structured methodologies is that they do not work well for schemas.

An alternative program development methodology that is coming into more widespread use is object-oriented analysis and design. It uses techniques that integrate the structure and behavior of problem and solution elements into objects. Because CIM's data model—and the schema design process described in this section—are based, in part, on object-oriented technology, object-oriented methodologies are especially well-suited for programs that interface with CIM Schemas.

Schema Development

A common methodology used for schema development is entity-relationship (E-R) modeling, whereby the entity-relationship data model is used with a process that concludes with a conceptual schema representing the desired schema design.

However, since most commercial schemas use a record or tuple-based data model, the E-R conceptual schema must be translated into the language of another schema model, such as relational. This process is usually manual and requires complex steps such as normalization. Furthermore, the translation causes the schema to lose semantics, which must be captured by programs or people.

CIM Schema Development

When you develop a CIM Schema, you can use E-R modeling and directly translate an E-R conceptual schema into a CIM Schema without losing semantics, because CIM directly supports basic E-R concepts such as entities, relationships, and attributes. However, CIM's data model is somewhat more advanced than the E-R data model (it supports extended concepts such as bidirectional relationships, generalization hierarchies, and general integrity constraints); therefore, you can more effectively develop a CIM Schema by directly incorporating its data model.

The schema design process we present in this section comprises a set of techniques that you can use to develop a CIM Schema. The process incorporates elements from E-R modeling, object-oriented techniques, and the semantic data model. Although this process does not constitute a complete methodology, it will help you to achieve a CIM Schema that meets the specific requirements of your application and reflects an effective use of the CIM Model.

Prototyping

Prototyping is widely accepted as a technique for evaluating and expressing a design. A prototype is a reduced version of the full implementation and typically contains a realistic implementation of the main elements of the application. Many nonessential features are omitted or simplified to enable the user to get a feel for how the application will function in practice and to allow for the evaluation of alternative algorithms and implementation strategies.

Prototypes are used to validate specific approaches to the design in the early phases of the project. A prototype may be used to explore all basic aspects of a design, including architecture, interfaces, and physical considerations such as capacity and performance; however, typically, some subset of these will be taken as the motivation of the prototype, the subset being used to determine which portions of the prototype will be developed.

Developing a prototype where the schema is the focus of the development effort is particularly appropriate as the prototype schema is likely to be useful with very little alteration in the final implementation. Once built, the schema can be used as the basis for either rough population strategies (enabling the exploration of aspects of the instrumentation or storage techniques) or for the formulation of queries and the rapid development of interface modules that illustrate the forms of access permitted by the design.

CIM is schema-based, so it is well suited for prototyping; it's a good idea to take advantage of this when you are exploring both small and large tasks in the management of your IT environment.

CIM Schema Design

In this section, we describe a process you can use to design a CIM Schema. The process comprises a series of steps intended to take you through the application development cycle outlined previously. Though it is not essential to perform the steps in the given order, it is important to recognize that the order is somewhat dictated by their internal dependencies. The most important point is, however, to be cognizant of the major issues you must cover through the design process.

Overview

You can begin schema design either when you are gathering requirements or when you begin your application development. Many requirements can be represented directly in CIM Schema constructs. (Note that when you develop a CIM Schema as a requirements task, you can still consider the process as schema design because the schema is a specification that can be directly implemented.) CIM can be useful as a vehicle for documentation and feedback in the early phases of the design cycle, and can function as a natural part of the implementation. Unless you are using some other systematic approach to capturing information requirements, we recommend that you use CIM as early as possible in the development cycle.

We divide CIM Schema design into three essential activities. Keep in mind that, potentially, there are different requirements applicable to each activity. Further, it is very important to keep the requirements as separate as possible. Mixing logical design and interface design or physical design and logical design will degrade both designs. Inherently, CIM provides such a separation, since CIM is a pure data model with no characteristics specific to either interface or implementation. The CIM concept of namespaces may be used to separate artifacts of the interface from the logical model, and CIM's qualifiers can be used to decorate the schema with any implementation-relevant data without compromising the structure of the schema itself. The schema design activities are as follows:

Logical design. This activity defines how to develop the logical schema. Logical design identifies elements of the information model, the definition of logical schema structure and semantics, and adherence to business rules and application requirements. This activity also focuses on schema structure and semantics.

Interface design. This activity describes how users and other consumers of the data will use the information provided by the logical schema. Interface design identifies queries and transactions that will be formulated against the schema, along with any additional information needed for access. The structure and semantics of the logical schema will be validated and refined as a result of this process. The interface design is an essential step in the validation of the logical schema, in the sense that the schema can only be assumed to be correct when it has been shown that it is usable.

Physical design. This activity defines how the logical schema will be mapped to a physical schema or data source. You should consider issues such as capacity, performance, operational, and schema evolution requirements during the physical design phase. You will be adding and refining various implementation-related qualifiers that will be used by the programs that access, maintain, and populate the schema.

These activities consist of a series of steps each of which has specific objectives and outcomes. Before you begin a new CIM Schema design, you should know how you plan to produce these outcomes and understand how they depend on each other. Do not expect to achieve a satisfactory outcome from a single pass through the steps; in fact, schedule a second or even a third pass. And be aware that different aspects of the application may be under development at the same time but in different phases, especially if you have several development teams working concurrently.

To illustrate this process, the following discussion uses a subset of the CIM Physical schema, which is shown in Figure 9.2.

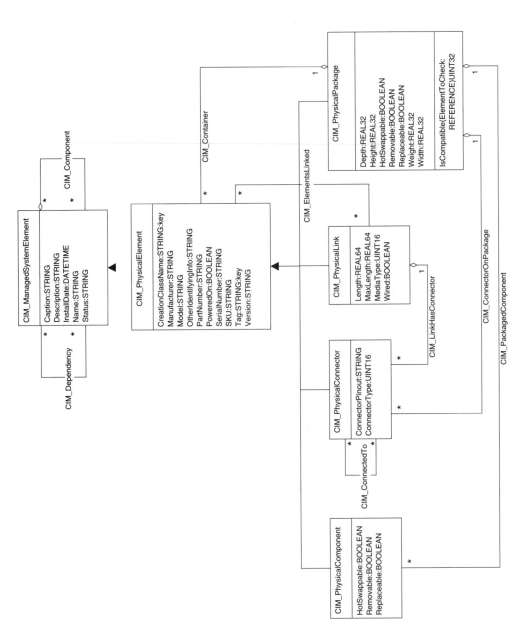

Figure 9.2   Extract of the CIM Physical schema.

NOTE
For the sample illustration, we assume that you have already gathered sufficient requirements so that you have a firm understanding of the area that you are modeling. We also assume you will perform the steps either during design or during a requirements-gathering process organized around an approach such as use cases.

The goal of logical design is to define the structure and semantics of the schema, which consists of the various constructs defined in the description of the CIM Model: classes, properties, associations, methods, events, and instances. The semantics of the domain you are modeling are expressed through the structure of the model and, where necessary, the integrity constraints required to augment the overt structural aspects of the model.

There are four principal steps involved in this activity:

1. Identify things and their properties.
2. Generalize and specialize.
3. Add semantics.
4. Evaluate and refine.

It is recommended that at least initially you follow this sequence; the first pass will establish a structure that you can use to organize information and ideas arising from subsequent activities. Following the steps will also help, for example, to add semantics without losing track of what you are doing, because you will have a basic set of classes and properties in place.

Step 1: Identify Things and Their Properties

The purpose of a schema is to provide a representation of the information that is required by an application. The basic unit of data in CIM is the instance. Ultimately, all data in CIM must be expressed as an instance and its properties. Instances are organized into classes, and during this step, you will identify the various classes or collections of instances that the application will deal with.

The primary focus in this step is representing instances, so it is very important that you have a clear understanding of those instances that will be used to populate any class you plan to propose. You must also ensure that any property has both a sensible relationship to the instance it characterizes and a clear source for its values.

To begin, think of the concepts of the model as the language that, you, the schema designer will use. You have to be fluent enough in that "language" to be able to accurately translate from the terms used by the customer to the terms of the model. (A good exercise to ensure this capability is to take sources, such as structures returned by API calls or the records of a database, and translate them into CIM terms.) The point is, be sure you can produce workable CIM Schemas before you attempt the kind of open-ended design exercise described here.

Identify Classes

In CIM, anything can be an object. Objects can be very concrete (such as a person or a telephone) or very abstract (such as an event, a time period, or a relationship instance). When identifying objects and classes, you must avoid the temptation to design how objects will be mapped or displayed. This is particularly important if you are accustomed to thinking in terms of records or program data structures that do not separate logic from implementation. Also be careful to avoid interface implications. If an object is a complex aggregation of many other objects, represent the full extent of the complexity without regard to how it might be displayed or manipulated. Defer interface and presentation issues until the interface design stage.

The schema does not usually define individual instances; it is generally read as a description of a collection of instance types or classes. The instance types are the actual data that will be consumed or produced by the applications that use the schema. Each type of object you identify should be represented as a class. Remember that in a subsequent step, classes will be eliminated where they are impractical or unnecessary, so don't be unduly concerned at this stage about the number of classes; just keep the size of the schema manageable.

There are many possible approaches to identifying potential objects. You can examine documents that describe the domain and obtain possible objects from the descriptions they contain. You can observe processes and procedures, such as shipping and staging hardware or taking incident reports, and extrapolate objects from your observations. Most important is that you get to know people who will be using the model, preferably those who will actually have to interface with the model, rather than their managers or others who may only be indirectly involved.

Keys

In the relational model, keys traditionally play two roles: one as an identifier for the row containing the key, the other as a way of providing a label for the row. Note that these two functions are separable, and so in some systems are supported by different features.

In the relational model, keys are collected into an index; however, the usage of terms is somewhat ambiguous, because the literature often refers to "the primary key" as meaning the collection of columns that have been marked as a key. In CIM, however, key may refer to either a single property marked as a key or to all the properties marked with the key qualifier. The specific meaning in each case must be inferred from the context.

The relational model also incorporates the idea of *candidate keys*. A candidate key is a property that could be used as a key, as it has unique values for all the instances in the class. In some contexts, candidate keys are used as primary keys, and in some constituencies, the candidate key may be used as the label, not the primary key. If the latter is the case, the schema designer must be careful not to be confused by the presence of two names for the same thing. Translating between the keys can cause some confusion; for example, if a user knows the candidate key value but does not know the primary key, he or she must have an efficient means of looking up the candidate key.

Keys in CIM provide a way of uniquely identifying an instance within the scope of a given namespace. Only properties and references may be used as keys (not qualifiers or methods). The fact that a property is a key is indicated by the presence of the key qualifier. In the following example, Name and Domain constitute the key of the class.

```
class UserAccount{
        [Read, Key]
      string Domain;
        [Read, Key]
      string Name;
    };
```

Given an instance of the Win32_SystemAccount class as follows, the keys would be used to build a path for the instance, such as:

```
\\root\cimv2\UserAccount.Domain = "FUNAZONKI",Name="BATCH"
```

The instance itself would appear as follows:

```
instance of UserAccount{
        Domain = "FUNAZONKI";
        Name = "BATCH";
    };
```

Keys may be propagated across an association; for example, the keys for CIM_Service are defined as follows:

```
class CIM_Service:CIM_LogicalElement{
        [Override ("Name") , Key]
    string Name;
        [Propagated ("CIM_System:Name") , Key]
    string SystemName;
        ...
    };
```

The CIM_Service class is related to the system on which the service is hosted by the CIM_HostedService association, which is declared as follows:

```
[Association ]
class CIM_HostedService:CIM_Dependency{
        [Override ("Antecedent") , Max (1) , Min (1)]
    CIM_System REF Antecedent;
        [Override ("Dependent") , Weak]
    CIM_Service REF Dependent;
    };
```

The association defines the dependent reference (the reference that points to the CIM_Service class) as "Weak." This implies that the keys of the antecedent class (CIM_System) should be copied to the dependent class. The propagated qualifier is used to indicate which of the properties were actually copied.

There are principles for designing keys beyond standard identifier specification. These principles are:

- Make sure that keys are unique within a namespace.
- Use propagated keys whenever keys must be qualified or where the object may be copied into other namespaces.

- Keep keys as small as possible. The key gets concatenated along with the class name and path to make the full identifier for the object. This is the value used in references and, usually, in relational mappings for identifying records. For example, if higher-level namespaces require more heavily qualified keys, consider leaving these off the list of keys in the lower namespace; they can always be added later during the import of the instance into the higher-level namespace.

- Make sure that every property is determined by the key, which is tantamount to saying that every property should be attached to the correct class. If this is true, and if the key properly identifies members of the class, the key should have a correct relationship to the other properties in the class.

- In the context of instrumentation and user interfaces, confirm that the key is an adequate mechanism for identifying the objects to which it applies. SCSI ID, for example, works as a key in the context of a system as long as there is only one SCSI bus. Plug-and-play (PnP) ID works as an identifier as long as you don't encounter machines that predate the PnP specification. You must be on the lookout for a number of factors, to ensure that keys provide an adequate identifier.

Identify Properties

A class should be characterized by a Description; it will also be defined by a distinctive set of features. The features will be some mix of properties, methods, and associations. Any class that does not have such distinguishing features is probably not worth keeping. If you are quite sure the class will not acquire some features through the design process, it can safely be discarded.

Properties can be thought of as follows:

- The characteristics that each instance of a class can have, such as identification (SerialNumber, Name), a feature (Height, Removable), or a relationship (Container, PackageComponent).

- Each property must have a name (such as PartNumber or Tag) and a type. A property's type indicates the range of values that the property can hold.

- Properties may be either ordinary data-valued properties or references. In CIM, references contain an object path that consists of a set of namespaces followed by a key clause (rather like an Internet URL). Data values are various self-contained types such as integers and strings. The main characteristic of these types is that they stand for themselves, whereas reference values are a handle on an object. CIM does not allow references to be used anywhere except in an association.

In defining the features of a class, there may be some ambiguity as to whether a property should be a data-valued property or a reference. This ambiguity typically arises from the decision as to whether a value in the model will be represented as a data type or as a class. For example, a simple string may represent an address, or it may be an object in its own right, with properties such as zip code and state. In the early stages of class definition, err on the side of making things classes wherever necessary. It is, for example, quite reasonable to have classes for address, location, owner, slot, media, and so on, even though it may later be possible to reduce these to simple types, and use properties to represent the relationship between the values and the things they characterize.

This distinction in CIM unfortunately obliges the schema designer to choose early between associations and properties. As a schema designer, bear in mind that in the early stages of the design process this distinction may be premature. Generally, whether something is an association or a property may depend on whether the type of the property is modeled as a simple string or an object. Let's pursue the address example: the following represents a "relationship" between Person and Address; the address is expressed as a property value:

```
Class Person{
      string Name;
      string Address;
   };
```

This is in contrast to the following where the address is expressed as an association to an instance of an Address class.

```
Class Person{
      string Name;
   };
Class Address{
```

```
     string Text;
};

Class PersonAddress{
    Person ref Person;
    Address ref Address;
};
```

The second case is much more flexible because it allows for Person to have zero or more addresses. The first approach allows only one address per person and has the awkward effect of having a blank value if there is no address; it is also difficult to determine whether two or more people have the same address and impossible to represent an address where no one lives. In practice of course, the Address class would have several properties such as Street, City, Zip Code, and so on, which are difficult to express in the case of a simple property. Therefore, at some point in the design cycle, you should plan to examine properties to determine whether they should be converted into classes and associations to make the model more expressive. You should also examine classes and decide whether to collapse them into properties to make the schema more concise, though less expressive.

Once you have defined a property's type, it is important to decide the cardinality of the property. Cardinality in this context means the number of property values it is reasonable for a single instance to have. For example, a PhysicalElement will only have one InstallDate, whereas PhysicalConnector might have more than one ConnectorType. We are actually defining dependency relations between the property and the instance. If it is possible for the instance to have more than one value, the given property is said to have a *multivalued dependency* on the instance (actually, on its key).

Other property characteristics, such as enumerations and whether the property is optional, may also be defined at the identify properties stage. These characteristics are not essential, however, because the class and its properties will be revisited at a later stage with these characteristics specifically in mind.

Apart from the property and class characteristics we have outlined, there are a number of other items you can address at this stage. But be careful not to spend too much time on these since they will be refined later; the recommendation is that if you come across information on these issues, you should record it. Specifically, watch for:

Hierarchies. In some cases, subclass relationships will be obvious, and they can help immensely in simplifying the relationship structure of the overall schema as you can put common associations over abstract classes, thus avoiding a proliferation of basically similar associations over concrete leaf classes. In short, use subclassing where possible but don't work too hard at getting it right.

Additional semantics. Included here are items such as key propagation, source information (as in MappingStrings), and Aggregation and Aggregate qualifiers used to indicate the strength of the association.

Interface considerations. You can capture a lot of information about how users are likely to implement the data represented by the model. The only caveat here is that the interface information should not be allowed to color the structure of the model. For example, the structure of the network is correctly a part of the model; how a specific administrator chooses to organize the systems he or she has to monitor and control is not.

If the requirements are obvious in these three areas, go ahead and gather them. But at this stage do not define how the model will be implemented. Keep issues around capacity, physical representation, or performance out of the discussion at this stage. The logical schema design must be correct before you consider these areas, and you could needlessly distort the logical schema if you attempt to address physical concerns too early.

A Modeling Example

To illustrate the principles described so far, we will extend the physical model in Figure 9.2 to track movement incidents. That is, each time certain types of equipment are moved, information about which piece was moved, where it came from, where it went to, who asked for it to be moved, who moved it, when it was moved, and any comments prior to or after the move will be tracked. Equipment may pass through a staging area; there are several staging areas, each of which is divided into additional areas. For example, when equipment is being organized for a large trade show, it will be gathered in a single staging area prior to final shipment.

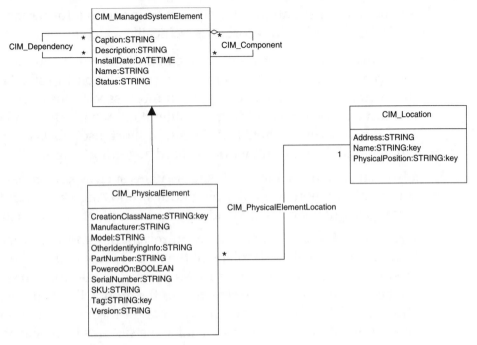

Figure 9.3 Physical element location.

Clearly, a major component of the model is the idea of location. A quick inspection of the standard CIM Schema reveals the existence of a Location class, defined as in Figure 9.3.

Note that the class comes complete with properties and an association to the PhysicalElement class. It is an important aspect of the CIM approach that only physical things can have locations. It is not sensible to ask "where are you?" of a CIM_LogicalElement. Logical elements do not have a location, in that they typically represent information of some kind. As such they can be located (in the sense of being requested and accessed through an interface of some kind), but they do not have a location.

The full text of the declaration for the Location class and its association to PhysicalElement is as follows:

```
      [Description (
      "The Location class specifies the position and address of a "
      "PhysicalElement.") ]
class CIM_Location
{
      [Key, MaxLen (256) , Description (
```

```
        "Name is a free-form string defining a label for the Location. It is a "
        "part of the key for the object.") ]
    string Name;
        [Key, MaxLen (256) , Description (
        "Position is a free-form string indicating the placement of a "
        "PhysicalElement. It can specify slot information on a HostingBoard, "
        "mounting site in a Cabinet, or latitude and longitude information, for "
        "example, from a GPS. It is part of the key of the Location object.") ]
    string PhysicalPosition;
        [MaxLen (1024) , Description (
        "Address is a free-form string indicating a street, building or other "
        "type of address for the PhysicalElement's Location.") ]
    string Address;
};
        [Association, Description (
        "PhysicalElementLocation associates a PhysicalElement with a Location "
        "object for inventory or replacement purposes.") ]
class CIM_PhysicalElementLocation
{
        [Description ("The PhysicalElement whose Location is specified.") ]
    CIM_PhysicalElement REF Element;
        [Max (1) , Description ("The PhysicalElement's Location.") ]
    CIM_Location REF PhysicalLocation;
};
```

Note that the class includes key declarations. Consequently, the way that the class will be populated and the circumstances under which it makes sense to use it are tightly constrained. In this example, the application requires items to be tracked as they are moved from one location to another. On further analysis, we discover that locations are locations in the sense implied by the CIM_Location class. And though it is reasonable to use building and room number as the PhysicalPosition value, some locations have actual names (for example the Kodiak room). In most cases, the type of the location makes a logical name; for example, an instance of CIM_Location might be:

```
Instance of CIM_Location
{
    Name = "office"
    PhysicalPosition = "24/1294
    Address = "One Microsoft Way, Redmond, WA, 98052"
};
```

Though there is no obvious CIM equivalent to the idea of equipment relocation, the description provided suggests something like:

```
class IT_EquipmentMove
{
```

```
        [Description("The date the move is scheduled to occur")]
    datetime ScheduledDate;
        [Description("Notes to the mover to indicate special "
        "restrictions or circumstances. This will also be used by "
        "the Mover to record any damage or  other relevant "
        "information discovered prior to moving the equipment.")]
    string PreComments;
        [Description("Notes used by the Mover to track information "
        "about the move itself for example damage in transit or "
        "problems effecting actual delivery")]
    string PostComments;
        [Description("Name of the individual responsible for "
        "requesting the move")]
    string Requestor;
        [Description("Name of the individual responsible for "
        "effecting the move")]
    string Mover;
    [Description("The location to be moved from")]
CIM_Location ref source;
    [Description("The location to be moved to")]
CIM_Location ref destination;
        [Description("The item to be moved")]
    CIM_PhysicalElement ref Equipment;
};
```

At this stage, the emphasis should be on gathering relevant facts. Accordingly, the schema focuses on properties and descriptions. Once a rough draft of the schema has been drawn, it is possible to refine it in various ways. For example, it seems fairly clear, even from the sparse description, that more than one pre- and postcomment might be provided, suggesting that the comments should be arrays of strings. The Requestor and Mover properties are questionable, in that they might be references to a Person class of some sort. The Source and Destination references are questionable in that only associations may contain references, implying that either the EquipmentMove class should be an association or the schema needs to include associations relating EquipmentMove objects to Source and Destination locations. Take a look at some instance data, shown in Figure 9.4, to get an idea what an instance of the EquipmentMove class might look like.

Notice that Figure 9.4 is an instance diagram, not a class diagram. The rectangles represent instances; the path for the instance is in the top portion of the rectangle, and the property values are in the bottom portion of the rectangle. Lines in the diagram represent associations between instances. In this case, we have a three-way association

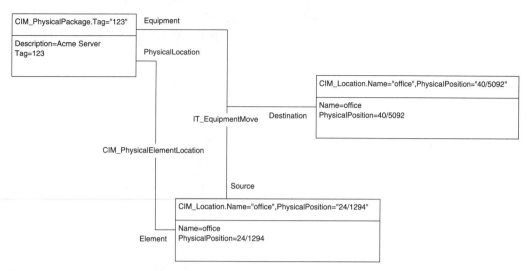

Figure 9.4 An instance of the EquipmentMove class.

between an instance of a PhysicalPackage, with Tag = 123; a Destination Location, with PhysicalPosition = 40/5092; and a Source Location, with PhysicalPosition = 24/1294.

Also notice another association, in this case, that relates the Physical-Package to the Source Location instance. It should be apparent that the source location for the equipment is necessarily the same as the current location for the equipment. In a sense, it is irrelevant what the source location might be as far as the move request is concerned, because the equipment can only be moved from the location it is currently at. It follows that the only thing the EquipmentMove class needs is an association between the EquipmentMove and the Destination, and an association between the EquipmentMove instance and the equipment to be moved.

It should also be apparent that the EquipmentMove instance could reasonably exist apart from a given destination. It may be known that a piece of equipment will have to be moved at some point in the future, even though it may not be known where it will be moved. A move cannot be reasonably scheduled without knowing what will be moved. This piece of information is required because the reference to the equipment is a part of the key. CIM has a technique for formalizing this: it propagates the key from the equipment. This technique involves the use of, first, the Propagated qualifier to indicate that a value has been propagated from another instance and, second, the Weak qualifier to indicate the association the value propagated across. This leads to the following schema:

```
class IT_Move
{
        [Key, Description("The date the move is scheduled to occur")]
    datetime ScheduledDate;
        [Description("Notes to the mover to indicate special "
        "restrictions or circumstances. This will also be used by "
        "the Mover to record any damage or  other relevant "
        "information discovered prior to moving the equipment.")]
    string PreComments;
        [Description("Notes used by the Mover to track information "
        "about the move itself for example damage in transit or "
        "problems effecting actual delivery")]
    string PostComments;
        [Description("Name of the individual responsible for "
        "requesting the move")]
    string Requestor;
        [Description("Name of the individual responsible for "
        "effecting the move")]
    string Mover;
        [Key, propogated("CIM_PhysicalElement.Tag")]
    string EquipmentTag;
};
    [Association]
class IT_MoveEquipment
{
        [Key, Weak]
    IT_Move ref Move;
        [Key]
    CIM_PhysicalPackage ref Equipment;
};
    [Association]
class IT_MoveDestination
{
        [Key]
    IT_Move ref Move;
        [Key]
    CIM_Location ref Destination;
};
```

Figure 9.5 contains a sample set of instances to illustrate how this model might be populated. Note that a similar set of arguments should almost certainly be applied to the Requestor and Mover properties, both of which should probably be associations to objects of an

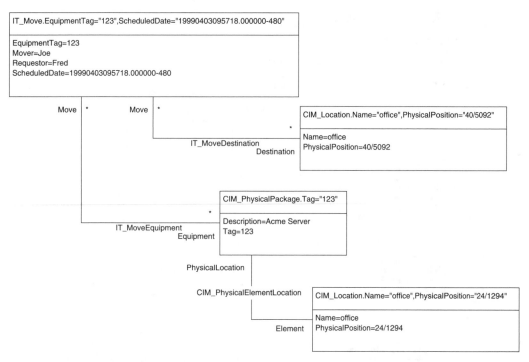

Figure 9.5 Move instance.

appropriate type. Also note that CIM has a rich user and organization schema that would be a useful point of departure for such a model.

```
    [Description("A staging location is a collection of staging areas "
    "used to gather equipment prior to final shipment")]
class IT_StagingLocation
{
};
    [Description("A staging area is a place where equipment is kept "
    "while In process of being moved from one location to another.")]
class IT_StagingArea
{
};
    [Association]
class IT_LocationAreas
{
IT_StagingLocation ref Location;
IT_StagingArea ref Area;
};
```

The model as it appears at this point is given in Figure 9.6.

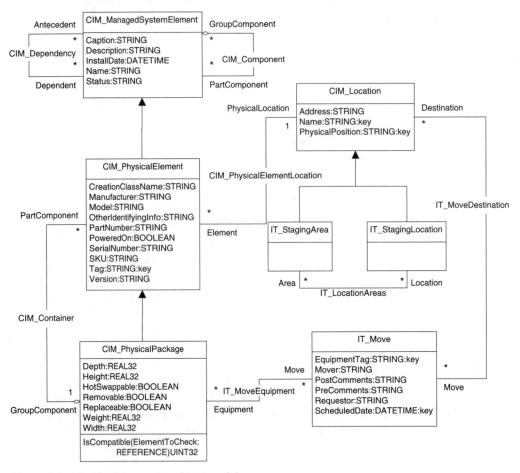

Figure 9.6   Draft of a move-tracking model.

Review of Step 1

We'll end this exploration of step 1 with some suggestions on specific topics pertinent to logical design.

Property Placement

Attach each property to the class that most clearly "owns" it. For example, project number is more accurately a property of projects than of employees. Some attributes can be temporarily repeated if necessary. For example, employee, president, and previous employee can each be given a name property. Later, this replication can be scrutinized to see if it should be eliminated.

Naming Conventions

The suggestions given here for choosing class and property names are intended to assist programmers and users who will construct queries against the schema.

■ Name classes in the singular (such as Project, Employee, and Department) to emphasize that attributes are properties of each entity in the class.

■ Use the singular form of property and reference names (such as Name, SerialNumber, and Size) to reiterate that each of these properties can only possess one value per instance.

■ Use the plural form for names of arrays or bit fields (such as System Roles and Printer PaperSizesSupported) to reflect that these properties can have several values per entity.

■ If there is no obvious role name for a reference, use the name of the target class. This is, however, a solution of last resort, as it is always a good idea to use meaningful role names.

■ For data-valued properties, make full use of the CIM-provided types (especially datetime and enumerated types through the use of Values and ValueMap qualifiers) because these types communicate more semantics. The type of a reference must be a class. Although the class is not required to exist at the time of definition, ultimately one must be specified for the schema to be meaningful.

Relationships

In CIM, every association establishes a bidirectional relationship. That is, each concrete association must have two or more references. We assume the association can be traversed in either direction, implying that the reference itself is bidirectional, since it must be possible to efficiently traverse from the target class to the association, as well as from the association to the target class.

Given that associations are always represented by classes, the location of properties is never an issue. A standard problem in relational schemas is the presence of properties, which is determined by a relationship between two tables rather than the key of any one table. Consider for example a purchasing scenario, as represented by the following schema:

```
Class Device{
        [Key]
    string Id;
    string Description;
    datetime PurchaseDate;
    string Purchaser;
};

Class Person{
        [Key]
    string Name;
};
```

Assume for a moment that Purchaser represents a foreign key to Person, and that a Device may or may not be purchased, and if it is purchased, the system must track the purchase date. Given these restrictions, it is perfectly reasonable to have a Device with an Id and Description but nothing else. Classes in which groups of properties have systematic relationships like those between Purchaser and PurchaseDate violate the spirit, if not the letter, of the rules provided by the normal forms. The point is that although PurchaseDate is dependent on Id, whether it has a value is determined by the combination of Id and Purchaser, not just Id alone. This leads to a more CIM-like schema as follows:

```
Class Device{
        [Key]
    string Id;
    string Description;
};

Class Purchase{
        [Key]
    Device reference PurchasedItem;
        [Key]
    Person reference Purchaser;
    datetime PurchaseDate;
};

Class Person{
        [Key]
    string Name;
};
```

Note here that it is important to be precise about dependencies and to take advantage of the liberal use of associations encouraged by CIM.

In CIM, everything is represented as a class; using a uniform approach will help you to avoid many of the typical problems associated with record-based models.

Step 2: Generalize and Specialize

The purpose of step 2 is to refine the rough classifications defined in the first step. One typical side effect of refining the inheritance tree is to simplify the schema by:

- Limiting the interpretations available for subclasses that have been introduced.

- Shifting numerous common properties and associations that run across many subclasses to a limited number of properties and associations that apply to a limited set of superclasses.

The first, limiting interpretations for subclasses, is known as *specialization*. The second, limiting properties and associations, is referred to as *generalization*.

Step 2 comprises a number of identifiable substeps; specifically, you will:

1. Look for commonality between classes to identify missing superclasses.

2. Look for properties that exist in multiple subclasses that can be moved to a common superclass.

3. Look for common references that target sibling subclasses and could be moved to a common superclass—these are generalizations.

4. Look for properties that do not apply to all the instances of a class but do apply to all the instances of a subclass; these should be moved down to the subclass.

5. Look for references that do not apply to all the instances of a class but do apply to all the instances of a subclass; these should be more accurately typed.

6. Look for subclasses that are not mutually exclusive—these are specializations.

Form Hierarchies

Recall that there are two ways to define a class: by giving a list of its members (or instances) or by giving a condition that can be used to recognize the members of the class.

To form generalization hierarchies, you examine each pair of classes and determine whether one is a subclass of the other, they are sibling classes, or they are unrelated. This amounts to comparing the class definitions, which is equivalent to theorem proving, an NP-complete problem. Thus it may be a very difficult task if, for example, you have a list of members for one class and a condition defining the other. For that matter comparing sets of instances may not be all that obvious either, especially if the sets were independently formulated and, for example, use different but equivalent keys. Therefore, here we attempt to clarify what it means to identify subclass, superclass, sibling, and unrelated classes. We also list some guidelines that will help you deal in a reasonable amount of time with imperfect and complex data.

Dealing with instances is not just cumbersome, in most cases it is impossible. The full instance definition may not be available at the time you are considering the hierarchy; and even if it were, it is very unlikely that you, the schema designer, would be in a position to definitively populate it. Given that the key uniquely identifies the instance, you can substitute a list of key values for the full instance definition, to slightly reduce the quantity of data. However, it is still unlikely that you would have a complete list of the instances.

One reasonable approach is to obtain a representative sample, although you must recognize that counter examples are definitive and that positive cases can only be taken as an indication. For example, assume you hypothesize that all services are applications; it would take only one instance of a service that is not an application to definitively prove that you are wrong. That means the counter example is definitive. On the other hand, if you produce a list of services all of which are applications, this does *not* prove that there is no counter example anywhere; at best, it only indicates that services are applications.

Dealing with class definitions in the form of conditions is also very problematic. For example, the definition of CIM_Process reads: "The

Process class is derived from LogicalElement. It is intended to represent a program in execution, running under an OperatingSystem; hence, it is weak to OperatingSystem. Processes are also known as "tasks." (See CIM standard schema CIM_Process declaration.) The key phrase presumably is "a program in execution . . ." Does this imply that anything executing is a process? Does it follow that programs executing in a virtual machine represent processes? What for that matter is a program or a task? Neither is defined elsewhere in the model. It is difficult, if not impossible, to tell how it should be interpreted, simply by examining the definition.

One approach to dealing with classes when there is no adequate definition or population available is to use the *signature* of the class as a definition. A class signature is the total set of features of the class; that is, its properties, associations, and methods (both immediate and inherited). The assumption is that any object that can support all of the features of the class is a member of the class; the class features become a kind of intensional definition for the class. This, however, is not a very satisfactory approach because the manipulation of the hierarchy involves changing the features of the class. Interactions between the design of the schema and the raw material used to drive the design process may instigate situations in which a design becomes a self-fulfilling prophecy. A class becomes a subclass of some other class, thereby acquiring the properties of that class; therefore, it can be considered a subclass of the class. This becomes a circular form of reasoning that is hard to justify but very easy to slip into.

Putting aside for the moment issues arising from the definition of the classes involved, take a look at the diagrams in Figure 9.7, which define the various possible relationships between classes with respect to the subclass-superclass relationship. There are four possibilities:

All As are Bs. In this case, it is possible to show that every instance of A is also an instance of B. It follows that A is a subclass of B.

As and Bs are Cs. Note that As and Bs have no instances in common, though every member of A and every member of B are also members of C. It follows that the schema will contain sibling classes A and B, both of which are subclasses of a third class, C.

Some As are Bs. In this case, some of the instances of A are also instances of B. If it is also the case that there are instances of A that

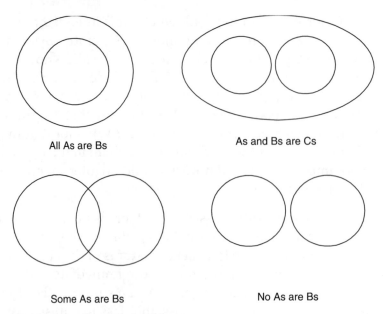

All As are Bs

As and Bs are Cs

Some As are Bs

No As are Bs

Figure 9.7 Class relationships.

are not instances of B and instances of B that are not instances of A, an association must be introduced between A and B to represent the mapping between the classes. In a model that supports multiple inheritance, this relationship would be represented by a subclass that inherits from both A and B. Since CIM does not support multiple inheritance, the association is required. Note that A and B cannot have a common superclass since they will, in some cases, have instances with the same key, and a superclass cannot have more than one instance with the same key.

No As are Bs. In this case, there are no instances of A that are also instances of B (this implies, of course, that no instances of B are also instances of A). It follows that the two classes are separate. Note the string assumption: Not only are A and B disjointed, they do not have a superclass in common either.

Avoid the pitfall of introducing multiple conflicting subclassing schemes below a single class. Consider, for example, the following:

```
Class Employee{
    [Key]
    string Id;
    // other properties
};
```

```
Class Manager: Employee{
};
    [Association]
Class DirectReports{
    Employee reference Employee;
    Manager reference Manager;
};
```

So far so good: the schema represents employees and managers, and provides an association that relates an employee to his or her manager. Now assume a requirement develops to track hourly workers and the number of hours they work; a quick search of the employee directory reveals that there are no hourly workers that are also managers. This leads to the following addition to the schema:

```
Class HourlyEmployee: Employee{
    uint32 Hours;
};
```

This works just fine until someone hires an hourly worker who has direct reports, meaning he or she is a manager. The schema breaks down at this point, as there is now an instance of Manager representing the worker with the direct reports and an instance of Hourly-Employee representing the same worker and the hours he or she works. As far as Employee is concerned, there are two instances with the same ID, which is likely to be an impossible situation in any implementation.

It can be very difficult to recognize these situations. Typically, they arise where a class is introduced as a subclass of another class without consideration of the complete set of subclasses that may ultimately have to be supported.

Redundant Data

In a normalized schema, each fact (class, property, or association) should be represented only once. The normal forms of the relational model are intended to preclude update anomalies, and the forms can all be explained in terms that circumvent anomalies that arise in the presence of various types of replicated data. What's important to note here is not that replicated data is bad but that update anomalies are bad. CIM can indicate the presence of replicated data via comments that describe the data. In the case of instrumentation data, the replication may be recognized and properly handled by the underlying instrumentation programs. In short, you must handle redundant data with care, but by no means do you have to regard it as an evil to avoid at all costs.

It is essential, however, that you do not confuse replicated data with duplicate properties. Consider the following schema:

```
Class PhysicalElement{
        [Key]
    string Tag;
};
Class PhysicalPackage: PhysicalElement{
    string Manufacturer;
};
Class PhysicalConnector: PhysicalElement{
    string Manufacturer;
};
```

We'll assume that Manufacturer means the same thing for both Package and Connector, so it can be moved up to PhysicalElement, resulting in the following schema:

```
Class PhysicalElement{
        [Key]
    string Tag;
    string Manufacturer;
};
Class PhysicalPackage: PhysicalElement{
};
Class PhysicalConnector: PhysicalElement{
};
```

The schema is more concise in that there are now just two properties, not three. The schema is also easier to interpret because PhysicalElements generally can be considered to have a Manufacturer property (hence the generalization label applied to the process).

Now assume that Packages have connectors and that connectors cannot exist without being attached to a Package. That means the Connector's manufacturer must be the same as the Package's manufacturer; therefore, the schema will contain duplicate data. Each Connector will have the same value for its manufacturer property and its associated Package. This redundancy may cause update anomalies, since it is possible for a Package's manufacturer to be changed without changing the corresponding values for the Connector's manufacturer. The obvi-

ous solution is to eliminate the Connector's Manufacturer property as
in the following example:

```
Class PhysicalElement{
        [Key]
    string Tag;
};
Class PhysicalPackage: PhysicalElement{
    string Manufacturer;
};
Class PhysicalConnector: PhysicalElement{
};
```

Note the difference between the two. The first, where the duplicated
property was eliminated by moving it up the hierarchy, did not
involve any update anomalies—though arguably it could lead to mis-
understandings because people might interpret the presence of two
different properties as different semantics, when in fact the two are the
same. The second—where the value of a property is derivable from the
value of some related property—does imply potential update anomalies and, as in the example, may even arise in the case of a single
inherited property.

Redundancies can arise in a number of different ways, including:

- The same data may exist in more than one property in the same
  class, or one property may be derived from or (in some systematic
  way) be related to the value of another property in the same class.

- Properties in different classes may have a derivation relationship. If
  the classes are unrelated, this may imply a missing association. The
  properties themselves may be used as the basis for a join between
  the classes, or they may require some type of association to support
  computation of the derivation expression. If the classes are related,
  the derivation may be eliminated by removing one of the properties, or the derivation may be documented to reduce the possibility
  of someone handling the properties incorrectly

- Properties in different classes may have the same set of values,
  though instances may not be derivable. If there is a common superclass, it may be possible to move the property up to the common
  superclass, eliminating the duplicate definition. If the classes have
  no common superclass, one may be needed. Note, given that the
  values do not overlap, you can assume the properties indicate the
  presence of an undiscovered association.

Some redundancies can be very subtle. Consider the standard example of fifth normal form described in Chapter 3. Basically, fifth normal form is violated when an association can be derived from two other associations. Presumably, one association being derived from another is not considered, as the two associations are simply duplicates, and one should be eliminated. Derivation from more than two other associations seems eminently reasonable. It may be possible to derive association A from a traversal of associations B, C, and D. Similarly, there may be systematic relationships between property values in any part of the schema, not just immediately associated classes.

Step 3: Add Semantics

The purpose of step 3 is to add qualifiers and documentation to the schema that establish additional constraints to help define the use and behavior of the schema.

At this time, you should also ensure that the appropriate security measures have been applied to restrict access to the schema. Currently, such measures cannot be specified directly through the CIM Schema, because CIM does not have the constructs for expressing security. Nevertheless, the implementation must support constraining access to the schema for it to be useful. For example, the Microsoft WMI (Windows Management Instrumentation) implementation of CIM uses pass-through security, whereby the security of the underlying interfaces is applied to any access through the schema. In this way, information the user does not have access to in the Windows Registry will not be accessible through WMI.

You can accomplish formal specification of additional semantics by using qualifiers. To help you with that, we list here the qualifiers approved by the DMTF at the time of writing, together with some comments on their correct use and interpretation:

Abstract. Indicates that the class is abstract and serves only as a base for new classes. It is not possible to create instances of abstract classes. Appropriate use of the Abstract qualifier can help to enforce the correct population of a class. The main point is that, for a given class, if all its superclasses are abstract and it has no sibling classes, then the class defines the complete population for the hierarchy as a whole.

Aggregation. Indicates that the association is an aggregation. In CIM, this does not imply existence dependency, but it does imply a loose part-of association whereby the subordinate in the relationship is a subcomponent of the superior. Aggregation relationships can be contrasted with dependency relationships, in that dependency relationships imply a functional relationship between the classes but not containment.

Alias. Establishes an alternate name for a property or method in the schema. An alternate name may be useful where there are several different constituencies using the same model, and they have different names for the same class or property. It is assumed that only one of these is recognized by the query processor and therefore has to observe uniqueness constraints and other naming restrictions.

ArrayType. Indicates the type of the qualified array. Valid values are Bag, Indexed, and Ordered. In a Bag, there is no guarantee that items will be returned in any specific order; therefore, the only solution is to enumerate the contents of the Bag. In an Indexed array, the items can be addressed using an index, and a given item always remains part of the same index in a given instance. In an Ordered array, there is no guarantee that items will be at the same index position, but they are guaranteed to be in the same order.

Description. Provides a description of a Named Element. The Description qualifier has no required format, but schema designers are encouraged to avoid the use of undefined terms (names that are not defined as classes or properties elsewhere in the schema). It is also considered bad practice to repeat in the description any information that is available elsewhere in the schema. For example, saying that a property can have the values *ok*, *bad*, and *unknown* when these values are given in the ValueMap causes the schema to become inconsistent.

Key. Indicates that the property is part of the overall key for the class. In CIM, the main implication of this is that the property, together with its value, will appear as a part of the "path" for the instance. If more than one property in a class has the Key qualifier, then all of the properties with their values will appear in the instance path. Note that Key cannot be overridden; once a property has been marked as a key, it cannot be unmarked by some subclass. Note also that once a class defines a key, other subclasses cannot add any new key properties. Key values are written once at object instantiation and must not be modified thereafter. Any two instances with different Key values are different instances; thus, it follows that modification of the Key values is equivalent to creating a new instance. Another way of expressing this is to say that Key values must be unique. No two instances can have the same Key values.

MappingStrings. One of the primary objectives of CIM is to provide a model that can be used for representing instrumentation as well as data storage. Instrumentation is the process of populating the model from the managed environment. One vital piece of information is the source of the instrumentation: Which Registry key, API call, or INI file entry was used as the source of the property value? Without this information, the model can be very difficult to interpret. The MappingStrings qualifier is an array of strings, because it may be the case that a given property may have several sources, not just one. In designing a schema it is essential that you supply values for this qualifier for every property you expect to populate.

Max. Indicates the maximum number of values a given multivalued reference can have. A value of Null implies no limit. Do not confuse Max with MaxLen, which implies a maximum size for a string. Max defines the number of instances of a given class that can be related to a given instance of another class. For example, in the schema fragment illustrated in Figure 9.8, there is a Container association between PhysicalElement and PhysicalPackage. The 0..1 notation on the Package end of the line indicates that any PhysicalElement can

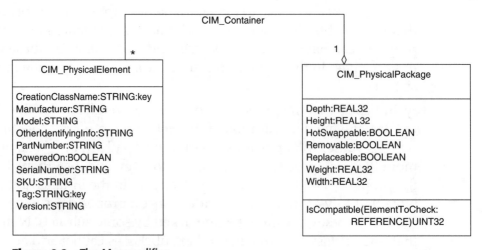

Figure 9.8 The Max qualifier.

have a Container association with zero or one instance of the Package class. This is represented by a Max qualifier value of 1 (implicitly by Min of 0, which is the default). The 0..* notation implies that a Package can contain zero or an unbounded number of PhysicalElements. This requires no qualifier value because the absence of a Max qualifier implies that there is no upper limit.

MaxLen. Indicates the maximum length of a string property. A value of Null implies an unlimited length.

Min. Indicates the minimum number of references a given instance can have referring to it. The default is 0, implying that the reference need not be present at all.

ModelCorrespondence. Indicates a correspondence between an object's property and other properties in the CIM Schema. Object properties are identified using the following syntax:

```
<schema name> "_" <class or association name> "." <property name>
```

This is not intended to be a derived property expression; it merely indicates that there is some kind of relationship between the two properties without saying exactly what. This qualifier has been used in the standard schema, but it is probably not very useful in extension schemas where the Syntax qualifier represents a better approach.

Override. Indicates that the property, method, or reference in the derived class overrides the similar construct in the parent class in the inheritance tree or in the specified parent class. The value of this qualifier *may* identify the parent class whose subordinate construct (property, method, or reference) is overridden. The format of the string to identify the parent class is:

```
[<class>.]<subordinate construct>
```

If the class name is omitted, the Override qualifier applies to the subordinate construct in the parent class in the inheritance tree. An overriding property or method may not expand the type; it can only restrict it. For example, in overriding a reference, it is acceptable to redefine the reference target as a subclass of the originally specified class, but it is not acceptable to make it a superclass of the originally specified class.

Propagated. A string-valued qualifier that contains the name of the key that is being propagated. Its use assumes the existence of exactly one Weak qualifier on a reference that has the containing class as its target. The associated property must have the same value as the property named by the qualifier in the class on the other side of the Weak association. The format of the string to accomplish this is:

```
[<class{.]<property name >
```

Read. Indicates that the property is readable. Read is true by default.

Required. Indicates that a non-Null value is required for the property. Although, required is false by default. It is necessarily true so far as keys are concerned. That is all keys must always have a value.

Units. Provides units in which the associated property is expressed. For example, a Size property might have Units (bytes). The CIM specification lists the complete set of units that are acceptable in a CIM Schema.

ValueMap. Defines the set of permissible values for a property. The ValueMap qualifier can be used alone or in combination with the Values qualifier. When used in combination with the Values qualifier, the location of the property value in the ValueMap array provides the location of the corresponding entry in the Values array. ValueMap may only be used with string and integer values. The syntax for representing an integer value in the ValueMap array is:

```
[+|-]digit[*digit]
```

The content, maximum number of digits, and represented value are constrained by the type of the associated property. For example, unit8 may not be signed, must be fewer than four digits, and must represent a value less than 256.

Values. Provides a translation between a value and an associated string. If a ValueMap qualifier is not present, the Values array is indexed (zero relative) using the value in the associated property. If a ValueMap qualifier is present, the Values index is defined by the location of the property value in the ValueMap. For example, in the following schema fragment, the values "A," "B," "C," "D," and "F" are mapped to "Honors," "Pass," and "Fail":

```
[Values{"Honors", "Honors", "Pass", "Pass", "Fail"},
ValueMap{"A", "B", "C", "D", "F"}]
```

Weak. Indicates that the keys of the referenced class include the keys of the other participants in the association. This qualifier is used when the identity of the referenced class depends on the identity of the other participants in the association. No more than one reference to any given class can be weak. The other classes in the association must define a key. The keys of the other classes in the association are repeated in the referenced class and tagged with a Propagated qualifier.

Write. Indicates that the property is writeable. The default is true.

Syntax. Allows the content of a property to be constrained in arbitrary ways. Syntax is a string-valued property and can contain any type of expression. The type of the expression must be provided in the SyntaxType qualifier. For example, a regular expression could be used to constrain the content of a Social Security number.

SyntaxType. Defines the format of the Syntax qualifier.

Step 4: Evaluate and Refine

After completing the first three steps for the first time, you will have an initial version of the schema. Now it is time to assess and refine the schema design and evaluate its completeness and accuracy. The main objective of the evaluate and refine stage is to make sure that no large-scale systematic biases have crept in and that the schema actually meets the requirements you set out to satisfy.

Matching Requirements to the Schema

If the application's schema requirements are formally documented, you should be able to track each application requirement to a feature in the schema. Note, however, that tracking may not be possible if the application designer failed to supply requirements at an adequate level of detail. If this is the case, you can take each of the features specified in the schema and describe the requirement met by that feature. For example, using some of the features of CIM_Card from the Physical schema:

- A Card represents a type of physical container that can be plugged into another Card or motherboard in a Chassis. The CIM_Card class includes any package capable of carrying signals and providing a mounting point for PhysicalComponents, such as Chips, or other PhysicalPackages, such as other Cards. A Card has a Boolean called HostingBoard, indicating that the Card is a Motherboard or, more generically, a baseboard in a Chassis.

- A Card has a string called SlotLayout that describes the slot positioning, typical usage, restrictions, individual slot spacings, as well as any other pertinent information for the slots in a Card.

- A Card has a Boolean called RequiresDaughterBoard, indicating that at least one daughterboard or auxiliary Card is required in order to function properly.

- A Card has a Boolean called Removable indicating whether it is designed to be taken in and out of the physical container in which it is normally found, without impairing the function of the overall packaging. A Package can still be Removable if power must be off in order to perform the removal. If power can be on when the Package is removed, then the Element is both Removable and HotSwappable. For example, an extra battery in a laptop is Removable, as is a disk drive Package that was inserted using SCA connectors. However, the latter is also HotSwappable. A laptop's display is not Removable, nor is a nonredundant power supply. Removing these components would impact the function of the overall packaging or would be impossible due to the tight integration of the Package.

Whichever approach you take in evaluating your schema, remember to use prototyping as a means to verify the important portions of your schema design as early as possible. Additional suggestions for evaluating and refining a CIM Schema are described in the following subsections.

Property/Reference Ratios

In most applications, all data in a schema is deeply interrelated. Consequently, in a properly designed CIM Schema, you should see numerous associations that represent relationships between classes. Precise ratios will depend on requirements of your particular application, but if your reference/property ratio is low, suspect redundant properties, improper merging of different entity types into a single class, relationships not expressed as associations, or other problems. All relationships should be expressed via associations, not with other techniques that would deprive the schema of semantic information.

Information Content

There is a simple formula to use to relate information to data and rules:

```
Information = Data Rules * C
```

where C is greater than 1.

The formula implies that information is an exponential function of Data and Rules. When you have two schema alternatives, compare the amount of information you can deduce from each approach. Here we characterize information as the number of facts reflected in the schema, where a fact is a data element plus a rule applied to that data. Consider the following schema:

```
CLASS Person{
        [MaxLen(20)]
      String Name;
     [Max(20)]
      String children[];
      uint32 EmployeeId;
      Person Reference EmployeeManager;
   );
```

From this schema we can deduce the following facts:

- The schema is to store Person entities.
- Some persons have a name, which is a String of a maximum of 20 characters.
- Some persons have one or more children, each of which is a String of a maximum of 20 characters.
- Some persons have an employee ID, which is an unsigned integer accommodated by 32 bits.
- Some persons have an EmployeeManager, a person (and, strictly speaking, a noncompliant schema, as only associations can contain references).

Now consider the following schema:

```
CLASS Person{
        [MaxLen(20), Required]
     String name;
};

Class Employee: Person{
```

```
        [Required, ValueMap{"1f99999"}]
    uint32 employee-id;
};

Class PreviousEmployee OF Person;
    [Association]
Class Management{
    Employee Reference Manager;
    Employee Reference Employee;
};
    [Association]
class Children{
     Person Reference children;
    [Max(2)]
    Person Reference parent;
};
```

Technically, this schema stores the same types of entities with the same attributes as the previous schema. However, look at the number of facts we can derive from this schema:

- The schema is to store Person entities.

- Persons can also be employees or previous employees.

- A person does not have to be an employee or a previous employee (Person is not abstract).

- A person can be an employee or a previous employee, but not both (no multiple inheritance).

- All persons must have a name, which is a String of a maximum of 20 characters.

- Some persons have one or more children, each of which is a person.

- The inverse of children is parents, meaning that if a person has children, the children have parents.

- Children/parents is a many-to-many relationship.

- A child cannot have more than two parents.

- When a person is an employee, he or she must have an employee ID, which is a uint32.

- Employee ID must be between 1 and 99999, inclusive.

- When a person is an employee, he or she can optionally have an Employee-Manager, which must be another employee.

- When a person is a previous employee, no information other than Person is stored.

The two schemas store the same amount of data, but the second schema has more rules and, as a result, far more information. Another way of expressing this is through implications; the real difference between the two schemas is that the second has far more implications than the first, evident in definite statements that can be made about the universe being modeled. The more statements that can be made, the more likely you are to find conflicts with observed events and the more likely the schema is to be refuted. The ability to refute is actually a good thing, since it means that the schema and its content are giving you information about the world in a meaningful way. Any schema that cannot in principle be refuted is necessarily devoid of meaning.

The situation is comparable to some recent bogus theories of psychological analysis. These theories stated that any individual who did not understand the theory needed analyzing and that once the analysis was successful the individual would understand the theory. The problem with such a theory is that it cannot be contradicted and therefore tells us nothing about the world. Contrast this with Newton's theory of motion. The theory had certain measurable consequences that were contradicted by observation and superseded by relativistic theories that had more precise rules and therefore greater information content. The point here is that it is very important that you formulate your schema in such a way that it confronts the universe being modeled. Ultimately, the confrontation depends on the interpretations and implementations brought by the user; these in turn will be critically dependent on the clarity and consistence brought to the schema design in the first place.

Unnecessary Classes

After allocating properties, methods, and references to classes you may find that some classes have no features or a limited feature set. Limited features may be characterized in terms of a lack of required properties or the absence of references using the class as the target of the references. The question here is at what point do the features justify the presence of the class it provides. There are some specific guidelines to find the answer:

- If the class can be used as a superclass by other schemas or anticipated evolutions of the current schema, the class should be kept.

- If the class properties can be moved to a superclass in which the property applies to a reasonable number of the instances of the superclass, the class may be eliminated.

- A reference may be changed to reference a superclass, in particular where the reference applies to a reasonable number of the instances of the superclass. If the reference can be changed to use a superclass, the original class may be eliminated.

Generally speaking, the price of moving a property up the hierarchy is the introduction of null values into the schema. The corresponding benefit is the simplification of the schema. Another criterion that may be available if the schema is being developed for a specific and well understood application is related to the use of the class in queries; that is, if the class is not used in any query, the class can be eliminated without any ill effect.

Nonrequired Attributes

A property that is not required can be null for some instances of the class. A Null property may indicate that a value is genuinely optional (such as children) or that it is not always knowable (such as birthplace). However, it may indicate that the property isn't applicable for some entities in the class, in which case, the property may actually belong to a subclass that may or may not be defined.

Making properties required makes it easier to query the schema. If properties are optional, any use of the property ultimately will have to examine the property and determine whether it has a value. This extra logic introduced into the interface substantially complicates the application and the user's experience of the schema and thus should be avoided if at all possible.

Issues related to information content also still apply: the more optional properties a schema contains, the less information it carries.

Boundary Conditions

You should test the schema for its capability to handle borderline conditions and exceptions. For example, you could ask the following questions of the Card class:

- Are all removable cards replaceable?

- Do all cards have weight, height, depth, and width?
- Can all cards be powered on?
- Can there be more than one card in a slot?
- Which components cannot be on a card?
- Can more than one card share the same cooling element? Are some cooling elements restricted to a single card?
- Can only hosting boards have package components?

Exception conditions are common and they should be represented in the schema. They may turn up as subclasses or as nonrequired associations or properties. These "consistent exceptions" should be documented in the early stages of schema design and revisited during final assessment of the schema with the intention of keeping the schema as simple as possible while meeting requirements as expressed in queries and other artifacts of the requirements-gathering process.

Many-to-Many Relationships

Many-to-many relationships between concrete classes are unusual. Often what appears to be a many-to-many relationship on closer examination turns out to have properties of its own or is restricted to a one-to-many association at the concrete class level. An association with properties is not a cause for concern in CIM since all associations are classes and can therefore have properties. But the life cycle of the association instance is a cause for concern. If the instance has properties and can exist independently of one or more of the instances it associates, the association may require special handling.

Consider the case of PhysicalPackage and its Container association to PhysicalElement in the context of an inventory-planning application. It may be possible to track the date at which a given element will be contained in a given package. For planning purposes, it may even be possible to know that some number of elements—though not exactly which elements—will be contained in a given package at a given date. If the reference to element is required, this cannot be represented.

Islands of Data

All data in the schema should be related to other data, so, theoretically, an isolated class or hierarchy (which has no relationships to other classes) should rarely occur. If you find such a situation, you may have failed to properly declare some relationships using associations, or the corresponding data may not belong in the schema; that is, it may be used by some literally unrelated application.

Trade-offs and Special Cases

This subsection offers suggestions for handling certain design alternatives and special situations.

Multiple inheritance. CIM does not support multiple inheritance. In the rare cases where multiple inheritance is indicated, however, specific modeling conventions should be employed. You must introduce a related class with the association between the classes as a one-to-one required association, which effectively supplies the "is-a" relationship without providing inheritance.

Embedded objects versus classes and associations. On occasion, you will find it convenient to represent the relationship between two classes by embedding the instance of the first class in the second, rather than using references. This is supported by CIM version 2.2, but is only used in one place, namely in modeling events. The requirement that prompts the use of the embedded object is the assumption that by the time the event is delivered, the original object may not be accessible (indeed, in the case of a delete, it may no longer exist).

Null attributes versus new subclasses. Although it is recommended that you specify as many attributes as possible as Required attributes, it is probably not useful to define a new subclass for each property merely to allow the property to be specified as Required. In fact, this technique can be viewed as merely moving the Not Required constraint to the relationship between the subclass and the superclass. The idea is to balance the need to reduce non-Required attributes with the proliferation of subclasses that are not really significant to the application.

Transitional constraints. Though CIM does not specify transaction semantics, probably most commercial implementations of CIM will use transactions to preserve consistency across the update process. In the presence of associations and behavior, a variety of complex constraints, beyond those directly expressible through the schema or simple query-based expressions, may arise. In particular watch out for constraints that limit changes to an object's state across time, as opposed to at some particular point in time. For example, a constraint might state that a router's configuration tables may not be updated more than once every five minutes. The enforcement of such a constraint requires knowledge outside any reasonable bounds for the transaction itself and so may be very difficult to enforce.

Historic data. Frequently, information regarding state changes must be maintained over time. There is a large and growing body of theoretical work being done on the subject of temporal databases because they pose unique problems with respect to indexing, searching, and storage. Some approaches to dealing with historical data in the context of a CIM Schema are outlined here:

- *Version attributes.* A property can be used to indicate version information for instances. Properties used might include revision number, entry date, release number, and so on. Each time a new revision is made, a new instance can be inserted with the appropriately updated version property. Queries can then be directed at the "latest" version (e.g., highest) value or a specific version level.

- *Special subclasses.* You can add obsolete entities to a special subclass that represents historic state, rather than deleting them. In conjunction, the obsolete entities may be deleted from subclasses where they are no longer needed. For example, in the Organization schema cited earlier, an employee who leaves the company is deleted from all subclasses but is retained in the Person class and added to the Previous-Employee subclass.

- *Separate hierarchies.* You can also handle historical data by completely deleting entities from the hierarchies that represent their "current" form and adding representative entities in a new class. For example, in the Organization schema, completed projects cause an Assignment entity to be created for each member on the project team.

Conflicting views. You may find that different users have conflicting takes on an application requirement; often this is an indication that the users in question have either a biased or an incomplete understanding of the area in question. One approach to solve this discrepancy is to create a schema that represents an intersection of all competing views, and then simplify the schema by reducing redundancy, moving attributes, and performing other refinements as usual. The resulting process should expose any inconsistencies and force a composite schema that adequately reflects all user requirements.

Interface Design

The purpose of the interface design phase is to focus on how the schema will be implemented by users and programs to determine whether additional schema refinements are necessary. When you consider the query and transaction processing requirements of your schema, you may identify essential schema additions or modifications. The interface design phase consists of the following steps:

1. Identify ad hoc query requirements.

2. Identify programmatic query requirements.

3. Evaluate and refine.

In steps 1 and 2, you will identify and specify how you expect ad hoc query users and application programs to use the schema. In both steps, you will define queries that represent the information required by programs and users. The purpose of step 3 is to verify these queries using any of several techniques. By formulating and verifying query statements, you will demonstrate that the schema adequately meets the needs of its defined user base.

CIM SQL

We use the word query here in a very broad sense, to cover both update and retrieval. We will not assume a full SQL implementation and so will not mention some of the more esoteric aspects of SQL (especially nested queries). As a result, certain operations that in principal are describable with SQL will be described using iterative programming against the schema. In systems management (and for that matter any reactive application) events inevitably play a prominent role in the way the application interacts with the environment; therefore, some aspects of event subscription and event handling will be covered in this section.

The CIM standard defines a simple subset of the SQL query language. There are three levels to the standard. The first requires support for filtered selection from a single table, the second requires support for updates, and the third requires support for joins between tables.

The CIM SQL subset supports queries in this form:

```
SELECT <row set>
FROM <table list>
WHERE <selection expression>
```

where a <row set> is a list of table columns, qualified if necessary, related to the tables specified in the FROM clause. A row set item may be a column name, qualified column (required if the name would otherwise be ambiguous), or an asterisk (*), a special character used to signify all the columns in the table—again, qualified if the use would otherwise be ambiguous.

The <table list> is a list of table names. Note that in level 1, only one table may be mentioned in the FROM clause. All tables must be connected either by a JOIN clause in the FROM clause or by a join condition in the WHERE clause. It is also possible to specify INNER JOIN or LEFT or RIGHT outer joins in the FROM clause. For example:

```
SELECT System.Name, System.Role, LogicalDevice.*
FROM System INNER JOIN SystemDevices ON System.__Path =
SystemDevices.GroupComponent INNER JOIN LogicalDevice ON
SystemDevices.PartComponent = LogicalDevice.__Path
WHERE System.Name="Bambazonki";
```

Returning to the previous code sample, the <selection expression> of the WHERE clause is limited to simple variable-constant comparison, with the exception of joins, where primary key-foreign key comparisons are allowed.

Using a query language is not essential but it is very convenient, because SQL is declarative, and as such allows you to express precisely what you want without having to describe how you will go about getting it. This is a great advantage when you are trying to build up an accurate and complete picture of what the schema is supposed to do. Beyond a certain point, the use of ordinary procedural code, such as Microsoft Visual Basic, will not help you or users to understand what the system has to do. True, SQL will probably not help your users very much but it may be a great aid as a concise expression of what would otherwise be either a vague natural language statement or an incomprehensible nested loop structure. For example, the Visual Basic equivalent (using the Microsoft WMI scripting interface) of the last SELECT statement would be:

```
Dim objs2 As SWbemObjectSet
Dim obj1 As SWbemObject
Dim obj2 As SWbemObject
Dim obj3 As SWbemObject
On Error Resume Next
Set obj1 = ns.Get("System.Name = " + Chr(34) + _
"Bambazonki" + Chr(34))
Set objs2 = ns.Get("SystemDevices")
For Each obj2 In objs2
    If obj2.GroupComponent = obj1.Path Then
    Set obj3 = ns.Get(obj2.PartComponent)
        If IsValidObj(obj3) Then
            List.AddItem obj3.Path
        End If
    End If
Next obj2
```

As you can see, it is far more difficult to tell what is going on here. An experienced programmer could readily identify that there is an association traversal, but it would be next to impossible to write a program that could detect the fact; as a result it would be very difficult to show that the association traversal is being performed correctly.

For the interface design steps, which comprise the rest of this section, we will use level 3 CIM SQL in the query examples.

NOTE

Implementations of CIM are free to support a full SQL implementation if they choose to. The minimal implementation is specified for interoperability and allows low-end devices such as routers and printers to support a full CIM implementation including level 1 CIM SQL.

Step 1: Identify Query Requirements

When you look at the interface for your application, two dominant facts emerge:

- First, the schema access requirements of every application must be expressed in the query language. It may take several statements and some intermediate storage to do it, but for every piece of data your program expects to get from the schema you must have a query that defines how the data will be retrieved. If you cannot come up with such a query, you must either change the schema or abandon the requirement.

- Second, every piece of information required by your users must be expressible as a query. This is a more extreme statement than the previous one, as it implies that you should always put information returned to your user in the schema. The alternative is to hold the information in intermediate internal structures, such as arrays or artifacts, of the interface, such as drop-down lists or other controls. The problem with any such approach is that it is not reusable and can't be queried. If you cannot express what the user wants as a query, the only readily available alternative is to actually build a functional prototype and demonstrate to the users what they will get. This is a potentially time-consuming, expensive, and unpredictable process.

Suggestions for discovering query requirements are detailed in the next subsections.

Capture Queries

The best way to capture ad hoc query requirements is to construct representative queries. Some of the techniques that you can use are summarized here:

Queries can be hand-written. This technique allows queries to be visually verified; the disadvantage is that it makes queries harder to execute against the schema.

Numerous SQL implementations are available that allow for the easy construction of test versions of a schema expressed as SQL tables rather than CIM classes. With a little care, these can be used as a basis for the development of queries and query results that have been shown to users and are known to provide the information required. Microsoft Windows Management Infrastructure Software Developer's Kit (SDK) makes it possible to develop and test CIM classes using static data; and it supports CIM SQL.

The advantage of using a functioning query system is that the queries are known to function correctly—at least over the instances known to the prototype. The important thing to bear in mind is that the databases used are prototypes; thus it should be possible to build the schema and populate it with minimal effort. If an implementation requires a lot of time and effort to establish, it is probably not an appropriate choice.

Update Queries

Where appropriate, you should use queries to update information. In particular queries should be used when the same update is to be applied to a range of objects. The normal object create, update, and delete life cycle does not have to be formally described; that is, when objects will be dealt with in isolation or individually, but in any event where objects are dealt with in groups (for example, a system and its attached devices) or where objects are dealt with as a set (for example, all the running services), queries should be used.

Retrieval Queries

The data returned from retrieval queries must include sufficient information so that the user can identify the referents of the query. Data in the schema is only useful if the user is able to relate the information to the environment in which he or she interacts. There is no point in issuing a trouble report if the engineer cannot determine which computer system he or she is supposed to repair.

Do not, however, confuse relating information to the environment with the use of keys. Keys may be useful as a mechanism for identifying the objects in the real world, but not necessarily. Keys are primarily intended for identifying objects within the system. They are used to establish object paths that can be used to locate a specific instance. These paths become the value for reference properties, and thereby establish relationships between instances.

In an ideal situation, users may be able to use keys for locating objects in the environments in which they work. This means that the user and the system both invoke the same properties to identify instances; consequently, there is no need to translate between one set of names and another. A major aspect of defining the retrieval query is, therefore, discovering which properties are useful to the user as a "label" for the data that he or she will see as a query result. If the label properties are not keys, you must ensure that they are still adequate identification mechanisms (the user should not be exposed to more than one instance with the same label); and it must be possible to translate keys into labels and labels into keys.

Step 2: Identify Programmatic Query Requirements

Keep in mind that CIM is an object-oriented model, and one of the main characteristics of the object-oriented model is that it is supposed to represent behavior as well as state. Behavior is represented in the model primarily via methods, but it may also be represented by the encapsulation provided by properties and associations. The traversal of an association may involve complex computations that in some systems would be represented by algorithms implemented in programs.

In implementing a management application using CIM, the application designer must choose between two distinct approaches to its design:

- The application may be implemented "on top of" CIM; that is, the application may provide significant capabilities that are not visible outside of the application's interfaces.

- The application may be implemented "underneath" CIM; that is, all of the significant features of the application are visible as methods, properties, or other features of the schema.

If you choose the second approach, all the significant capabilities of the application become visible using the standard features of CIM. There are tremendous advantages to this option:

- The capabilities necessarily become visible to other applications and users.

- The capabilities are accessible using the standard capabilities of your CIM implementation, such as querying.

- There is a natural integration with other applications that are provided in the same way.

Let's say you provide an application that supports trouble tickets. One temptation in such a case is to have the trouble ticket available as a separate stored item. Persistence for trouble tickets might be provided in a separate database with no connection to CIM and no interfaces apart from those supported by the application itself. But if the trouble ticket is surfaced through CIM, it becomes possible, for example, using ordinary CIM associations, to establish a relationship between systems and the trouble tickets that are applicable to the systems.

When implementing "underneath the schema," any time procedural processing is required to augment a query, you should consider adding features that allow the information to be retrieved using a single simple query. It follows that a major part of the documentation of the processing to be performed against the schema will be represented by a combination of queries, algorithms, and schema features such as methods, properties, associations, and classes, which together provide the infrastructure necessary to allow the data to be retrieved using single simple queries. The best way to capture programmatic query requirements is to use SQL queries.

Update Queries

Integrity is the primary focus of update queries. Transaction integrity is usually defined using what's called the ACID test. ACID is an acronym for atomic, consistent, isolated, and durable. Its four parts are defined here:

Atomic. The transaction happens entirely or not at all.

Consistent. The transaction takes the system from one consistent state to another.

Isolated. Partial results are not exposed to other users.

Durable. Once committed, the transaction will not subsequently disappear.

Though there are a number of different possible mechanisms for providing ACID transactions, two standard techniques are used to ensure that updates are performed correctly: *locking* and *two-phase commits*. Locking ensures that the effects of an update are not partially visible. For example, assume the manufacturer of a LogicalDevice must be the same as the manufacturer of the LogicalDevice's corresponding PhysicalElement. When changing the manufacturer, it is possible to have different values in the two locations. The standard way of avoiding this problem is to lock both locations first, thereby preventing access to them; the locations are unlocked once the changes have been made.

Two-phase commits are implemented in the context of distributed transactions, where the elements of the transaction are distributed across several processes or systems. The basic problem is figuring out how to ensure that all the elements of a transaction will take place. Even though these elements may individually behave consistently, the potential exists that some of the elements may detect a logical error in the input or encounter an unrecoverable error in processing the transaction. The solution is to invoke a protocol that essentially asks each element of the transaction, "Can you complete the transaction?" When an element has responded positively, it is then told, "Okay, finish the transaction." The question is referred to as "prepare to commit"; the directive to finish the transaction is referred to as "commit". You can think of the transaction as happening in two phases: First, the various elements of the transaction are given some work to prepare (they are basically responsible for ensuring that the work can be done; they don't necessarily actually do it. In the second phase, the elements of the transaction are either told to forget the transaction—an element was not able to commit—or they are asked to go ahead and make the commitment.

Currently, CIM does not support a locking mechanism or a specific technique for specifying transaction boundaries (for example a Begin-Transaction or Commit-Transaction function). These incapabilities constitute substantial restrictions on CIM, to be sure, but there are also advantages to their absence from the CIM specification. The principal advantage is that the application designer is obliged to develop applications *underneath* the schema rather than on top of it, because application boundaries and two-phase commits can then be hidden behind method calls.

To a great extent, you can deal with atomicity, consistency, and isolation by encapsulating their implementation within appropriate methods. Durability must be a part of the underlying implementation. You can deal with it by using a persistent store, such as a commercial database. However, persistent storage may not be an option if, for example, the application is dealing with instrumentation over a dynamic system such as a network router and its routing tables.

To capture update queries, you must define adequate interfaces for transforming the state of the system as required by the user. Each transformation must be definable as a single atomic operation on the model. That means the transformations must be one of the following:

Instance creation. It must be possible to create a valid instance, including all the instance dependencies or other required associations, in a single operation.

Instance deletion. It must be possible to delete an instance in such a way that any objects dependent on the instance are also deleted; or the delete should be disallowed.

Instance update. It must be possible to update the instance in such a way that all of the updates take place within the scope of a single operation; that is, a "put" operation on a single instance. Generally speaking, property operations are not atomic and only take effect at the time of the instance put.

Method call. If all else fails, a method call with appropriate parameters may be used to encapsulate any of the preceding.

NOTE

Refer to Chapter 11 for more on the subject of method design and usage.

Data Types and Formats

Not all programming languages will be able to accommodate all of the data types that CIM supports. For example, some languages may not support NUMBERs (which are expressed in fixed-point, 4-bit BCD format) or KANJI STRINGs (which contain 16-bit characters). Therefore, you must ensure either that all attributes that are to be updated and/or retrieved by an application program have data types that are usable by the corresponding programming language or that some technique will be used to map CIM data formats into formats usable by the program. Note that some CIM data types (such as DATE, TIME, SYMBOLIC, and SUBROLE) can be expressed in a numeric or string format for a given query, depending upon the options used when the query is compiled.

Also be aware of precision. Application programs may be required to process data with different arithmetic precisions than are required in the schema. For example, a program may process all dollar amounts using a NUMBER [10, 2] format, while the schema is designed to store dollar amounts only in a NUMBER [8, 2] format. STRING sizes could also differ between application programs and the schema. Though these differences may not be significant, depending on how data is moved between the schema and the application program, in some cases you will want to consider adjusting the precision of certain attributes stored in the schema to match the precision used by application programs.

Step 3: Evaluate and Refine

After you have identified the various queries and operations that will be performed against the schema, it is time to build a prototype of the schema. You will populate this prototype with sample data to ensure that the queries and functions actually work, that they are properly understood, and that they deliver the data as expected. This may be a time-consuming exercise but it is an essential step to complete, for without it, you will have a very difficult time determining the exact characteristics of a query and schema.

You can think of queries algorithmically, as a series of nested loops. To demonstrate this concept, consider a query to return all the services on a given system that are currently initiated and stopped under an account with administrator privileges (i.e., it is a member of the administration group). Here's the code:

```
For each service in the system
    If the service is stopped
        For each service account
            For each group the account belongs to
                If the group is the administration group
                    Return the service
                End if
            Next group
        Next account
    End if
Next service
```

If you knew that administration services were interesting and would often be requested, it would make sense to duplicate the information available in the inner nested loop in the service instance. The query could then be reduced to the following:

```
For each service in the system
    If the service is stopped and is an administration service
    Return the service
    End if
Next service
```

Denormalization (that is introducing redundancy or properties that sometimes do not have a value) is acceptable as long as it is intentional and is maintained properly. The obvious risk with the arrangement in this example is that the service may cease to be a member of the administration group, but the value in the service instance may not be updated to reflect that fact. This is a major concern with stored data (if your CIM Schema is mapped to an ordinary SQL database, for example). In contrast, it is typically not a problem with instrumentation data, where the data is being reconstructed every time someone asks for it. In any event, as a schema designer you must be aware of the queries to be processed against the schema, and you should relocate and refine the schema to enable the queries to be supported efficiently and accurately.

Expect to do the following types of refinement at this stage:

- Duplicate and relocate properties to reflect query patterns.
- Remove classes and properties to reflect the absence of any query that makes use of them.
- Add classes, properties, and associations to support requirements revealed by the queries, which were previously unrecognized.

The second item is the one most commonly ignored. It is usually a very simple matter to add a class or property to a schema, but very difficult to take it out. The decision to remove it can only be made if it is reasonably certain that there is no use for it, and establishing this without a comprehensive set of queries is practically impossible. If classes and properties are not removed at this stage in the design process, it is unlikely that they will ever be removed. This will come at a cost, incurred because they will have to be populated and tested even though there is no known use for them.

Physical Design

Whereas the logical and interface design phases focus entirely on the logical structure of the schema, the physical design phase deals with physical requirements, such as mapping to data sources, distributed access, discovery, capacity, performance, and maintenance. The CIM specification goes to great lengths to ensure that the physical and logical aspects of the schema are kept as separate as possible. The physical side of the schema is defined through the appropriate use of qualifiers. Though there are sets of reserved qualifier names that are documented as system qualifiers in the specification, CIM gives you, the schema designer, a free hand as to which qualifiers to add to the schema.

Qualifiers have been used in various ways by different CIM implementations. For example, the Microsoft Windows Management Instrumentation uses the Provider qualifier to indicate which code will handle which class. The point is, the qualifiers you use for the physical design will inevitably be highly implementation-dependent.

It is very important that you define a logically correct schema before trying to address physical issues. That said, be aware that there are intractable problems associated with defining a good logical schema, apart from the very complex issues associated with physical mappings for the classes defined in the logical schema. It is much easier to optimize a schema that represents a correct logical design than to try and program correctly against a schema that is a poor reflection of the logical structure of the data the application is expected to deal with. Optimizing an invalid program will just have the effect of delivering bad results faster.

The physical design phase is divided into the following steps:

1. Identify capacity requirements.
2. Identify performance requirements.
3. Identify operational requirements.
4. Evaluate and refine.

Before taking on the physical design of the system, you must have an implementation of the CIM Schema available. This can be provided by conventions on top of an SQL database (how to map classes, properties, associations and so on) or by a system such as Microsoft's Windows Management Infrastructure.

Step 1: Identify Capacity Requirements

There are two aspects of capacity requirements to consider. First, identify the size of the population you anticipate for each class. Second, verify that you have the bandwidth available for delivering the information and, if the information is to be persisted, storage capacity for holding it.

Take special note of the cumulative effects of instrumentation data across an enterprise. Much of CIM is intended to represent instrumentation data, and, therefore, it is not computed unless specifically requested. For example, the CIM Schema represents logical files as follows:

```
class CIM_LogicalFile:CIM_LogicalElement
{
    uint64 InUseCount ;
    boolean Archive ;
    boolean Compressed ;
    datetime CreationDate ;
    boolean Encrypted ;
    string FSName ;
    datetime LastAccessed ;
    datetime LastModified ;
    boolean Readable ;
    uint64 FileSize ;
    boolean Writeable ;
    string CompressionMethod ;
    string EncryptionMethod ;
    string Name ;
};
```

A typical Microsoft Windows NT system directory will have as many as 4,000 files in it; the system as a whole might have 20,000 files. Given a corporation with 20,000 desktops, this would amount to 400,000,000 instances, each approximately 300 bytes, resulting in a total of 120 gigabytes of data. Furthermore, the data would be very volatile, approximately half of which can be expected to change regularly. If only 1 percent of the files on the system were to change on a daily basis, this would mean daily traffic of 1.2 gigabytes. Clearly, over a T1 link (1 megabyte per second) this would be unacceptable, as it would mean the link would be entirely occupied with transferring file information for 20 minutes every day. Even over a T10 (10 megabytes per second) the link would still be occupied for 2 minutes every day. Over a 100-megabits-per-second link, the data could be handled in approximately 12 seconds, a penalty that might be acceptable depending on the quality and timeliness required of the information.

The caching policy associated with management information is a primary determinant in the performance characteristics of the overall system. All of the information available about the management environment is, by definition, cached data, as it represents the state of the environment being managed and, presumably, could be discovered by examining the environment itself. The cache could take one of three forms:

- A pass-through cache in which changes to the cache would be passed through to the underlying data.
- A push cache, in which information would be delivered to the cache as a result of events in the environment being managed.
- A pull cache in which case information is retrieved from the environment either on a regular basis or as a result of a request for data where the data is known to have become stale.

When you are designing the schema and the implementations behind it, pay careful attention to these considerations, because they will be the primary determinants of the implementation effort required and the infrastructure needed to support the application.

Step 2: Identify Performance Requirements

There are several aspects of schema performance for which your application may have requirements:

- Application programs may be required to perform a certain amount of work in a given time period (e.g., a certain number of transactions of a specific type per hour).
- Application programs may be required to respond with the results of a query within a certain amount of time (e.g., a search must respond within a given number of seconds).
- The system may be required to recover after a system failure within a certain amount of time.

The schema is not completely responsible for each of these performance criteria, but each of these performance criteria can be affected by various aspects of the schema implementation (they are necessarily implementation-specific and therefore beyond the scope of the CIM standard).

Step 3: Identify Operational Requirements

In addition to performance and capacity requirements, you must consider certain operational aspects of your schema, involving how to maintain and manage the schema. Some topics in this category follow.

Backup and Recovery

Every schema should be backed up periodically so that it can be recovered in case of a failure. Similarly, audit trails generated by the schema must be saved in case they are needed for later reprocessing. It is recommended that you make backups to media that is physically stored away from the computer system to reduce the chance of losing all copies of the schema in a single disaster.

Distribution and Migration

Any structured data source must have some mechanism for delivering schema to the various locations that maintain the data source and for changing the "shape" of the schema over time. For example, it may be necessary to add classes or properties, add associations, or change method implementations. It is important to think through the scenarios where these types of events may occur and to consider, for example, how properties can be added to a class where the class already has instances.

Step 4: Evaluate and Refine

As with any change you make to your schema, verify the adequacy of any physical schema change you make. If you modify the schema to accommodate capacity, performance, or operational requirement, verify that the change accomplished what it was intended to. But note that criteria such as performance or disk space utilization often cannot be completely verified until at least a prototype test is performed.

If you use a prototype to verify the design of your schema, be sure to confirm physical requirements as well. For example, populate key classes to their intended capacities, including average populations for subclasses and properties. Similarly, verify the performance of critical update or retrieval queries during prototyping so that you can identify any problems early in the development cycle. In particular, use the queries that you developed in the internal design phase to test schema performance.

Populating the Schema

A vital part of any prototyping effort is providing suitable sample data for the schema. There are two possibilities: you can implement the prototype over a database or over an instrumentation source. Using instrumentation is advantageous because it allows the prototype to deal with realistic data at a reasonable cost. There are two obvious sources for the sample data:

- Legacy instrumentation systems represented by SNMP and DMI. These are fairly widely available, though the quality of the data is somewhat variable.
- The Microsoft Windows Management Instrumentation. It is a close implementation of CIM and provides a wide range of data from computers running Microsoft operating systems.

The ability to establish and populate prototype schemas is critical to the success of any serious attempt to use CIM and, thus, should be a prerequisite for any project based upon the model.

The CIM Data Model: Beyond Systems Management

As you know by now, the CIM data model provides an expressive and efficient mechanism for designing management schemas. What you might not know is that the CIM data model can be used for designing other application components as well. Its rich modeling features, such as hierarchies, complex relationships, and integrity constraints, mean that the CIM data model can be used to express problem and solution elements in many functional areas, even if those elements do not correspond to management data as they do in a CIM Schema.

For example, CIM's data model can be used to represent nonpersistent data held in application programs. Program elements that can be modeled using Managed Object Format (MOF) include:

- *Data structures such as tables, queues, lists, and stacks.* Classes can be used to represent the overall data structure and the types of entries therein. Properties can indicate fields or variables within each entry or references to other entries. Integrity constraints can be used to express the semantics of classes and attributes within the data structure.

- *Interfaces including entry-points, parameters, and results.* A class can be used to represent an entry-point. Its attributes can indicate the parameters given to the entry-point and the results returned by the entry-point. Complex parameters or results can appear as references to new classes that represent the structure of the parameter or result.

- *User interfaces such as windows.* A class can be used to represent a display, data-entry, pop-up, or other type of window. Attributes of the class can represent window characteristics such as position, color, and contents. References can represent relationships to other windows or other data structures within the program.

- *Reports.* A class can be used to represent either a printed or displayed report. Attributes can represent report contents, layout, and relationships to other data structures.

There are many advantages of using a common data model for as many components as possible when developing a complete application system. Besides reducing the number of models that developers must learn and communicate with, a common data model also increases the integration of individual application components. When the CIM data model is used as a documentation standard in both requirements and design documents, you improve communication between each development phase and reduce loss of semantics as compared to structured development techniques, for example.

Another advantage of using CIM's data model as a common data representation model throughout your application is that you can continue to take advantage of various tools. Using this "extended" approach, the CIM data model can be used as the basis for a complete object-oriented development methodology. Object-oriented analysis and design can be used for all application components, including the CIM Schema.

The Mechanics of Schema Extension

The following is a list of supported schema modifications. Note that use of some of these modifications will result in changes to application behavior, and that all changes are subject to security restrictions. In particular, schema modifications can only be made by the owner of the schema or someone authorized by the owner.

TRANSFORMATIONS*

A class can be added to a schema.*

A class can be deleted from a schema.

A property can be added to a class.*

A property can be deleted from a class.

A class may be added as a subtype of an existing class.*

The Override attribute may be added to a property or reference.*

The Override attribute may be removed from a property or reference.

A class may alias a property (or reference) using the Alias attribute.

Both inherited and immediate properties of the class may be aliased.*

A method may be added to a class.*

A method may override an inherited method.*

Methods can be deleted, and the signature of a method can be changed.

A trigger may be added to or deleted from a class.*

Fully qualified class names must be globally unique.

A qualifier may be added to a class, property, or method.*

A qualifier may be deleted from a class, property, or method.

An existing class can change its subtype relationships by movement down the inheritance hierarchy; that is, a class may be made a subtypeof one of its superclass subtypes.*

A property may be deleted where the class inherits a property with the same name and type (the class interface remains unchanged).*

The range class of a reference may be changed to a superclass of the Range class.*

The type of a property defined by a subclass may be made more, but less, restrictive (this is analogous to the ability to define subtypes of associations).

*Transformations marked with an asterisk can be applied to a schema with minimal impact on existing applications.

How does a program to determine whether the schema encountered is consistent with the schema the program was written against? Although CIM does support the notion of a version (for example, at the time of writing, the current version of the schema is 2.1), it is really directed to the schema designer not to the programmer. From the viewpoint of the designer, extensions to a schema are typically expressed as extensions of a specific version of the schema. The programmer is faced with a very different problem, which presents itself in the form of two questions:

- Is the current schema consistent with the schema the program was compiled against?
- Is the content of the schema consistent with the expectations of the program's designer?

The first question can be answered easily by looking at the queries the program expects to process against the schema. If the queries compile, the schema is acceptable.

The second question is much more difficult to address. In some cases, the content will be defined by the presence of a specific schema in a specific namespace. For example, in the Microsoft WMI CIM implementation, the state of the current environment is provided by the \\<machine name>\root\cimv2 namespace. You can expect other well-known namespaces to emerge as the standard matures. Another approach to answering the second question is to have the program interrogate the content for certain classes and compare the content with expected results. Note that the schema is acceptable only if certain objects are present.

Restrictions

The following is a list of restrictions on the objects that make up the schema:

- Property names must be unique within the owning class; that is, a class may not have two properties with the same name. But note, a class can have a property that has the same name as an inherited property.

- If a property has the same name as an inherited property and Override is specified, the signature of the property must be compatible; that is, the type and cardinality must be the same as or a subset of the overridden property.

- A reference has an owner and a range class. For example, in the association:

```
class Uses
{
        [Many]
    Device ref Used_Device;
        [Many]
    Soft_Component ref Using_Component;
}
```

The reference Used_Device is owned by the association Uses and has the class Device as its range or type. The reference name must be unique within the owning class or association. A class can have a reference name that is the same as an inherited reference name.

- A descendent of a class containing a reference may use "Override" to redefine the reference specified by its superclass. For example:

```
class Hardware_Binding

{
        [Override(Used_Device), Many]
    Interface_Device ref Bound_Device;
        [Override(Using_Component), Many]
    Kernel_Driver ref Bound_Driver;
}
```

The effect of this specification is to limit the value of Used_Device for any instance of Uses that is also an instance of Hardware_Binding to an Interface_Device. The specification effectively says that a Used_Device of a Hardware_Binding must be an Interface_Device and is known as (has an alias) Bound_Device.

- The range class (or type) of an overriding reference must be the same as, or a subtype of, the range class of the reference being overridden.

- Any object referenced in the specification of a class, reference, or property specification must exist at the time of the specification; that is, forward references are not allowed.

- A class descendant may rename a property (or reference if the class is a descendant of association) using the Alias attribute. Alias may apply to an existing property, allowing the following scenario:

```
Time 1
add class MyDev: superclass Device
{
STRING Temp[50]
}
Time 2
modify class Device: superclass Physical_Component
{
STRING Temperature[60]
}
modify class MyDev: Device
{
[Alias("Temperature")] STRING Temp
}
```

The effect is to allow additions to the superclass that represent generalizations of multiple properties without requiring that all properties have the same name. The effect, as far as MyDev is concerned, is that Temp is a synonym for Temperature, and thus, a provider for Temp is no longer required.

We have covered various design related topics. Specifically, schema design, interface design, and physical design. These three areas taken together make up the range of design activities that have to be dealt with in putting a CIM Schema together. The important thing to appreciate is that the schema alone is not enough. There must also be some clear idea of how the schema will be used and how the schema will be populated and distributed. Without these it is unlikely that the schema will ever be successfully used.

In the next chapter we will summarize the analysis process, looking at a series of questions you can use to ensure that you cover all of the complex issues that have been covered in the various discussions around schema analysis and design.

References

Much of the material for this chapter is based on work done by R.L. Guck and J.P. Thompson associated with the development of the Unisys Semantic Information Manager. For a detailed discussion of these and other topics around model based approaches to application design see:

Thompson, J.P. 1989. *Data With Semantics: Data Models and Data Management*. New York: Van Nostrand Reinhold.

Analysis

This chapter summarizes much of the information contained in the rest of the book regarding analysis. To this point, we have described how the CIM Model itself was designed and how it should be used. In this chapter, you'll learn specific questions you should ask yourself while designing a CIM Schema.

For example, when defining a property for a class, you should ask:

Is it possible for each member of the class to have the given property?

If the answer is no, it follows that certain instances of the class will not have a value for the property. This can be eliminated by the introduction of a subclass that contains the property whose subclass members are exactly those instances that have the property. Clearly, this may cause a problem if an additional subclass dimension is thereby introduced or, in other words, if a given instance may appear as an instance of more than one class at the same level.

The discussion around this question and the issues raised by it are intended to encapsulate the rest of the book and provide a summary the schema designer can use as the basis for ensuring that the modeling language is being used appropriately and to its fullest advantage.

The analysis questions and their explanations are grouped under the following headings:

CIM Classes

Features

Properties

Associations

Methods

Classes

Each class has a definition that you can think of as a condition that distinguishes objects that belong to the class from those that do not. For example, the question to ask regarding the membership condition for the Managed System Element class is:

Is the object a potential component of a system?

It may be necessary to conform to a series of conditions to qualify as a member of the class. Managed System Element can be further characterized by answering the question:

Is the object likely to be significant to any management application?

The process of extending the schema consists of walking through the various conditions to identify the most concrete class available that is a superset of the class to be added to the schema. One of the items that has to be supplied as a part of the definition of the new class is the membership condition that specifies which objects should belong to the class. The question to ask is:

How do I recognize members of this class?

Two questions emerge from this one. The first addresses the way that instances of the class are recognized as members of the class:

Is there a way I can provide a list of the members of the class?

The second derives from the idea that members of a class can be recognized by virtue of having some property in common; for example, all big, red, rock eaters are large, red, and eat rocks.

Is there a way I can recognize an instance of the class when I encounter it (without having to refer to an explicit list)?

Every class must have a way to distinguish its instances. The distinguishing property for an instance is referred to as the key for the instance. Actually, this term is a bit of a misnomer, because the key for a class is really the concatenation of all the properties that have the Key qualifier. For every class, you must ask the question:

What is the distinguishing property (or properties) for the class?

Then, after you have considered keys and how to recognize instances of the class, you should ask:

Is there a clear definition for the class?

If a clear definition exists, you can proceed. If not, you need to go back and reexamine how to recognize instances of the class. If you cannot come up with a reasonable definition, and you are sure the class is relevant to the application, try to define the class by specifying what its properties and other features are.

Having arrived at a definition, you must ask:

Is the membership indicated by the definition a subset of the membership of any other class?

If the answer to this question is yes, one class is a subclass of the other. Though the shape of the subclass hierarchy may shift markedly as the design evolves, this should mainly be around a basic set of subset relationships between classes that are discoverable at a fairly early stage of the analysis process.

Having established any subclasses relationships, ask:

Is the definition consistent with that of any superclasses?

If the answer to this question is no, it may mean that the subclass is actually a sibling class, not a direct subclass; it may mean that the superclass is incorrectly classified; or it may mean that the subclass definition or the definition of one of the superclasses is invalid. In any event, it should never be the case that an instance of some subclass is not a valid instance of one of the superclasses of the subclass. Ensuring that this is always true causes much of the hierarchy rearrangement that occurs throughout the schema design process.

Always be on the lookout for overlaps between class memberships, as they will tell you a lot about the structure of the schema and will often help you to identify where the schema has been designed incorrectly. Every time the definition or position of a class changes, ask:

Do the instances overlap with those of some other class?

Another important area to watch is operations on the class. As far as the definition of the class is concerned, operations can help tremendously in identifying situations where the schema design is impractical or will not be able to satisfy the requirements of the application. Ask:

How are instances created, deleted, and modified?

The way that instances are created, deleted, and modified may have profound impact on your perception of what the instance is. In particular, watch for situations where the key properties have to be modified (you will probably have to select something else as a key) or where the defining characteristics of the instance change. For example, in a university database, you might define a Person class with subclasses Student and Teacher. This works until you realize that students may become teachers or that a person may even be both a student and a teacher at the same time. A better approach is to have Student and Teacher as role classes and to represent the fact that a person is a student by having an instance of the Student Role class with an association to the Person instance.

Returning to the subject of keys: It is a good idea to determine whether there are any other possible distinguishing properties. Often, there are several possible candidates. It is important to understand how these are used and then to provide a mechanism that will allow one key to be translated into another. For example employee number can be translated into social security number given there are lists of employees and their social security number ordered by both the employee number and social security number between different candidate keys if necessary. For example, if one group uses SKU as the value to identify parts, and another uses a concatenation of serial number and system serial number, and data has to be exchanged between them, it will be necessary to identify the part with a given SKU that corresponds to the part with a given serial number. The questions to ask in this situation are:

Are there any candidate keys?

How do they relate to each other?

Candidate keys may be important as alternative identifiers or as labels for the class. A class label is a value, typically too large to use as a key by the people who invoke the system to identify the objects in the real world. For example, people rarely refer to other people by Social Security number or employee number, using instead their personal names. Names, however, though essential as a means of social interaction, are a very poor mechanism for identifying instances. They tend to be long, and more problematic, they do not have a canonical form: spelling, capitalization, format, and other factors vary. Nonetheless, it is important to ask:

Does the class have both a label and an identifier?

If the class has both a label and identifier, the label must be treated as a candidate key, with some appropriate mechanism for locating an instance of the class, given a value for a label property. Note: The mechanism may be very expensive to provide and may be a major part of the application used to access the system.

When designing keys, it is very important to know the scope of the key. You must determine under what circumstances the key is unique. You might argue, for example, that a 128-bit *Globally Unique Identifier (GUID)* is always unique because of the way that it is generated. But assume that you use GUIDs to identify trouble tickets and that every trouble ticket is uniquely identified by the GUID generated at the time the ticket is created. What if the ticket changes, and the application has to track both versions of the change? The GUID would no longer be unique; in fact, the GUID would be unique only at a particular point in time; in this case, it is not unique across time. To take a more limited example, devices on a SCSI bus are allocated an index that is guaranteed to be unique within the scope of the bus; that is, no two devices on the same bus will have the same identifier. However, across different busses, the identifier will not be unique. The bus index is scoped by the bus. Similarly, different companies have different schemes for allocating serial numbers; within a company, you might reasonably expect serial numbers to be unique, but across companies this would not be a good assumption. Serial numbers in this case are scoped by company. In this category, therefore, always ask:

What is the scope of the identifier?
And make sure you clearly understand where it is appropriate to use the identifier.

Features

A feature is either a property, a method, or a relationship; features characterize classes. A property is a mapping between a class and a set of values that characterize the members of that class. A relationship is a mapping between a class and members of other classes in the system that characterize the members of the class. Consider for example a process. A process has an associated executable, which is the file containing the instructions being executed by the process. This executable file associated with the process may be represented in a number of different ways, as shown in Figure 10.1.

In this representation, the mapping between the process and the file is provided by a string-valued property, where the property contains the file path. An alternative representation is provided in Figure 10.2.

In this second representation, an association provides the mapping between the process and the file. The executable path is provided by the Path property inherited from the Logical File class. In a sense, the two examples are not comparable, because the second provides far more information than the first; however, they are comparable with respect to the idea that they both represent a mapping between a process and its associated executable. During schema design, it is important to recognize that something initially identified as a property may, on closer examination, turn out to be an association. Similarly, there are cases where it is desirable to *collapse* an association, by taking properties out a class and providing them in the associated class.

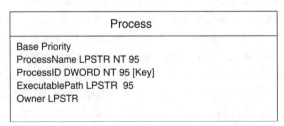

Process
Base Priority ProcessName LPSTR NT 95 ProcessID DWORD NT 95 [Key] ExecutablePath LPSTR 95 Owner LPSTR

Figure 10.1 Process properties.

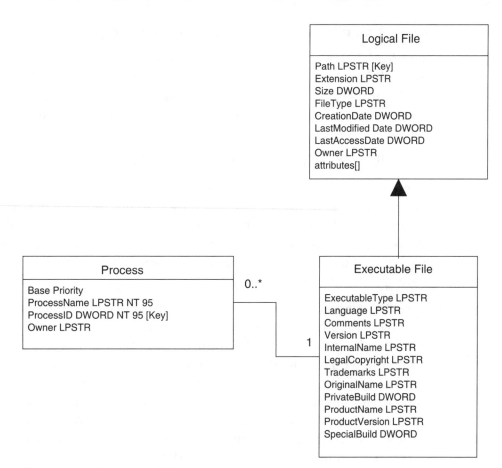

Figure 10.2 Process and file.

The question to ask when approaching a topic for the first time is:

What are the features of this class?

Initially, don't be too concerned about how to represent the features. The main point is to capture the ideas behind the class; worry later about the details of how they will be represented in the schema.

Properties

A property provides a characteristic of a class; therefore, a primary task in adding a property is determining which class the property characterizes. Think of the property as a part of the membership condition of a class. This implies the question:

Does each member of the class have the given property?

If the property is known to be required, you have a strong membership condition. If a member of the class can be identified that does not have the property, this strongly implies that the property must be moved to a more specialized class. If the property is not known to be required, it is still reasonable to ask:

Is it possible for each member of the class to have the given property?

If some members of the class can have the given property, but at a point in time or under some circumstances, do not have a value for the property, the inclusion of the property in the class may be reasonable. If, however, some members of the class can never have the given property (that is, the property is inapplicable to some members of the class) a more specialized subclass may be required.

Beyond the association between them and their class, properties also have a type that limits the kinds of values the property provides. The most general type is a string of unlimited size; that said, it is recommended that you restrict the type to the minimal possible set of values consistent with the predicted use of the type. This, however, is easier said than done, as it involves guesstimating how the property will be used over time within the class and how any classes that are added as specializations of the class might use it. Therefore, it is essential that the correct definition of the property address the question:

What is the set of values that the property can assume?

This is somewhat different from the notion of a primitive type, which is really related to how the value for the property will be represented in a record (8-bit ASCII string, 4-bit number, and so on). Type as used here relates more to the rule that restricts the set of values assumable by the property. As such, type should not be confused with the idea of a display format. Consequently, you must, at some point, ask:

What is the basic type of the property?

Two related questions examine the structure of the property:

Is it possible for an object in the class to have more than one value for a given property?

Is the property a scalar (a single value) or a vector (a set of values—possibly structured as in an array or unstructured as in a bag)?

The fundamental objective is to accurately identify the primitive type or class that will supply the values for the property. The distinction between primitive type and class is particularly important as it is a vital source of information on the design of associations. Many associations will first surface as primitive types when the primary candidate key for the association target is placed as a property in the class being defined. For example, the design of a device class might include the name of the driver used to handle the device. Some subsequent iteration of the schema design may identify drivers as objects in their own right, at which point the driver name in the device class becomes an association.

As a result, when identifying the type, you should also be concerned with identifying any similar types used elsewhere in the schema, because these may be relevant to the need for additional structure (more on this shortly in the section "Identifying Associations.")

Beyond a property's type, another critical characteristic is the uniqueness of the property. Uniqueness is one of a general class of rules that define the valid states of the system. These rules apply across more than one object in the system, and are sometimes referred to as *aggregation rules*; they apply to aggregates, or sets, of objects rather than to single objects. A unique property is identified by asking and answering the question:

Is it possible for more than one object to have the same value for the given property?

This question must be addressed *after* the placement of the property has been established. Perhaps a property, as defined by a superclass, need not be unique across the set of objects that may be members of the superclass; however, the same property as inherited by a subclass might be unique with respect to the members of the subclass. This infers that the question of property uniqueness should be revisited any time a property is moved or a subclass is added to a hierarchy. Adding rules by the subclass is typical of the object-based models with inheritance.

Other aggregate functions may imply rules that span multiple objects; for example, A SCSI bus may not have more than eight devices attached simultaneously. Here the rule can be thought of as applying to a property of the bus (Number of Attached Devices), which itself is derived using a Count function. Similar rules can be derived for each of the common aggregate functions, namely average, Maximum, Minimum, Count, and Sum.

A special case of aggregate functions is provided by the $\forall$ ("for all," or universal quantifier) and the $\exists$ ("for each," or existential quantifier) operators of the predicate calculus. These operators take a condition and a set of objects as parameters and apply the condition to all of the members of the set; the first, $\forall$, returns true if the condition is true of all of the members of the set, and $\exists$ returns true if the condition applies to at least one member of the set. The use of existential and universal quantifiers at some point is an essential step in defining the rules applicable to properties.

Another essential area to address is the life cycle of the property. You must at some point ask:

Under what circumstances can the property be read and written?

Each property in the schema has to be defined as readable and or writeable; in particular, the circumstances under which properties that are writeable can be updated must be clearly defined.

Associations

Associations are a major source of design decisions and this is reflected in the variety of questions that may have to be dealt with here. The issues are grouped under three headings, Identifying Associations, Refining Associations, and Types of Associations versus Types of References.

Identifying Associations

When adding a feature to a class, the first task is to identify the type (or range) of the feature. The feature type will largely determine whether the feature is a property or an association. Given the type is a class, it follows that the feature is an association. If the type is a simple data value (such as a string or integer), it is important to consider the domain of the type. The domain of a type is the set of values that can be assumed by the type. For example, the domain for the Standard-Month type is a value from 1 to 12. The domain of the type Win32 file name is a specific set of strings defined by a set of syntax rules to which the strings must conform.

Relationships between objects can be inferred from the presence of properties that share domains. This is the same as the primary key-foreign key relationship of the relational model. In this case, it is important to determine whether the domain of the property matches the domain of some other property in a potentially related class. But be aware that these types of relationships can be very difficult to define accurately from a simple identification of overlapping domains. For example, the ExecutablePath property of the Process class may be taken to indicate the existence of a relationship between Logical File and Process, whereas it is a relationship between Executable File and Process. The limitation of the relationship to a subclass of Logical File, in some cases, may be very difficult to infer from the simple identification of the domains. With that caveat in mind, it is important to ask:

Are there any other properties in the schema that have the same set of values as the property being defined?

If there are, this raises a series of additional questions:

Is the set of values defined by the properties the same?

Another way of expressing this is to ask:

For every value in the first property, is there a corresponding value in the second?

Is one set a subset of the other?

Do the sets simply intersect?

If the properties are the same, a simple relationship is indicated. If one is a subset of the other, a partial mapping is indicated, with a possible additional subclass on the subset side. If they intersect, probably a class is missing that contains the complete value set.

Refining Associations

A CIM relationship can be divided into five aspects, as defined here and illustrated in Figure 10.3.

- An object type on each end of the relationship, labeled in the figure Class1 and Class2. If the relationship is reflexive, they may be the same class.

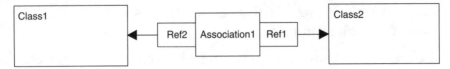

Figure 10.3   Parts of an association.

- An association that sits between the two related classes, labeled in the figure Association1.
- A reference on each end of the relationship, naming and characterizing that end of the relationship, labeled in the figure Ref1 and Ref2.

The two objects, two references and the association itself make up the five aspects of an association. For example, in a file directory context, the diagram might be labeled as in Figure 10.4.

The differences between relationship types are related to certain key characteristics of the classes and references, and can be discerned by asking and answering the following questions:

Are the roles required?

Is it reasonable for a directory not to have a subdirectory?

Are the roles multi- or single-valued?

Can a directory have more than one subdirectory?

Can the instances of the roles be enumerated? Or, to put it another way, can the relationship be traversed from the end represented by the role?

Given a directory is it possible to get its parent?

Can the instances of the class be enumerated?

Is it possible to iterate over the set of all instances of the class? For example, is it possible to enumerate all files and directories without regard to the directories that contain them?

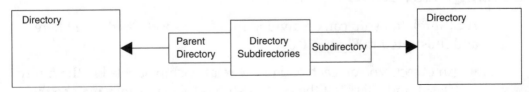

Figure 10.4   Subdirectory association.

Certain sets of objects cannot be enumerated; for example, it is not possible to iterate over all the names that have ever been used by anyone in the United States.

What happens to the instance of the class when the relationship gets deleted or the reference is reassigned?

If the parent directory is deleted do the subdirectories disappear?

Taken together, these characteristics give a wide range of relationship types:

References may be required or not: two possibilities.

Both sides may be required or not: two possibilities.

Both sides may be single- or multivalued (i.e., 1:1, 1:M, M:1, M:M): four possibilities.

Relationship may be traversible or not, in both directions: four possibilities.

Both the target classes (Class1 and Class2) may or may not be traversible: four possibilities.

Automatic delete may or may not apply on both ends: four possibilities.

This list results in potentially 2^{10} possible association types (for example, an association type might be Required:Optional, 1:M, traversible both directions, random-access both ends, no automatic delete).

The addition of an association must take into account each of these possible association attributes. To the designer, each property implies a decision. Thus, for each association, you must ask:

What are the characteristics of this association?

Notably, you should at least ask:

Are the roles required?

Are the roles multi- or single-valued?

Can the instances of the roles be enumerated?

Can the instances of the association class be enumerated?

What happens to the instance of the class when the relationship gets deleted or the reference is reassigned?

You must carefully evaluate the applicability of any restrictions and keep in mind that though it is possible for a subclass to restrict the definition of an association, it is not possible to relax the definition. For example, once an association has been declared as required, it must remain required for all descendants of the declaring class. Abstract associations will be many to many, nonrequired, and associate abstract classes. As the definition process moves to more concrete classes, associations will become many-to-one or one-to-one, required in at least one direction, traversible in a specific direction, and defined between concrete classes.

In defining an extension to (a subclass of) an existing association, you should evaluate each of the association attributes to take advantage of the associations that have been declared so far. If necessary, you can add an association as an abstract supertype of an existing association and declare the new association as a subtype of this new supertype. This may or may not be feasible, depending on whether the extending designer owns all of the associations involved. In any event, the addition of associations may result in generalization as well as specialization of classes, thus requiring you to go through the same generalization and specialization process with associations as required for classes themselves.

Note that an association is a class and a reference is a property, so all the class and property questions apply.

Types of Associations versus Types of References

Names are frequently assigned to certain types of association. Common types include: Containment, Aggregation, Part-of, Unary Association, and Simple Association. The precise interpretation of these terms is problematic. From a purely pragmatic standpoint, CIM has taken the position that Aggregation is a relationship type that defines a parent-child hierarchy that spans the whole system. The intention of the hierarchy is to allow a browser to enumerate all the components of the system by a traversal of the hierarchy. To satisfy this requirement, there must be a mechanism that enables a browser to discover an association that spans all the components of a system and that has references that can easily be identified as parent and child.

The names associated with the roles have no significance as far as the system is concerned, and other role names may be attached to the reference. The parent reference is labeled with the Aggregate qualifier.

Figure 10.5 Inverses.

Inverse References

Figure 10.3 identified five elements: two associated classes, the association class, and two references. This is very different from the case illustrated in Figure 10.5. Here there are two independent references, Class1.Ref1 and Class2.Ref2. There is no guarantee that Class1.Ref1.Ref2 = Class1, which is very clearly the intent of the case illustrated in Figure 10.3.

One very important aspect of the analysis that is required for the correct specification of associations is the identification of any cases where references are inverses. In such cases, it is essential that either one of the references be eliminated or that the reference pair be converted into an association, to ensure the referential integrity of the system. Given that CIM mandates the use of references, this is somewhat less likely than in a reference-based model (in which associations are not represented as objects). Still, the possibility exists that a feature of a class may be converted into an association without the schema designer realizing that there is a corresponding feature in another class that is actually its inverse. Therefore, a very important question to ask when designing associations is:

Does this association duplicate an association or reference that already exists in the schema?

Methods

Methods represent the behavior available for a class. In the context of an information model, you can think of methods as the set of transactions supported by the class. This is true both with respect to changes in state, in which the method can be expected to transform the object from one valid state to another, and in reporting state, in which a method can be expected to provide the state of the object in a consistent fashion.

This perspective differs somewhat from the usual object-oriented concept of a method, in which a method is an arbitrary piece of code provided by an interface. The distinction between the code and the interface is often made using the terms *method* and *operation*, where method refers to the code and operation refers to the interface.

Your first task as a designer is to define the operations supported by each class. You define the operations in terms of their signature, pre- and postconditions. The operations supported by the class, considered in these terms together with its properties, represent the public interface of the class.

In the CIM Model, method and operation are distinguished by the operation declarations as found in the MOF and the implementation of the body of the method as supported by the provider of the method.

As a schema designer, you must provide each of the significant elements of class behavior. These elements are gleaned from the responses to the following questions:

Are there any state changes applicable to the object that involve changes in the value of more than one property?

Each such state change implies the existence of a method that supports the change.

Are there sets of values pertinent to the object that contain properties from more than one object or value computed from more than one property?

Each such set implies the existence of a method, without side effects, that computes a result set in such a way that if the result set is not computed as a unit, the returned data might be invalid.

Are there any operations (with or without side effects) that can only take place in the presence of the object?

For each method it is important to ask:

Is there an inherited method that has similar pre and postconditions or that returns a similar result set?

The method body may imply a different algorithm for the state transformation or result set computation. The key issue is to recognize situations where polymorphic methods are being supported by a subclass. Failure to do so may lead to anomalies in applications that utilize the schema. The semantics of the schema will become entangled with the semantics of the application. Therefore, the application programmer will need knowledge of the schema to take account of the fact that a subclass is providing an implementation or a method declared in the superclass, but is not overridden by the subclass.

The long-term impact of such application anomalies will be corruption of the integrity of the schema, since application developers will either have to abandon the schema as a source of information or become acquainted with the various applications that use and maintain it.

With respect to the definition of the method itself, you should address the following questions:

What are the method parameters?

What is the method return type?

Are there any pre- or postconditions; does the method have any invariants?

Is the method a function or an operation?

Is the method a constructor or a destructor?

This chapter has provided a summary of the various approaches to schema analysis and design in the form a set of questions you can use to check that you haven't omitted any vital step in the process of putting a schema together. It would be inaccurate to assume that the questions provided here are complete or in some way definitive. What needs to be asked will vary from case to case and you will develop a personal style in which some questions will be much more important than others. The main thing to appreciate is that the design task is complex enough that you need some way to ensure that pieces of it do not get left out.

Chapter 11 will cover some issues that are specific to designing methods and events. These issues have been excluded from the general discussion of schema design on the grounds that method design is really a separate topic and one that has been addressed at length by the object-oriented community. The design of events is a topic that has had very little attention as a programming technique and is important enough to warrant some separate coverage of its own. The next chapter is a guide to some of the important issues with special reference to the design and use of methods and events in the context of a schema.

Methods and Events

The objective of this chapter is to delve into the subject of methods and how to design them. To that end, it covers common approaches to dealing with parameters, the distinction between operations and functions, overriding and polymorphism, and the fragile base class problem. To answer the questions what is an event and where is it appropriate to use one, this chapter explores event design. It also addresses dealing with time-sensitive data and the bridge between events and log entries and details how the use of events can be described in terms of providers and subscribers. The important topics of polling, filtering, and aggregation are also examined.

Method Design Issues

A number of fundamental issues and choices are associated with the design of methods in an object model. To begin with, method design is similar to property design, in that methods must be of an appropriate type (and signature). Methods must be attached to the appropriate class both in terms of placement in an association graph and in an inheritance tree. It is very important to determine whether the Format method belongs on the Disk or its related Partition (what is being for-matted: disks or partitions), or whether Format belongs to the Disk or some higher-level abstraction such as Storage Extent.

Issues peculiar to method design fall under these headings:

- Passing objects versus passing parameters
- Operations versus functions
- Overriding and polymorphism
- Fragile base-class problem

Passing Objects versus Passing Parameters

The following schema fragment illustrates an approach to defining a function; here, the function always has one input parameter represent-ing the input to the method. In the event of the method returning more than a simple status result, it may have one output parameter as well (but see the discussion of operations versus functions). The single input parameter is an object representing the various values required by the method (note that the use of the In qualifier is nonstandard, as its scope is limited to parameters).

```
class InitializeServiceParameter{
    [IN]   string Name;
    [IN]   string CreationClassName;
    [IN]   string SystemCreationClassName;
    [IN]   string SystemName;
    [Values ("Automatic", "Manual", "System", "Boot", "Disabled", "Unknown" ) , IN]
        string StartMode;
    [IN]   boolean AcceptPause;
    [IN]   boolean AcceptStop;
    [IN]   boolean DesktopInteract;
    [IN]   string DisplayName;
    [IN]   string ErrorControl;
    [IN]   string PathName;
    [IN]   string ServiceType;
    [IN]   string StartName;
    [IN]   uint32 TagId;
};
class Service{
        [key]
    string Name;
        [key]
    string CreationClassName;
    boolean Started;
        [key]
```

```
        string SystemCreationClassName;
            [key]
        string SystemName;
            [Values ("Automatic", "Manual", "System", "Boot",
            "Disabled", "Unknown" )]
        string StartMode;
        boolean AcceptPause;
        boolean AcceptStop;
        boolean DesktopInteract;
        string DisplayName;
        string ErrorControl;
        string PathName;
        string ServiceType;
        string StartName;
        uint32 TagId;
        uint32 InitializeService(
            [In] InitializeServiceParameters Parameters);
    };
```

The obvious (and more typical) alternative is to define the method
with a series of parameters corresponding to the properties of the
parameter class, resulting in a Service class defined with an Initialize-
Service operation, as follows:

```
class Service{
    // properties omitted
    uint32 InitializeService(
        [IN]   string Name ,
        [IN]   string CreationClassName ,
        [IN]   boolean Started ,
        [IN]   string SystemCreationClassName ,
        [IN]   string SystemName ,
        [Values ("Automatic", "Manual", "System", "Boot",
        "Disabled", "Unknown" ) , IN]
            string StartMode  ,
        [IN]   boolean AcceptPause ,
        [IN]   boolean AcceptStop ,
        [IN]   boolean DesktopInteract ,
        [IN]   string DisplayName ,
        [IN]   string ErrorControl ,
        [IN]   string PathName ,
        [IN]   string ServiceType ,
        [IN]   string StartName ,
        [IN]   uint32 TagId );
    };
```

Arguably, the declaration of the Parameter class is much easier to
understand. It also permits the specification of default values and
other aspects of the parameters not allowed in the direct parameter

declaration. A further advantage of this approach is that the method can be extended (through overriding or schema evolution, for example) by the addition of properties or subtypes to the Parameter class without impacting existing applications. In general, consider using a Parameter class if a method has a large number of parameters or has parameters that may have to be extended over time.

Operations versus Functions

Methods have two aspects: a *signature* and a method *body*. The signature consists of the method name; the parameter names, types, and their order; and the method return type. The method body consists of a sequence of instructions. Methods usually behave as though they have a hidden parameter (in C++, referred to as "this") that represents the object against which the method is called. Static methods are considered to apply to the whole class, and as such do not have a "this" parameter.

Methods are usually classified as either *operations* or *functions*. Operations have input parameters, return a status, and have side effects. Functions either have output parameters or return a result (which may be a complex object such as a string, as opposed to the simple status value returned by an operation). Functions usually do not have side effects because they are used to access values; if accessing the value produces a side effect, repeated accesses will change the state of the system and can lead to unpredictable consequences.

You can view a property as the combination of a Get function used to access the property value with a Set operation used to set the property value.

When designing methods, be clearly of the distinction between operations and functions, and never mix the two. That is, operations should never return values, and functions should never have side effects.

Overriding and Polymorphism

Two main concepts are used to describe the definition of a method within the context of a class-subclass hierarchy, namely *overriding* and *polymorphism*.

Overriding is used where some aspect of the method (or property, for that matter) is to be changed by the subclass; for example, the subclass may change the method description or other informational qualifier on the method. Overriding is accomplished by restating the definition of the feature, thus altering the aspect that is to be changed by the subclass. Note that in CIM, what gets overridden is controlled by the subclass. This contrasts with C++, where the superclass definition determines whether the subclass definition will be overridden (by use of the *virtual* keyword).

Polymorphism is the process whereby a subclass overrides an inherited feature and supplies an alternative implementation for the feature. The declaration (that is, the signature) remains unchanged, but the body of the method is different (the concept applies equally to properties).

In general, overriding is used to restrict the type, while polymorphism is used to expand the domain. For example:

```
class CIM_Service
{
        [key, volatile, read]
    string Name;
        [Description (
        "The StopService method places the Service in the stopped "
        state. It returns an integer value of 0 if the Service was "
            "successfully stopped, 1 if the request is not supported and "
            "any other number to indicate an error.") ]
    uint32 StopService();
};


class Acme_Service:CIM_Service
{
        [Description("Attempts to pause the service. If the service "
        "does not pause within the PauseTimeOut time an error is "
      "returned")]
    uint32 Pause();
    uint32 PauseTimeOut;
};
```

The Pause operation defined by the Acme_Service class replaces the Pause function defined by CIM_Service. The CIM_Service Pause function does not specify what it will do if it is unable to pause the service. The Acme subclass specifies a time-out value and directs what the

Pause function should do if it is not possible to pause the service within the established time-out interval.

Another common concept is that of *overloading,* whereby a new method that is only distinguished from some other method by its parameter types is defined. Overloading is not supported by CIM, as all methods must either be distinct in terms of method name or identical in terms of method signature.

When you are designing methods, occasionally you will find it necessary to override inherited methods or properties and to provide polymorphic functions or properties. Always do this with the greatest of care, as both of these features introduce substantial complexity into a model.

Fragile Base-Class Problem

The fragile base-class problem (FBC) can be reduced to the question: Can a subclass be added to a schema without breaking independently developed subclasses? The problem takes two forms: *syntactical* and *semantic FBC.*

The syntactical FBC arises where the implementation requires unrelated subclasses to be recompiled when a subclass is added to a hierarchy. This is a prominent feature of C++, in which a virtual function table is used to represent the structure of the C++ object. The order of the entries in the table is affected by changes in unrelated classes, and therefore minor changes require broad recompilation. The CIM schema is expressed in such a way that there are no essential dependencies between superclass and subclass declarations. Thus, there is no inherent reason why any CIM implementation should be subject to the syntactical fragile base-class problem.

The semantic FBC problem can best be illustrated using an example.

```
class A{
    uint32 DataSize;
    string Data;
    sint32 AddData(str string);
    sint32 Fill(str string, uint32 copies);
    string GetData();
};
class B:A{
    sint32 AddData(str string);
};
```

In this case the A:AddData function has been defined to place a string into the Data property and update DataSize to reflect the number of characters in the string. When the string value is reassigned, the string allocated in Data is not deallocated; instead, the DataSize value is updated to reflect the number of characters in use. Fill supplies Data with its string parameter, up to the current DataSize value.

Consider what happens when B:AddData is defined and does not update DataSize: Both GetData and Fill will fail to function properly, as they are dependent on DataSize being correctly maintained. In this case, a subclass has broken its superclass by failing to observe conventions required by the superclass functions. This is the essence of the semantic FBC problem. It is not possible to simply override an operation. The full side effects of the operation must be understood before this can be safely done. The problem is mitigated in CIM by virtue of the fact that the subclass controls overriding, meaning that accidental override is unlikely. Every time an override occurs, it is a result of a conscious decision on the part of the person defining the subclass; it is not an unintended consequence of an action on the part of someone specifying a superclass.

Designing Event Classes

An event is anything that occurs, for example:

- A new class is created.
- An instance is deleted.
- A 'ping' packet arrives.
- A network break-in is attempted.

Thus, an event (also known as an *indication* in CIM) is an object created as a result of the occurrence in the managed environment.

Events are classes; they can have properties and methods, and be arranged in a type hierarchy. But event classes differ from ordinary classes in that they do not have an enumerable set of instances. The Event class instance is only generated on the occurrence of the event. Effectively, once the event has occurred, the instance no longer exists; put another way, the event only exists at a moment in time, so asking for all events is not meaningful. If there is a requirement to track and report on events across time, it has to be met using an application that captures appropriate events and records them in a normal (nonevent) class that can be queried and enumerated in the usual way.

Two types of parties are involved in an event: *producers* and *consumers*. Producers publicize events, and consumers subscribe to events.

- Producers are pieces of code that have inside knowledge about events. It is their responsibility to report events. They should know nothing about consumers.
- Consumers receive events. They should know nothing about producers. The consumer of an event should only be concerned with the definition of the event as expressed by the event class.

Event Representation

Events are represented as instances of event classes; that is, a class derived from the CIM_Event class. For example, the PrinterJammed-Event illustrated in the next code sample would get an instance each time a printer became jammed.

```
class PrinterJammedEvent : CIM_ExtrinsicEvent
{
    string PrinterName;
    string ProblemDescription;
};
```

Another example is an event supported directly by the system, in this case, an event being generated when an instance is modified.

```
    [Abstract, Description("A subclass of Event indicating "
    "state changes of objects defined in the CIM model.")]
class CIM_IntrinsicEvent : CIM_Event
{
        [Description ("The TargetInstance is the object that gave "
        "rise to the event.")]
    CIM_Object TargetInstance;
};
    [Description("A subclass of IntrinsicEvent indicating the "
    "modification of an existing object instance in the environment. "
    "Note, that this can indicate changes of more than one property.")]
class CIM_InstanceModificationEvent : CIM_IntrinsicEvent
{
        [Description("Object that reflects the state after the "
        "modification. Note that implementations are not required to "
        "report all of the object's properties but may choose to "
```

```
            "return only those that have changed.")]
        CIM_Object PreviousInstance;
    };
```

Intrinsic Events

The Object Manager provides support for intrinsic events that reflect changes that occur to the system. Each time an object is created, updated, or deleted, an intrinsic event is generated. This applies to instances, classes, and namespaces (that is, all of the objects known to the system). This is not to say that these events are always generated, rather that the events are generated only on demand. For example, files are represented in CIM by the CIM_LogicalFile class. In theory, every time any file changes in any way, an event is generated; therefore, the potential volume of events is vast and can only be provided on an as-needed basis.

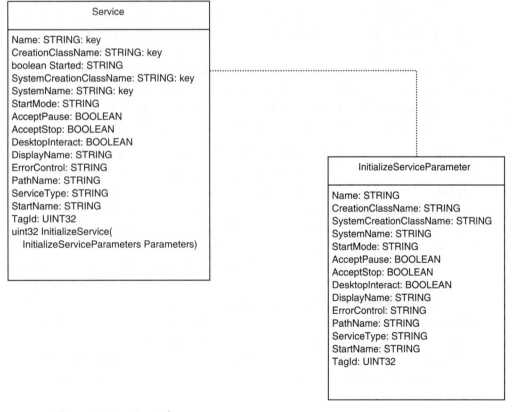

Figure 11.1 Event classes.

The system classes involved in the intrinsic events are illustrated in Figure 11.1. Note the TargetInstance property on the various intrinsic events: It provides the information about the instance being modified. The PreviousInstance property provides information about the previous state of the object on a modification, to enable the detection of events such as "decrease in available free space by more than 10 percent."

When designing events, consider first whether an intrinsic event already exists that will be triggered on the occurrence of the event. If a suitable intrinsic event does exist, and has a suitable implementation, always use it rather than inventing a new event class to serve the same purpose.

Implementing Events

There are two basic strategies for implementing events: The event may be provided natively by the underlying event source or polling may simulate the event. If the event is provided natively by the underlying source, this implies that the source of the event has built-in mechanisms that allow events to be detected. For example, a file system might have the capability to produce an event anytime a specific file is updated. The support for this event may be intricately tied to the file system's update control mechanisms and may be provided efficiently with very little overhead for the caller or the file system.

By contrast, if there is no support for the event in the underlying system, the event can be simulated by polling. In this case, the object manager or some other process must periodically examine the state of the object and infer the occurrence of the event from the observed state. For example, a file update could be inferred from the update timestamp. The polling process would be required to remember the last timestamp and compare the old and new timestamp on a periodic basis. The length of the period is known as the *polling interval*. Polling is a reasonable approach given that the polling interval is large and the amount of data involved is small. For example if there is a requirement to report when operating systems are changed and the change need only be detected at weekly intervals, the overhead of a polling based event may be a matter of a few bytes of data and a few seconds of CPU time once a week.

Aggregation, Correlation, and Throttling

The principal problem to be dealt with in designing an event based management system is ensuring that the events generated by the system do not become a performance problem. Consider for example the events that might be produced from the normal life-cycle events in the system model. These are intrinsic events in that they are produced as a by-product of creating, deleting or modifying objects in the system. Every time a process or thread is created or destroyed, every time a file changes state in anyway, there is a potential event. The possible number runs into thousands per second, and any attempt to subscribe to all of them would bring the system immediately to a standstill. A variety of strategies has evolved that are aimed at reducing the impact of the event stream on the performance of the system being managed. These strategies are described here as "Aggregation, Correlation, and Throttling."

Event aggregation is a process by which a number of events are aggregated into a single event. Aggregation is usually based on an assumption of uniformity among the events being aggregated. It can be described using an interpretation of the SQL "group by" clause. For example

```
Select Count(*), Average(TargetInstance.UserModeTime)
From InstanceDeletionEvent
Where TargetInstance Isa CIM_Process
Group By Priority
```

This query can be thought of as resulting in a single event, which will consist of a count of the number of events and the average of the User-ModeTime for the events involved. The piece missing is the period over which the average will be computed. This is provided as a part of the event subscription. See the CIM standard for a description of the exact mechanisms involved.

With aggregation a simple summarization is used in order to reduce the size of the event stream. Aggregation can use any summarization function – such as average, sum, min and max. More complex scenarios arise where a number of different events can be reduced to a single event based on the occurrence of a pattern of events over time. This is correlation. For example, a system may be considered in a critical condition if it is running a production database, more than 100 transactions per second occur over a period of 2 minutes (an aggregation), and database backup starts. The correlation of multiple events in these types of scenarios essentially involves the use of a state machine with various states within the state machine being taken as the occurrence of an event that needs to be reported (such as "system is in a critical state").

In practice most of the events used by a management application for managing a system are likely to be aggregation or correlation events. The simple, primitive type of event represented by most intrinsic events are simply to fine grained to be useful across a broad management environment.

Aggregation and correlation are techniques for reducing the size of the event stream and thereby controlling the impact of the event stream on the overall performance of the system. Throttling is more a brute force approach to the same problem, whereby the event stream is limited to a certain percentage of the available system resources. There are various possible throttling strategies; for example, events may be limited to a certain percentage of the available network bandwidth, events may only be transmitted when the system utilization is below some threshold. Given the use of throttling, events must be prioritized in some way to allow a sensible determination of which events are to be delayed or discarded.

It should be clearly understood that CIM does not directly address correlation, aggregation, and throttling. The use of CIM as an event source is dependent on the existence of architectural levels that do aggregation, correlation, and throttling. Clearly these can be expressed using CIM classes, but in designing a management application you should understand that these are not a part of the base standard. In constructing a management application you should expect to provide aggregated and correlated event classes that represent a distillation of the events on the system that are specifically relevant to what your application is trying to do.

References

There is very little accessible literature on designing events. The DMTF white paper mentioned below describes much of the terminology and motivation behind the CIM approach to event definition.

DMTF, Events White Paper, Nov 1999. obtainable from www.dmtf.org

Implementation Theory

B y now you realize that the DMTF Common Information Model contains a significant number of classes that capture useful design patterns for management tools. This, the final, chapter shifts the focus from the model to how it is to be implemented. In short, if you do not understand the implementation theory intended by CIM, you cannot appreciate its value and contribution to the industry.

Implementation Independence

With the exception of the XML tags defined for CIM, the DMTF has not prescribed a particular implementation of the model, rather it is not intended to enable the exchange of information among various implementations. Let us see why.

The Common Information Model is just that, an information model. It organizes the information that a disparate group of IT workers needs to perform its tasks. Such an organization needs applications to help it plan future changes, model and evaluate complex configurations, track the operational environment to ensure all systems are up and

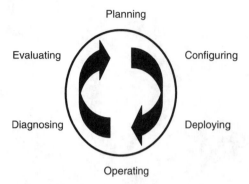

Planning

Evaluating

Configuring

Diagnosing

Deploying

Operating

Figure 12.1   Resource life cycle.

running, and so on. Thus, these are different tools for different parts of the resource life cycle (see Figure 12.1).

Many of the previous efforts in the industry that developed management information models primarily focused on an implementation that dealt with the operational environment. There were implementations like SNMP that were designed to provide a window into a resource's actual configuration and its current operational state. While this is important, models tuned for one of part of the resource life cycle tend not to work well in other parts.

Most database theory prescribes that an information model be mapped to a particular technology and tuned for a particular set of applications. Since the DMTF recognizes that the CIM is appropriate for many applications it has elected not to either pick a particular technology or to map to existing popular ones. Part of the reason is that it is not possible to answer the following type of questions without very specific information about the expected set of applications:

- Should each CIM class be mapped to a unique relational table for a RDBMS implementation?
- Is the naming hierarchy implied by the scoping objects (non-weak participant of a weak association) the appropriate access path for a directory implementation?

The answer to questions like these is always the same: It depends on the application and what you are trying to do. So the motivation for being implementation-independent is to maximize the opportunities to actually use the model. Let's look at different ways the model could be used.

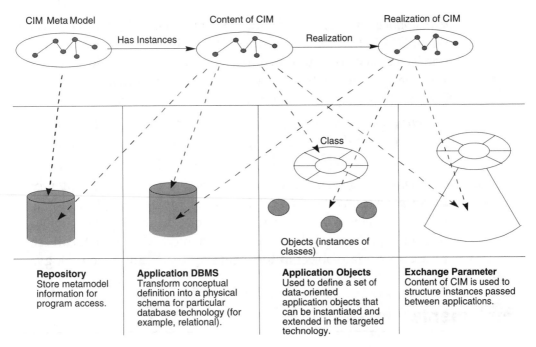

Figure 12.2 Four ways to use CIM.

Because CIM is not bound to a particular technology or implementation, it promises to facilitate the sharing of management information among a variety of management platforms. The CIM Naming mechanism was defined to address enterprise-wide identification of objects, as well as the sharing of management information. As stated, because CIM is a conceptual model that is not bound to a particular implementation, it can be used in various types of implementation. Four types are illustrated in Figure 12.2. These four types can be used within the same management system or between management applications in different management systems. The four implementations are described here:

- *As a repository.* The constructs defined in the model are stored in a database. These constructs are not instances of the object, relationship, and so on, but are definitions for someone to use in establishing objects and relationships. The metamodel used by CIM is stored in a repository that becomes a representation of the metamodel. This is accomplished by first mapping the metamodel constructs into the physical schema of the targeted repository, then populating the repository with the classes and properties expressed in the model.

- *For an application DBMS, the CIM is mapped to the physical schema of a targeted DBMS (for example, relational).* The information stored in the database consists of actual instances of the constructs. Applications can exchange information when they have access to a common DBMS and the mapping occurs in a predictable way.

- *For application objects, the CIM is used to create a set of application objects in a particular language.* Applications can exchange information when they can bind to the application objects.

- *For exchange parameters, the CIM—expressed in some agreed-to syntax— is a neutral form used to exchange management information by way of a standard set of object APIs.* The exchange can be accomplished via a direct set of API calls or by exchange-oriented APIs, which can create the appropriate object in the local implementation technology.

Implementation Model

Figure 12.3 summarizes the implementation model intended for the CIM that allows for management information exchange scenarios. For example, the way instances of classes are named was chosen with this architecture in mind. The figure shows two different implementations with the major components of the architecture. The left side is using an application DBMS and the right side is using an application object implementation. Each implementation must provide the equivalent of a Data Interchange Engine.

Briefly, the major components of the architecture that form the Data Interchange Engine are defined in the following. Later, each of these components is examined in greater depth.

Identity Mapper. This component is responsible for keeping track of how to map the identity of the incoming and outgoing classes to and from the native identity scheme.

Extractor. This component knows how to retrieve the instance information from the namespace and form the information into a valid MOF or XML stream. The Extractor must be able to create unique key for each distinct object, and it records the ordered pair of the assigned key and the native identity with the Identity Mapper component.

Optimizer. This component knows how to extract the instance information from the MOF or XML stream and store it in the native format.

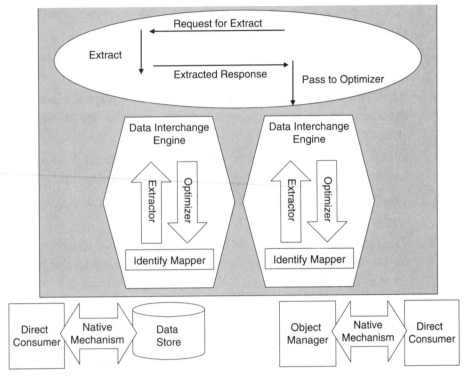

Figure 12.3.   Implementation architecture.

The native implementation behind the Data Interchange Engine can be just about anything: an instrumented SNMP MIB, a relational database, an LDAP directory, or a set of CORBA objects.

Processing Flow

When two different management platforms want to exchange management information, the process starts with one of the platforms contacting the other. The contacting platform or initiator makes contact because of an external event like a user request. When two Data Interchange Engines interact as a result of an external event, you can expect the following to occur:

1. The Initiator uses the Namespace type of the target platform to select the proper protocol and/or API it is to use to interact with the Data Interchange Engine of the target.

2. With this information about the access protocol, the Initiator uses the Namespace handle to make contact with the target.

3. Based on the access protocol, the Initiator requests a set of information about some objects.

4. The targeted Data Interface Engine routes the request to the Extractor to translate it into a native operation.

5. After the native operation completes, the Extractor interacts with the identity-mapping components to create either an MOF or XML stream.

6. When the stream has been formed, the Data Interchange Engine hands the results to the initiating Data Interchange Engine.

7. The initiating Data Interchange Engine routes the results to the Optimizer.

8. The Optimizer works with the Identity Mapper to construct the native operations that will store the information in the Initiator's native format.

Interchange Format

There are three types of interchanges that can occur between two management systems. These include:

1. One management system can pass a set of definitions that the receiving management system compiles into its system.

2. One management system can pass instance information that the receiving management can import or load into its system.

3. One management system can pass definitions and instances to a receiving management system that compiles the definitions and loads the instances.

Given the different types of interchanges, the CIM MOF and XML provide an exchange format that can handle the three situations shown in the Figure 12.4; model definitions only, model definitions and instances, and instances only.

Data Interchange Engine Components

The Data Interchange Engine is used to explain the implementation theory for the CIM. This subsection examines in greater detail the major components of the Data Interchange Engine.

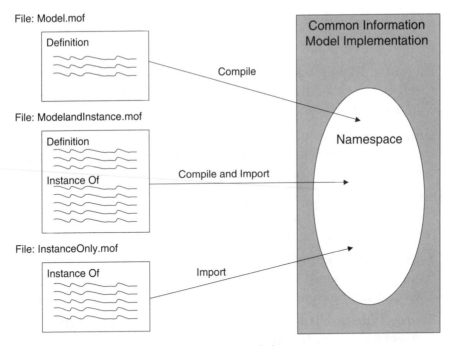

File: Model.mof

Definition

File: ModelandInstance.mof

Definition

Instance Of

File: InstanceOnly.mof

Instance Of

Common Information
Model Implementation

Namespace

Compile

Compile and Import

Import

Figure 12.4. Exchange Format: Instances and classes.

Identity Mapper

The Identity Mapper's major function to is to extract the name of the objects as they flow into the implementation and to remap the names when they flow out. The Identity Mapper must pay close attention to both model path and the namespace portions of an object's name. The easiest part to deal with is the model path (The set of property values marked with the key qualifier, including the one propagated from a scoping object if one is used) since this information can be extracted from each object instance directly.

The more difficult task is keeping track of the Namespace Path since it can be specified in various ways. The Namespace path is composed of two parts:

- *The Namespace type identifies the implementation type.* Each implementation has its own access protocol or API. Fundamentally, a Namespace type implies an access protocol or API set that can be used to manipulate objects.

- *The Namespace handle identifies a particular instance of the type of implementation.* This handle must resolve to a namespace within an implementation. The details of the handle are implementation-specific.

The difficulty in tracking the Namespace path is that its parts can be specified several different ways. For example, in an MOF file, the Namespace path can specified as:

Source pragma. Contains the complete namespace path. This value can be used with any objects that do not have any namespace information specified locally.

Source qualifier. Contains the complete Namespace path for the object scoped by the qualifier. The value of this qualifier overrides a Source pragma if one existed.

Source Type pragma. Contains only the Namespace type, so the Namespace handle is specified locally. The Namespace handle for association references will be specified as a part of the reference.

Source Type qualifier. Contains only the Namespace type for the object scoped by the qualifier.

Nonlocal instance qualifier. Contains the Namespace type for association references when it resolves to a management system other than the source.

The specific details depend on whether you are processing an object or an association. The Identity Mapper must be able to extract the details for inward-bound MOFs and to create "equivalent" names for outward-bound MOFs.

Extractor

The Extractor must transform the native form of the information into a well-formed MOF or XML stream. To properly design the transform, implementors must decide which of the following two mapping strategies they want to use: recast or domain mapping.

Recast Mapping. Provides a mapping of the source's meta constructs to the targeted meta constructs, so that a model expressed in the source can be translated into the target. The major design work is to develop a mapping between the source's metamodel and the CIM metamodel. Once this has been done, the source expressions are recast, as in Figure 12.5.

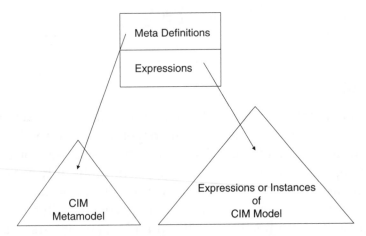

Figure 12.5. Recast mapping.

Domain Mapping. Takes a source expressed in a particular technique and maps the content to CIM. This mapping does not rely heavily on a meta-to-meta mapping; it is primarily a content-to-content mapping. In one case, the mapping is actually a re-expression of content using a more familiar and expressive technique.

Optimizer

The Optimizer must take an incoming XML or MOF stream and map it to the native implementation. The design of the Optimizer, like the Extractor, must establish a mapping strategy.

When an MOF file is consumed by a particular Optimizer, two operations are performed, depending on the file's content. First, a compile or definition operation is performed to establish the structure of the model. Second, an import operation is performed to insert instances to the platform or tool.

Once the compile and import have been completed, the actual instances are manipulated using the native capabilities of the platform or tool. In other words, to manipulate an object (for example, change the value of a property), you must know the type of platform to which the information was imported, the APIs or operations used to access the imported information, and the name of the platform instance that was actually imported. For example, the semantics become:

```
Set the Version property of the Logical Element object with
Name="Resource A" in the relational database named LastWeeksData to
"1.4.0".
```

Types of Exchanges

The CIM architecture provides the basic building blocks for exchanging management information between management platform. Earlier, we discussed the fact that the details of an exchange transaction can vary. For example, you can exchange model definitions only or you can exchange instance details only. This section discusses some of the finer points relating to exchanging information. As you will see, when two management platforms interact, it is important to understand the nature or context of the information being exchanged. The following subsections describe types of exchanges that can occur between various management information sources.

Before reviewing these, let's look at the following example so we understand why it is important to understand the characteristics of the source. Suppose that someone hands you a printout with the following information about Jason Lauler's workstation or that this information is exchanged between two applications:

Lotus 123

4 Megs of RAM

300 MB of hard drive space

Word

What is this a list of? The answer depends on where it came from and when. Here are some possible answers:

- It is the desired configuration for Jason's desktop machine.
- It is the configuration of Jason's machine last week when an inventory scan was performed.
- It is the set of resources being monitored on Jason's machine.
- It is the items that need to be added to Jason's machine for his new job (change management).
- It is the resources that were in action when a problem occurred (diagnostics).

So, the exchange types discussed in the following subsection emphasize transactions between different types of sources.

Scan Exchange

A scan exchange is the process of an application moving information from configuration or control files to another information source. The source is the persistent information that actually controls the configuration (i.e., behavior) of a particular resource or system. That is, if the persistent state of the source changes, then the behavior or capability of the IT resources change. In this case, the application for the source information is likely to be an editor that created the file used to configure the resource. For example, when an application scans information from Microsoft's WMI cimv2 namespace it is performing a scan exchange.

Discovery Exchange

Discovery exchange is the process of an application moving information from an active resource to another information source. This information is obtainable only when the resource is actually up/active/running (for example, current number of active users).

Populate Exchange

Populate exchange is when an application moves information from one passive management database to another passive database. The source does not actually control the resource; it is typically stored in a database associated with a management application. The populate exchange generally targets a database that has a broad or more complex scope (e.g., manager of managers).

Deploy Exchange

Deploy exchange is when an application moves information from a passive source to the control or configuration file of a set of resources; it is the opposite of scan exchange. This type of exchange is the only one that results in a change of state to the actual system.

Multiple Exchanges between Applications

So far, the discussion has implied that there can be only a single type of exchange between applications. In fact, the ability to scale a particular namespace really stems from the fact that applications deal with a variety of domains. So, within a particular namespace, applications may have different types of exchanges going on at the same time in different directions, enabling collaboration.

Complementary Applications

The first situation in which a multiple exchange can occur is when two or more applications complement each other. For example, consider an operational console application, a help desk application, and an inventory application. The operational console wants to include information about the last time a resource changed so that there is a quick way for the user to determine whether a status change is driven by a relatively recent change. The help desk application wants to record the current operational information about a resource when a problem record is open. The help desk application also wants to capture a snapshot of the software currently installed on the machine. In this case, the exchange details are different for each application.

Synchronized Applications

There are several situations where two or more applications produce the same information. In this case, it is desirable to get the information synchronized, in essence, to build a two-way bridge between the information sources. This can be accomplished by having two exchange transactions for the same information. The legitimate combinations of the element types for collaboration are two populates, a discover and deploy, or a scan and deploy. These are shown in Figure 12.6.

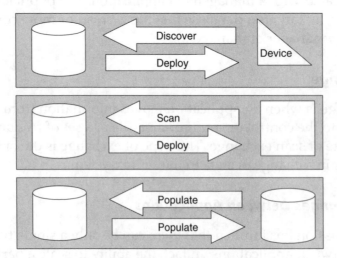

Figure 12.6 Exchange type combinations.

Summary

The implementation theory for the CIM is rooted in a set of principles that maximizes its ability to influence the industry. Rather than driving a particular implementation that favors a particular application/technology combination, the intent is to drive implementations that can exchange information.

Since the CIM is an information model, standard database theory methodologies can be used to map the logical design implied by CIM into a physical design. While this is useful, the real value for the industry is that the CIM can be used to build data interchange engines that compliment these traditional implementation techniques. A data interchange engine is composed of three parts: identify mapper, extractor, and optimizer.

When designing a data interchange engine it is important to realize the purpose of the interchange must be clearly understood. Formats like MOF and XML allow for interchanges that result in compiling new definitions into a system, that result in loading instances, or both. Also, when designing for repeatable interchanges between two systems, it is important to understand the nature of the source and target. This will determine whether the exchange is a scan, a discovery, a populate, or a deploy transaction.

K

Keys, 45–46, 196–198, 219–220, 236. *See also* Candidate keys; Foreign key; Primary key; Table key.
  qualifier, 257

L

Labels. *See* Classes.
  properties, 236, 259
Languages, 21
LANs, 176
Large-scale systematic biases, 223
Late binding, 27
LDAP. *See* Lightweight Directory Access Protocol.
Leaf class, 81
Legacy instrumentation, 247
Library ports, 98
Life cycle, 186. *See also* Applications; Resource life cycle.
Lightweight Directory Access Protocol (LDAP), 179, 180
  directory, 289
Linked-list class, 60
Linux, 2, 5
Lists, 247
Load balancing, 114, 130
Locations. *See* Common Information Model.
  concepts, 137
Locking mechanism, 239
Locking techniques, 238
Logical connectivity, 177
Logical containment, 177
Logical design, 192, 208
Logical device, 145
Logical Element class, 8
Logical elements, 202
Logical entity, 84, 145
Logical schema structure, 192
Logical splits, 84–86
LogicalDevice, 238
LogicalElement, 36
  class, 83
Logical/physical split, 131
Logs, 43–44

Loose coupling, 22
Lower-level extents, 123
Lower-level storage extents, 123
Low-level component information, modeling process, 141
Low-level configuration details, 104
Low-level devices, 106
Low-level storage extents, 122
LUN, 126. *See also* Target LUN.

M

Maintenance cycle, 188
Manageable components, 80–84, 89
  capturing techniques. *See* Decomposable manageable components.
Managed Object File (MOF), 5
Managed Object Format (MOF), 10–11, 60, 247
  compiler, 62
specification, 11
Managed system, 3
Managed System Element (MSE), 5, 8, 10, 82–84, 256
ManagedSystemElement, 53
Management. *See* Accounting management; Configuration management; Fault management; Performance management; Security.
  applications, 11, 256
industry, CIM usage, 11–20
protocols, 3
tools, 152
Management information, 109
  representation, 75
Management Information Base (MIB), 4, 10, 132, 181, 289
Management Information Format (MIF), 2, 4, 132
Management Information System (MIS), 22
Management Type Definition (MTD), 14
Management-significant system elements, 5
Manager, 3
Manager/agent paradigm, 2–3
Manager-to-manager, 11